Hearing God Day by Day

A Daily Devotional
by
Les Wheeldon

Foreword

This daily devotional 'Hearing The Heart Of God, is exactly that. After reading the daily teachings one comes away feeling you have caught something of the heart of God. Rev. Les Wheeldon has produced a truly Holy Spirit inspired devotional that will greatly help each reader in their spiritual growth and daily walk with the Lord.

Today there are many books and writings that focus on how Christians can be successful in themselves, however the daily devotionals in 'Hearing The Heart Of God' highlight the sure and lasting ways to a successful Christian life, that is in seeking the presence of God, knowing Him intimately, and loving and feeding on His Word. 'As the deer pants for the water brooks, so pants my soul for You, O God' (Psalm 42:1 NKJV) is a true reflection of the teaching and exhortations this daily devotional. In the stream of God's presence our deepest thirst is quenched, our wounds are healed, our strength is renewed, and we are placed beyond the reach of the enemy.

I am confident that your reading and application of the daily truths found in 'Hearing The Heart Of God' devotional, will bring you to a more exciting intimacy and heart knowledge of our God and Saviour.

John Elliott - Director World Outreach International

www.world-outreach.com

About Les Wheeldon

Les Wheeldon began ministry in January 1979. He and his wife Vicki served first in a pioneer situation in French speaking Cameroon in West Africa, for 8 years.

Since then he has pastored several Churches in the UK and has travelled extensively in many nations preaching and teaching the Word of God.

Les has been the Head of Biblical Studies at the Marketplace Bible Institute in Singapore since 2006.

Les and Vicki currently live in Epsom near London, England.

LesWheeldon.com

January 1

"Therefore, having been justified by faith, we have peace with God..." [Romans 5:1]

Remembering this is the best way to start each new day and each New Year. This gift of justification is the foundation of all life for those who follow Jesus. It means that I am no longer living in the shadow of yesterday's failures, nor in the fear of how I shall live in the future. It is God's gift to me, and all I need do is to believe in God. My past is as bright and clear as the sunrise on the ocean. My future is as safe as the mountains that catch the earliest rays of the rising sun. My past, my present and my future are in the hands of Jesus, who speaks my name before the throne of grace. By His death and resurrection, I am worthy to receive His Spirit. By this justification and His Spirit, I have access to the Father's heart; I have confidence that my prayers are heard; I have the joy-strength I need to do His will. Start each day knowing that, before you say or do anything, you are declared right with God by the blood of His Son.

January 2

"And the Lord has laid on Him the iniquity of us all." [Isaiah 53:6]

Our faith in Christ does not begin with DO, but with DONE. This verse in Isaiah is written in the past tense, as the Lord speaks of His finished work, through the mouthpiece of the prophet. Our walk with God is only ever possible because we have been forgiven, and this is something we must realise has already been done. We are to enter into the good of it, not by doing but by believing. The work that God has already done is to produce in me the life of Christ Himself. I have in me the acceptance of God through the work of His Son. But more than that, I have the life that has already fully pleased God; *"...you are complete in Him"* [Colossians 2:10]. I am only able to live this life from the position of rest, where all striving has ceased and I worship and thank Him. If we can keep our eyes on this great DONE, then we will never again live as those who are the bottom of the class, who struggle to pass, whose best is never quite enough. We have the life in us that has satisfied the Father's heart, and because of this we have 'passed the exam' with distinction from the beginning. Are you looking at yourself and what you have to achieve today? Then stop and look at

5

Calvary, and then step joyfully into the day, with the spring in your step of knowing that you are accepted in Christ. Let your doing be a song of praise to Him.

January 3

"Judge not, that you be not judged." [Matthew 7:1]

Have you fully realised the evil of judging others? When we judge another person, we are at the same time expressing a judgment about ourselves. We are declaring that we were never in need of forgiveness or grace; we have never fallen or been in danger of falling; we have always had the purest motives. In short, we have never repented because we have never needed to! The heart that judges looks down; the heart that judges has not yet seen its own sin; the heart that judges is unrepentant. When once we begin to look at ourselves, we become aware of the plank in our own eye, and we realise what fools we have made of ourselves. When once we truly repent, our eyes are washed, and we begin to look with understanding and mercy on others who fail; we begin to esteem others as higher than ourselves. This is not an attitude we can adopt by our own will - it is the result of the grace that comes to wash and refresh us when we humble ourselves. Think of different ones you have been tempted to criticise or look down on, and let the Holy Spirit give you love for them. Repentance is a word of refreshing to those who know its power. By it we discover afresh the love of God in us; and it is not far off, though it may cost us our dignity and pride to stoop and drink of the Lord's mercies afresh today. There is always a stream of living water flowing for those who will kneel and drink.

January 4

"...dwelling in unapproachable light, whom no man has seen or can see..."
     [1 Timothy 6:16]

It is common to us all to want to be in control of our lives and of all that is around us. We want to be able to oversee our lives – so that nothing is out of sight or out of reach. But this is precisely what makes our lives so dry and empty. It is the qualities in God that are beyond us that make Him so exciting. It is not just that He is saying wonderful things about us. It is He HIMSELF that is the delight. To begin to pin God down is like pretending I've known something all my life. *"Oh, I've always known that"* or *"I've known that for years."* There is a side to God which will never be known to us, simply because God is so much greater than we can ever say. Just imagine that there could be ten new colours in heaven that you have never seen. No-one can describe them because no-one has anything to compare them with on earth. Similarly, there are things in God's love, power and holiness that are beyond our power even to guess at. This should cause us to think more worthily of Him and to worship Him. He is God, and He alone. If we can lift our minds for only a few minutes each day to consider Him as He truly is, then some of that glory will be reflected in our lives. We will be nobler, better people. The best thought we can ever think is God. There is no higher, more mind-stretching, more beautiful activity than to worship Him.

January 5

"For His anger is but for a moment,
His favour is for life;
Weeping may endure for a night,
But joy comes in the morning." [Psalm 30:5]

One great need of our hearts is for hope. Life carries us on a wave of the next new exciting thing, but then these things run out. Sometimes life's joys are cut short in tragedy. The result is the same, and we have a 'night of weeping'. The darkness of the night seems so deep because we lose hope - we lose sight of God's intervention. The night presses in and becomes stronger than the promises of God. It can seem to have a permanent quality. Here the Psalmist is giving prophetic insight into the oppressive darkness and depression that sometimes crushes the souls of believers. Get perspective, he says - the dark days are but for a moment. Press through! Declare to the storm, *"I will trust in the Lord!"* It may seem as if God is angry, but this will only last for the time it takes for a candle to flicker, compared with His favour, which is on us for all of life, both now, and in eternity. 'Joy is coming....' Don't let the night get hold of you - that is what happens when we lose hope. Keep your heart fixed on the promise of God: 'Joy is coming...' Don't mix the concrete of despair with the tears of the night. Instead let your tears water the tender plant of God's word, for a new day is on its way. As surely and unstoppably as the earth turns into the sun for a new day, there will be a new dawning of grace and favour on your life.

January 6

"My Presence will go with you, and I will give you rest."
[Exodus 33:14]

The Presence of God can be sensed and experienced. If this were not the case, then our experience of God would be merely theoretical. If the Presence of God made no difference, then all the great promises of God would be empty talk. The truth is that there is a spiritual dimension to all our lives. We live with an underlying sense of 'something'. For the sinner, there is a sense of futility, of emptiness, of meaninglessness; he or she feels these things, sometimes strongly, sometimes very weakly. Often such feelings lie in the subconscious, but they are never far from the surface, and can sometimes well up and sweep us away. But here God's promise is that His Presence can become the great bedrock of our existence. This Presence will be our constant companion, but also there will be moments when this Presence will sweep us away into indescribable joy. This is the joy that is without any sting in its tail. It is a joy without a crash to follow it, because it is of a completely different order from all other joys. 'Presence' implies that it covers and drowns out other 'presences'. This means that I am not the centre, He is. This is the Christian's secret, our hidden source of hope and faith, which are constantly nourished from within. Moses understood this when he replied, in effect, *'If your Presence does not go with us, then what is the purpose of going anywhere?'* Let God be your life; let Him swallow you up in the consciousness of who He is.

January 7

"Today, if you will hear His voice..." [Psalm 95:7]

One great aspect of the Holy Spirit's ministry is the sense of 'here' and 'now'. This is because God is, above all, in the present tense. The devil loves the words 'tomorrow', or 'later' - constantly building a wall of time between us and God. The devil is also very fond of the word 'yesterday' - making us sometimes full of regret, and at other times full of nostalgia. The past has personal horrors that can ruin the present, and it has golden ages to look back on nostalgically and make us feel that we will never know all the blessings that past generations have known. But thank God that the Holy Spirit comes with a resounding 'Today!' He brings God to us here and now. The veil has been torn - the veil of sin, the veil of past failures, the veil of my own lacks, the veil of idealism, in fact every barrier between us and God. The Holy Spirit has the art of making God real to us today. Believe, and then look for Him now. Stop asking when, and begin to see His hand in ways that you were previously blinded to. Above all, dare to step out of unbelief and spiritual dullness, into His direct wonderful Presence.

January 8

"...let us go on to perfection" [Hebrews 6:1]

Go on! The idea of mastering something to perfection is daunting. We start to learn a language, never expecting that we could really be fluent. We start to learn a musical instrument, never expecting we could play in an orchestra. Similarly, we follow Jesus with the expectation that we will always be handicapped by sin and unbelief. But in this verse we are confronted with the challenge to lift up our eyes to God's goal - that we should be perfect. Of course, we all accept that one day in heaven we shall be perfect, but the emphasis here is that we should get off the 'merry-go-round' that turns around the same spot for ever. Salvation is the first step through an open door. Now there is the opportunity to know God and the power of heaven. So we must go on. The first obstacle is our habits. God has changed our hearts, but we have habits of unbelief, of negative thinking. These habits are like mountains in our path, like trees with deep roots in our lives. The Holy Spirit challenges us to look the obstacle in the face and calmly declare: "This mountain shall be removed." Then we must step forward into the day, looking to the Holy Spirit to give us hope that these habits shall dissolve and disappear as we confront them. God says we will be like Jesus, in our faith, our love, our holiness, our thinking, our habits - in all things. Don't be fainthearted! Go on!

January 9

"Let us therefore be diligent to enter..."
[Hebrews 4:11]

Go in! The Holy Spirit is constantly challenging us to take things into account that we cannot know naturally - the 'natural man' has no knowledge of them [1 Corinthians 2:14]. Here in

Hebrews the Spirit is speaking a great word to believers, revealing a realm that is within our reach. We will not drift into it by accident - we must enter in by faith. It is not a realm of more information - it is the realm of powerful Presence, of holiness, of righteousness, peace and joy. This realm is shut off to the sinner till he repents and believes. This realm is of a different order from everything we know naturally. There is nothing like it. It is a realm where God is revealed, where He is King, where other laws operate. It can be consciously entered, or else how should we ever know we had entered? The saved man or woman is made for this realm - it is our inheritance. We were saved when we became as little children, and we must enter into the holy Presence of God with the humility of little children. The point is that children must be taught. The child of God must never lose the childlike wonder of discovering God's love and the realm of Father's touch. Don't wait to be better! Go in, and you will find things at work immediately that make you a better person. The Presence of God makes us better than our best, because it is not us, it is Him in us.

January 10

"...run with endurance the race that is set before us..."
    [Hebrews 12:1]

Go through! The Christian life has mountain-tops - moments of exhilaration. But these are interspersed with periods of ordinary things, and sometimes with times of grief, pain and loss. If we moan in the midst of ordinary things, we unravel the rainbow that was woven on the mountain-top. We are called to enter into the holiest of all, and then to take that glory into the dullest corners of the universe. Glory made flesh does not dazzle by the spectacular, but by the extraordinary patience and endurance that is exhibited by the sons of God. The Christian life is not a 100-metre dash; it is a 26-mile marathon! Thank God we are not racing against each other - all who finish win the race. The temptation is to forget what we have seen in the Holy Place. We are to run with endurance, knowing that the hardest moments will come when our own bodies are screaming at us to give up. We acquire likeness to Christ as we steadfastly keep our eyes on Jesus. It is through endurance that we acquire the essential Christlike quality of ruggedness. We partake of His sufferings, His loneliness, His unselfishness, and thereby His holiness is made enduring and unfading in us.

ist..." [Galatians 2:20.]

nost sublime ever written. They
iat, by the grace of God, we are
: God's love reached its greatest
ally secure because we are made
of God's life. The amazing fact
ind such a love that empties itself,
The child of God has been rooted
makes God so amazing. In other
us. It is not only that we have
ve have the purest love - the love
his is what makes the child of God
vas even in Eden. He had the
vith God, and thus to let God fill
iner can **only** be saved by the love
ior, and then we discover that it is
id that we are called to fellowship
ove, and to manifest it. God does
Calvary; He has given us that love
lieve and let that love flow.

January 12

"I have been crucified with Christ." [Galatians 2:20]

This means that the believer has a cross in his or her heart. By this I do not mean cruel nails and a crown of thorns, but that there is in the heart of the believer the instinct of self-emptying - of esteeming others higher than ourselves, of taking the lower seat, of washing the disciples' feet. No-one can ever hope to fulfil the royal law unless there is a mighty urge inside to do so. No-one can love grudgingly. The miracle of the cross is that, by it, I am made one with God. This is the true miracle of the baptism with the Spirit. Never lose sight of it. Don't be deflected from it. You were made one with God by the death of Jesus and the gift of the Holy Spirit. This should revolutionise your whole thinking about yourself and God. He is in you -not some extension of God, not some remote distant outpost in the Kingdom of God. No, God Himself is in you in His essence and in His greatest form. You have been empowered by the Presence of the uncreated God in your heart. Dare to believe it; wonder and worship and let your heart rejoice in what He has

11

made you.

January 13

"Is it well with you? ...And she answered, 'It is well'."
  [2 Kings 4:26]

When Elisha asked the poor bereaved mother this question, he must have clearly sensed the turmoil of her soul. Her response to the prophet was spontaneous and not contrived. Her words were of the same quality and stature as Job's. Her heart was torn with grief and sorrow, but she answered these remarkable words of faith and trust that God was over all. How vital it is that we never let go of faith, no matter how deep the trial. These words opened the door for a miracle, and such words of trust always do. God is the God of miracles, and whether that miracle is a sudden healing of a broken body, or a sudden flood of heaven's light on a grieving soul, a miracle will always come to the heart that truly believes. This woman was shaken to the core, but out of the awful pressure came the confession of her faith that all was well. This is the faith that rises to touch the throne, and that defies the waves and storms which threaten to overwhelm. God is faithful, and all is well. Confess it, believe it, and make this faith yours. Circumstances vary, but God is unchanging and faithful. All is well now - not merely some day, but right now. Tomorrow will bring resurrection, but we will not give up faith while waiting for resurrection - we must touch the throne today.

January 14

"Everyone went to his own house. But Jesus went to the Mount of Olives." [John 7:53-8:1]

Jesus went from the Temple, where He taught during the day, to the Mount of Olives, and then back again the next day to the Temple to teach. He went to the Mount of Olives for solitude and rest, and most of all to pray and wait on God. That was His home, and only when prayer becomes our home, our centre, our reference point, the focal point of all we do, only then do we fully enter into what prayer is. We assume that this was easier for Jesus than for us. True, He was the Son of God; true, He was sinless; but He was also tempted in all points like we are. He must have felt weak and sometimes dull, but He waited on His Father. We must press through the dull times and settle our hearts so deeply in His Presence that we stop looking over our shoulder at the pressing demands of life - this must be reversed. We must look steadfastly at the Father and listen to His voice. Jesus' teaching in the Temple must have brought the Father's touch to His hearers, and we must learn this pattern for our lives and ministry. We can keep ministering, witnessing, preaching and teaching, but the difference will come when we have learned to go home each night to Father, and wait on Him for fresh bread for each new day.

January 15

"...each one (of the seraphim) *had six wings: with two he covered his face..."* [Isaiah 6:2]

These mighty angels have been sinless and faithful to God since the day of their creation. When they cover their faces, it is not because of guilt or shame, remorse or repentance. There is nothing remotely negative in this act. They have no sense of unworthiness or need, since such things are the fruits of sin and separation from God. Their beings are filled with the wonder of the majestic holiness and beauty of God, and their response is to shield their faces from the brightness which is so overwhelming. We can learn from their response something of the hidden wonder of God, whom we know in part. He is matchless in love and mercy but also in holiness. He loves you more than you can ever imagine or guess, and He burns with deeper fires of holiness than the human mind can conceive. The effect of God's Presence on those beings who have surrounded him since eternity past, is to cause them to cover their faces in worship and wonder. The cry of those who love Him is that they may know Him as He is.

January 16

"Now it came to pass, in the morning watch, that the Lord looked down upon the army of the Egyptians through the pillar of fire and cloud..." [Exodus 14:24]

This is the climax of the confrontation between Yahweh and Pharaoh. Pharaoh continued his insane opposition to God and to the deliverance of the people of Israel. God stood majestically between Israel and the Egyptians, but Pharaoh's armies entered the sea, where they were held back by the pillar of cloud and fire. Perhaps they saw the dim outline of God's face, looking at them. Certainly they must have sensed His

13

indignation. What was on God's face? Perhaps it was the same absolute, restful authority of God which confronted the devil at Calvary. God was saying, by His look, *"How dare you come here to this place of salvation?"* God troubled the Egyptians through His majestic gaze. God looked on the devil as he sought to destroy Jesus on Calvary. Jesus persisted in ceaseless love, and destroyed the powers of darkness, swallowing them up in the floods of wrath against sin, and mercy for sinners. With what terror of total defeat the enemy fled from Calvary! The wonderful truth is made known in verses like these, that God was in Christ reconciling the world to Himself and spoiling principalities and powers - He made an open show of them.

January 17

"God is love, and he who abides in love abides in God, and God in him." [1 John 4:16]

The beauty of the Lord is His love. His face is beyond description because it is the face of love. We often seek to be content, to be blessed, and to possess the things we want. The best of all is love, which is not a mere feeling - it is a quality of character that directs our being outward to notice others, to care for them and touch them with the kindness and tenderness of God. Love is the most refreshing and invigorating work of the Spirit in our lives. If you seek to be refreshed, seek to love. Let the love of God soften your heart and your thoughts, and you will find that your physical body is refreshed and released from burdens that wear you down. The selfish heart is cursed with the burden of a self-centred life. The only answer is to be released from that inward-looking self-obsession. It is often the case that a depressed person has no reason for their depression. If they had, they would be sorrowful, not depressed. It is often the case that there is nothing wrong with us; it is simply that we will not allow our lives to be taken up as tools in the hands of a loving Father. Abandon yourself to love; look with compassion on those around you. Ask yourself how you can touch them with the love of Jesus today, and the fountains of love will flow from within and you will find to your surprise that you are free from the burden of your own needs.

January 18

"...do not let your left hand know what your right hand is doing." [Matthew 6:3]

Religious practices so easily become a theatrical performance, and Jesus is the enemy of religious posing - in prayer, in giving, and in every area of spiritual life. Here in this verse Jesus goes to the heart of this whole area of temptation, and exposes who the audience is that we so often play to - ourselves! Jesus is saying, when you do something generous or kind, when you have a victory in some area, when your faith rises in some great flow of utterance or supernatural power, then beware of the danger of continually congratulating yourself, of patting yourself on the back and telling yourself how well you did. If you indulge in this, the result will be a feeling of exultation that is self-centred, and you will rob God of the glory. Taking our eyes off ourselves is the vital heart of worship, and hence of spiritual life. It is only possible by keeping our eyes firmly on the Lord Jesus Christ. Love Him, with all that you are and all that you have. Pour out your precious anointing oil on Him. Love Him, refresh Him. Don't think of an audience, and don't even be the audience yourself. Look up to Him and worship Him alone.

January 19

"There is another who bears witness of Me...And the Father Himself, who sent Me, has testified of Me."
    [John 5:32, 37]

At first sight, the 'witness of the Father' might seem to be much the same as the witness of Jesus, since He is the One telling us of the Father. But Jesus is here explaining something that comes to our hearts directly from God. When we hear the truth preached, when we hear the gospel of Christ, something stirs in our hearts and assures us that it is true. It is more than our own conscience, and Jesus tells us that this is the Father Himself, bearing witness to the Son. Later in John, Jesus says the Father's activity is essential, since no-one can come to Him unless the Father draws them [John 6:44]. These words open our understanding to the way the Holy Spirit works in stirring our hearts. The Father's voice produces an inner assurance, perhaps describable as a tug on the heart. The Father is drawing us, which is more than our own conscience; this is the longing to know God, and to be in fellowship with the Son. In these verses Christ is speaking to us in the language of heaven. People speak of arguments, of methods and plans, of numbers and statistics. Christ speaks in terms of the indescribable and most wonderful touch of the Father in our hearts. We must learn to obey this

15

prompting, as it makes sense of everything as we obey and follow the leading of that touch.

January 20

"...the hour is coming, and now is, when the dead will hear the voice of the Son of God; and those who hear will live."
[John 5:25]

The power to raise the dead is in the voice of the Son of God. This is a key to spiritual life. We do not receive a vague anointing or power to change our lives. We hear the voice that calls us from the grave. That voice is loving, caring and compassionate. It is majestic and powerful; it is authoritative to the point that there is no power that can withstand that voice. It is the voice of the Creator, who calls forth things that are not, and suddenly they are. The voice is not impersonal, not shouting for the sake of merely making a noise. This is the voice of the most wonderful Person imaginable. There is personality because the Creator is Himself a Person, and defines what personality is. It is in hearing this voice that we are raised from the dead, and life is imparted to our weak, lifeless souls. So incline your heart to hear. He has spoken and He is speaking, and those who hear will live. He is speaking to your heart, and He will awaken you from the deepest 'soul sleep', called spiritual death, and raise you to the relationship of friend to friend with Jesus.

January 21

"He who is without sin…" [John 8:7]

There is criminal law and there is spiritual law. It is in this statement that Jesus reveals the difference. Not everyone has broken the letter of the law, but everyone has sinned. It is the trick of the religious mind to believe that it is better than others because it has not committed the sins of the common people. But the sword of the Spirit cuts away this fog and shows us that sin is a spiritual power that has destroyed human ability to claim moral power in ourselves. There is no power in humanity to overcome sin, either at the level of the individual or at the level of governments or religions. Sin is spiritual and has infected the whole race. All of us need a Saviour. Never forget this. As soon as we forget it we begin to judge others and to trust in our own righteousness. It is not long before we are picking up stones to condemn others. Allow the Holy Spirit to keep before your eyes the conviction of sin. It will not crush or condemn you, but will keep you in the place of trusting in grace. It will keep your spirit loving and fragrant before the Lord, and compassionate towards those who fail.

January 22

"But Daniel purposed in his heart that he would not defile himself ...." [Daniel 1:8]

Daniel was a young man, probably in his teens, when he was taken by force into exile. His stay in Babylon was to be life-long, and his course was to be marked with uncompromising godliness and holiness. He was to be a prophet who would change the course of the king's life and bring hope to the captive remnant of the Israelites in Babylon. His course was set at this moment, when he formed a purpose in his heart to be different and set apart in obedience to God's will for his life. This may seem a small thing for us to do, especially given the seeming insignificance of the person making this decision, but the consequences are life-long. It does not matter what you have done with your life and opportunities until this moment; it matters what you purpose to do with the rest of your days. Settle things in your heart; purpose to be obedient and different. Set your course in godliness and rest assured that, whether or not you rise to be a famous person on earth, your life will reverberate throughout eternity, because you followed the call of God to belong to Another.

January 23

"...thus you shall eat it (the Passover)*: with a belt on your waist, your sandals on your feet, and your staff in your hand."*
    [Exodus 12:11]

This is one of the details of God's marvellous salvation of His people. It is really obvious, but easy to overlook. The Passover lamb must be eaten wearing clothes and shoes ready for a journey. The result of faith in Christ is that a door opens for us to begin our journey, and that is the great meaning of the Passover - it is the first vital step in a journey. It would be madness to be delivered from slavery and then continue as if nothing had happened. So, too, when we put our faith in Christ, we are set free to follow Him, to leave the ways of sin, and begin the

17

discovery of the Person of God. Dress yourself for the journey today, with shoes that are comfortable for a long walk, and no unnecessary burdens that will tire you and make you discouraged, or even make you turn back. Take a good staff to lean on, a cross that will support you over steep inclines or rocky terrain. Never forget you are on a journey of discovery.

January 24

"....God .... rested" [Genesis 2:3]

God finished all His work and then rested. We are transported by this word to the cross, when Christ cried, *"It is finished"* and then entered into rest. On both occasions the emphasis is not on physical rest, for, as the Bible reveals, God does not grow tired or old! Here the emphasis is on the rest of satisfaction, of fulfilled longing. A man who falls in love is restless, but not tired. So, too, God could only rest after He had created human beings, who were the whole reason the world had come into being. Then sin entered the human race, and God had a restless longing to make a way back for humanity. Through the cross, God has entered into the rest of the fulfilment of His deepest longings. He has done everything to win us back; and every time we enter His Presence it is as if we hear music, singing, joy and delight, for the rest of God is not sleepy, but full of joy. God has done it, and He welcomes us in. Enter into His rest today.

January 25

"Lord, I knew you to be a hard man..."
    [Matthew 25:24]

Many religions of the world have taught that God is implacable, and that there is nothing we can do to change God's will or move Him to compassion. The result is a deadly passivity, a state of resignation - believing in fate and an utter powerlessness to change anything. This, of course, is most of all a slanderous insult to God. God cares about us; He loves us all, and watches over us tirelessly to seek to awaken things in our hearts that will reach out to Him. It is true that God alone is sovereign. No person can claim that they are equal to God in respect of free will. But God is not hard; He is generous and shares freedom of will with His beloved human race. We are not treated as brute beasts or even amusing pets. We are treated by God with loving, generous respect. He shares freedom of will with us; it is

18

one of His great gifts to us. So reach out to Him and find that He is waiting for a response, so that He may lavish His loving bounty on you. You are beloved and precious, and He is tender and kind.

January 26

"You have asked a hard thing." [2 Kings 2:10]

Elisha was invited by Elijah to present his petition, before Elijah was taken up into heaven in a whirlwind. So Elisha asked for a double portion of the prophet's spirit. This was no mean prayer, because it was bound up with the ruggedness and fearless righteousness that undergirded Elijah's life and witness. Elisha could have asked for something really easy, such as a quiet life, or a retirement bungalow, or lots of money. Often our praying centres on the desire for an easy life - bless me and my family, and make us comfortable! We might not pray like that directly, but that is the implication. God is challenging us to step out of the consciousness of our little world that we do not want anyone to disturb. We are to step onto the stage of the grand plan of the ages, and pray a prayer that is worthy of the One to whom we pray. We might start by asking for a good portion of His character and Spirit, but God would surely take us much further than we can guess. Get a larger perspective, and start asking God something really hard. Perhaps there is a prayer tucked in the back of your heart that you have not dared pray because it is just too big for you. That is God's speciality - hard things, impossible things - dare to pray for them. God loves a challenge!

January 27

"Our Father in heaven, hallowed be your name."
     [Matthew 6:9]

This is where all prayer begins - not for our problems, but for the glory of God. Yes, there is a prayer of getting right with God - that is a prayer of confession, repentance and faith. But the Christian life is not a life-long struggle to get right with God, though that is what it seems to be for some people! When we turn to Him and believe, we are totally accepted. From then on, our prayers should no longer be focused on ourselves in the same sort of way. We need to learn quickly that prayer is not primarily about polishing our spirituality, or for ever bringing our problems to God. Prayer is about the glory of God, the honour of His name. Prayer is for *Him*. In your praying, take time to consider God and pray for His glory. This will impact all of your praying and thinking. You will see problems as much smaller and easier to solve, if only God Himself is glorified. There is something so depressing about focusing on problem-solving. It is like a wedding feast without a bride. The focus is wrong and there is no reason to be glad. Once we get our focus right, delight enters in, for God is jealous of His glory.

January 28

"The Spirit Himself bears witness with our spirit that we are children of God."
    [Romans 8:16]

The witness of the Spirit in our hearts is our most precious possession. It is the key to the treasure-house, for by that witness we know God and have assurance of eternal life. The witness is not an audible voice, but it is a quiet certainty. It is so quiet that it can easily be ignored, but it is so clear and persistent that we can only ignore it by wilful neglect or rebellion. The witness of the Spirit is an inner quiet joy, but if we stray from the Father's will, a cloud darkens our inner life and we feel a grief of heart that all is not well. This is the grief of the Spirit, and it is good that we feel it. Just as we feel pain if we get too close to the fire, and so are saved from harm, so too we feel inner grief if we stray from Father's will. The witness of the Spirit is the means by which we are alerted to the fact that there is danger. Guard the witness. If your heart says stop, then stop and wait on God. We cannot live by logic; we live by our relationship with God, and the foundation of that is the witness of the Holy Spirit. Commune with God and the witness is refreshed and renewed, and your joy of salvation rises like a fountain.

January 29

"By faith he forsook Egypt..." [Hebrews 11:27]
"Do not love the world..." [1 John 2:15]

The key word here is 'forsake'. It conveys the radical nature of the action - total and irreversible. Such a powerful turning away from the world can only be done by faith. It requires a miracle from God for us to utterly abandon Egypt and cut every link with

20

it. What does this mean practically? It means that we are to forsake every lust that draws us to worldly pursuits and pleasures that are inconsistent with our walk with God. We bring those lusts to the place of execution - the cross. We condemn them to death, and by faith we see their power broken. Our hearts are liberated to enjoy Christ and His Presence to the extent to which they are unentangled with the world. So pilgrim, stand up, shake off the world and get on your journey. Your eyes are on Christ and His kingdom, and to gain that, you are willing to suffer the loss of all things. We lose our life that we may gain a better one.

January 30

"...the Spirit and the bride say, 'Come!'... And let him who thirsts come." [Revelation 22:17]

The Holy Spirit is constantly speaking to us to come to Jesus; and the bride - those who love Him - says the same thing. Sometimes we react to their pleading with hesitation, wondering if we are worthy; sometimes we hold back because of hurts. We look down on ourselves and into ourselves. The result is that we say in our hearts, *"I can't come"*. The turning point is reached when we speak to ourselves, and give ourselves a push towards the waters of life. There can be a thousand reasons presented to us as to why we should turn to Jesus and drink of His life this day, but the only thing that will make it happen is when we at last agree with the Spirit and the bride, and appeal to our inner selves. This is true in so many areas of spiritual life. People have told us what we must do, we know it, but we pray for a word from God and hang back. Speak to yourself and exhort yourself, rise up in faith and do what God has been telling you to do.

January 31

"Give me the little book." [Revelation 10:9]

The prophet/apostle was commanded to take and eat the little book that was open in the mighty angel's hand. God is commanding us to take and eat the little book that is open in God's hand. Have you realised this - that to understand the Bible, you have to take it from God's hand in reverence and with faith? John asked for the book, and we must also ask God to give us the Bible. In answer to prayer, the Bible will be given to us in a completely new way. It will become three-dimensional instead of two-dimensional. For many people, the Bible is like a picture on a wall, perhaps our favourite picture. In answer to prayer, the Bible becomes three-dimensional, and the hand of God comes out of the picture and touches our hearts and changes our lives. The Bible rightly received is explosive; it has the power to revolutionise our lives. Go, take the book and devour it.

February 1

"...the Comforter,... the Holy Spirit..."
[John 14:26, TLB]

The word 'Comforter' is the Greek word *paraclete* which can also be translated 'exhorter'. The danger with the word 'Comforter' is that we may think of someone who smoothes our ruffled feathers, and lulls us to sleep. No doubt He can do that, if that is our need. However, the great work of the Spirit through His ministers the apostles was one of powerful exhortation. The Holy Spirit is the one who reveals Christ, and then tells us what we can do because of who Christ is, and because of what Christ has done. The Holy Spirit challenges us to think and do the impossible. He declares to us our sonship; He declares to us our freedom and power; and He declares to us our spiritual position - seated with Christ in heaven! Then He gathers us up and tells us to sin no more. He tells us to pray without ceasing. He tells us to believe for great miracles. He bids us rise up and be completely different from the former person we were just minutes ago. He sings to us with incredible joy, and appeals to us not to let sin reign in our bodies. He bids us enter into unspeakable joy! The exhorter brings strong comfort to the people of God.

February 2

"Wait on the Lord" [Psalm 27:14]

The Holy Spirit is Himself the servant Spirit of heaven. He waits on God and serves the people of God. We do not wait on God because we like quietness, but because we have deeply agreed with the mind of the Spirit, that wills to exalt Christ and the Father. The Holy Spirit is invisible in form, but also it is His will to be unnoticed. The delight of all who wait on God is that they are filled with God's servant Spirit, and absorbed into God's serving life. This is the unspeakable joy of the person who waits on God. It is given to him or her to look on God and serve Him. It is not the quietness of meditation, but the hush of concentrated gaze on the living God. Waiting on God is full of the joy of self-denial so that God's Presence may fill everything, His will prevail, and His rule and kingdom come. Waiting on God is the Spirit of heaven, and it must be the Spirit of God's people.

February 3

"And they overcame him by the blood of the Lamb..."
[Revelation 12:11]

This is one of the great keys in the believer's life to victory over the powers of darkness. Some people have emphasised the actual mention of the word 'blood' as the key to this victory - the thing that Satan cannot stand. But the truth is that the blood really refers to God's own Being and life - undiluted, uncreated, and poured out in love at Calvary upon sinful humanity. The result was that God, by His Being, swallowed up and destroyed the whole spirit of human rebellion. We overcome Satan by drinking spiritually of that raw, undiluted, living, uncreated Presence of God. The effect in us is as dynamic as it was on the cross. It cannot be otherwise, since the blood will never lose its power to wash away and destroy the power of sin, and take away the grounds for Satan to work in a person's life. So don't just sing about the blood, don't just use the word when you pray. Drink in the Presence of Him who has overcome for us. Satan is terrified of Christ in us. The blood does not mean that Christ is in us merely as a guest. No, He is in us - in our minds, our wills, and our affections. The picture is powerful, and the results are astounding. We overcome Satan by the blood of the Lamb.

February 4

"...they overcame him by the word of their testimony..."
[Revelation 12:11]

This verse is not exalting the power of our mere words or claims as the source of our victory. We can 'claim' to be on the moon, but a thousand years of testimony will not move us one inch closer to that delusion! The power of true testimony is that it involves the aligning of my mind with what God says, and this is not just true, it is the foundation of truth! There is power in strongly reminding myself of what God has done and who He has made me. There is power in declaring the work of God through the cross and the resurrection. Satan is totally defeated, and that is a fact that is brought into my experience when I believe God's Word, and confess with my mouth what He has done. I am making that victory mine. Remember that the testimony of the prophets was always in the past tense when speaking of the cross. *"And the Lord has laid on Him the iniquity of us all."* [Isaiah 53:6]. The prophet needed to be bold to declare something that he had never thought of before. Similarly, we need boldness to declare something so incredible that we never hear such things from any other source than the Word of God. *"...as He is, so are we in this world"* [1 John 4:17]. This is to be the testimony of all God's people, and by this we will be released to know the power of the truth.

February 5

"... they overcame him ... (for) they did not love their lives to the death." [Revelation 12:11]

One of the greatest tests of your motivation is to ask, *'For whose glory do I live?'* Most of us at some time or other have prayed and sweated to obtain a comfortable life. We want victory over the things that bother **us**, not the things that 'bother' God. But here is another secret of victory over Satan - that we count our own lives as dispensable so that God may be glorified. This means that we are willing to sacrifice comfort, blessings, peaceful circumstances, everything, so that God's purposes are advanced. It may seem strange that we are to sacrifice blessing to advance God's kingdom! Of course the two are not mutually exclusive - we can have both. But all too often we are actually willing to sacrifice God's eternal purposes so that we might have an easier time of it down here. The sure sign of this is petulance when things do not go our way. The true overcomer is really willing to endure hardship when the glory of God is at stake. This does not mean throwing your life away as a fanatic, but it does mean being free from self and living for a higher purpose. Satan has no access to the Christian who is free from self.

February 6

"Then fear came upon every soul..." [Acts 2:43]

This blessing of godly fear came upon all who were present on that great Day of Pentecost, including the apostles. Of course, the new converts were touched with fear because of the great Unknown that had just invaded their lives. They had been pierced to the heart with a terrible conviction of sin, and then had passed into the joy of forgiveness and into the Kingdom of God, through being filled with the Holy Spirit. But the apostles, too, were filled with fear. This indicates that they were also suddenly aware that they had misjudged Jesus Christ - they had underestimated Him, they had been caught off-guard by the

25

greatness, the holiness, the majesty and the wonder of the risen Christ. They had known Him briefly after He was resurrected, but now they knew Him from the inside, and the realisation filled them with godly fear. Fear of God is awe coupled with deepest reverence. The effect of the same fear in an unbeliever who does not know God is sheer terror. There is so much about God that we do not know. Sometimes we act as though we knew so much, when to heaven we must appear like complete beginners. Let the fear of God touch your heart today, and you will receive wisdom and understanding that will wash your thoughts and direct your steps.

February 7

"Thinking he was in their company, they travelled on for a day. Then they began looking for him among their relatives and friends. When they did not find him, they went back to Jerusalem to look for him. After three days they found him in the temple courts..." [Luke 2:44-46, NIV]

How astonishing that Jesus' mother and stepfather could have overlooked Him for a whole day! But then they missed Him, and set off to search for Him. They overlooked Him because they assumed they knew all about Him; their hearts were not troubled, and they assumed He was where He should be. So they continued in their daily routine for a day before they missed Him. Then they began searching, and they spent three whole days without understanding how and where they should find Him. How long can we continue in our daily routine, even of prayer and Bible reading, before we suddenly sense that He is not in it in that unmistakable way? Suddenly, we long for Him. This is a sign of love, for it is only those who love Jesus who miss His Presence. We ache for that something that only His Presence can supply. This is not the aching sense of lostness that engulfs the sinner - it is the ache of a heart that longs for the loving touch and affirmation of our great Friend. There is no word to describe Him; He is closer than a friend, yet He is Master too. He is majestic in His authority, and yet He washes our feet with a positive kindness that does not shame us, but makes us believe we can be like Him. Come, Lord Jesus, I long for you.

February 8

"Also for Adam and his wife the Lord God made tunics of skin, and clothed them." [Genesis 3:21]

There is extreme tenderness and love in the way God dealt with the sinful pair. He applied correction and yet at the same time reached out to show them love and protection. Behind these words lies the fact that God killed animals in order to clothe Adam and Eve with skins to protect them from the cold. God's face must have been bathed with tears as He shed the animals' blood. Father, Son and Holy Spirit were declaring through this act that there was a plan to clothe sinners with righteousness. Was it lambs that were slain to clothe them? Perhaps. Certainly, God was moved by all the events. How our sins grieve His heart and hinder His plans for the human race. Yet how wonderful is His love, that reacts with such concern over His loved ones having to feel all the lostness and pain of their new condition. God demonstrated that His love was not exhausted by their sin. Let God demonstrate His love for you. He longs to clothe you with His love, with His best robe, with a ring on your finger. If He loved a guilty pair like this, what will He not do for His returning children who reach out in brokenness and repentance to know Him? God has many garments to clothe us with - garments of praise, joy and power. Let Him take away the garments of mourning, and fill you with joy.

February 9

" 'Your words have been harsh against Me', says the Lord..."
    [Malachi 3:13]

God takes us seriously when we speak; we would be shocked if we realised how seriously. When we say we feel let down by people, or by life, and that we really feel like giving up, God listens. God takes note of every casual word, and sometimes it is the casual asides we say under our breath that come from the deepest part of us. God reasoned with His people in Malachi's day, to let them know He could hear them. Isaiah cried out because of his unclean lips, and God touched them with burning coals [Isaiah 6:5]. And God can touch our lips today and cause us to speak faith - in the same way that Caleb did when he trusted that God would enable him to conquer the giants in Hebron [Joshua 14:12]. It is only such childlike confidence in God that can really please Him. Look at the giants in your life, and thank God for the opportunity they present to prove His power and grace today. Speak faith under your breath. Let it become the habit of your tongue, and the instinct of your heart.

February 10

"Then those who feared the Lord spoke to one another, and the Lord listened..." [Malachi 3:16]

God takes us seriously when we speak encouraging words to one another - words that build each other up and glorify Him. Today you may be longing for a word or sign of encouragement from someone - a letter, a smile, a phone call. You may long for someone to say something to you that will encourage you in your walk with God. And God will surely send someone, for He loves you. But have you thought about being sent yourself? Go into the day and bring God's touch to people. The act of bringing God to others will itself strengthen you. When you speak the love of God to someone, you are privileged to overhear what God is saying to someone in need. It is so liberating to speak to people about His love and to know that He is listening and He will make what you say real to them, and let you share in that refreshing that they feel. Go out into the day carrying precious seed. You will return rejoicing.

February 11

"Come up here..." [Revelation 4:1]

John had just seen the Churches in Asia through the eyes of Christ [Revelation 2-3]. The seven Churches of Asia were his home Churches. John lived in Ephesus, and doubtless visited all of them regularly before his imprisonment on the island of Patmos. Now he had just seen some of the Churches as quite cold, lifeless, formal and declining, while others were in better shape but undergoing persecution. How grieved John must have felt. Then God showed him heaven, and caused him to know that nothing had changed on the eternal level. It doesn't matter whether our problems are big or small, they can overwhelm us if we lose sight of heaven. Come up here! Rise to hear the heavenly choir. Look up to see the throne and the sovereign Lord ruling the world. It is sometimes easier to recognise God's will and plan for others than for ourselves. God is in charge of all things affecting you. Trust Him, worship Him, love and adore Him.   Let your song today be the song of triumph.

February 12

"These all wait for You, that You may give them their food in due season." [Psalm 104:27]

Jehovah Jireh [Genesis 22:14] means 'the Lord will provide'. His people can be confident in Him - He will provide. Have we ever really paused to understand that this is not a blessing He extends to a few who have enough faith?   God provides for all that He has made.   He provides water and sunshine for every living thing, food for every bird, ant, lion, whale and shrimp. Every cup of water in the ocean, every thimbleful of earth is filled with living creatures.   All depend on a supply of sustenance, and God is the provider.   God is so bountiful and abundant in His ways, and He has created the world to live in abandoned dependence upon Him.   The birds cannot provide for themselves - they don't sow and reap, for they cannot. Mankind must sow and reap, but we must do so in joyous dependence on God. He cannot fail us, for to do that He would have to cease to be God.   No more can He forget you or fail you than He can cease to uphold the whole world of living things that He has made.   The creation waits on Him unconsciously, but to us is given the bliss of consciousness - of acting not by instinct, but by choice, and with full appreciation of God's greatness. Delight yourself in God, who cares for you this day.

February 13

"....yet without sin." [Hebrews 4:15]

This is one of the most well-known truths among God's people - that Jesus is the sinless One.   But have we grasped the implications? Jesus is without blemish, for no worry or fear ever crosses His brow, no shadow of a depressive thought ever darkens His heart. He never thinks a mean or vindictive thought about anyone. He is never selfish or hurt. All of these things are impossible to Him, for He cannot think evil. Jesus is holy, and He has been tested beyond our imagination and has stood the test. He is holy through and through. It is with such a One that we have fellowship.   He pities us, but does not extend to us sympathy, but hope.   He says to us quite simply: *'Follow Me'!* He knows the way through the maze, through the snares and temptations. He offers us the wonder of fellowship with a sinless life. We may not be sinless in this world, but we can turn away from our constant fellowship with mean, sinful thoughts and behaviour, and have fellowship with the most amazing Person and life imaginable. Holiness cannot be attained by striving, nor by teaching. Holiness is imparted to us as we fellowship with Jesus. What a moral strength can be ours if we will open our hearts to commune with Him.

February 14

"...desire the pure milk of the word, that you may grow thereby..." [1 Peter 2:2]

It is a strange exhortation: desire God's Word! It might seem that we should first be encouraged to read the Word, so that then we may come to desire it. But it is only if we first desire God's Word that we will ever read it. Here the Holy Spirit speaks to us that our desires are subject to the involvement of our will. God commands us to desire, therefore the possibility exists that I can stir myself up and do exactly what God says. This means that I am not to accept my moods, and resign myself to any state of mind or heart, as though it were all-powerful and sovereign. No! God's Word is over all, and if God tells me to desire something, then as I turn to Him in obedience, I will find that it is true. So stir yourself and yield yourself to what God says. To the lukewarm Church of Laodicea Jesus gave the command, "be zealous" [Revelation 3:19]. So much of what we expect the Holy Spirit to do is within our reach, if only we will stir ourselves and obey.

February 15

"There is another who bears witness of Me, and I know that the witness which He witnesses of Me is true." [John 5:32]

At first sight, this verse could seem as if Jesus was claiming that another proof He was from God is that God had told him so! Obviously, this is building one proof on another and so would constitute only one proof, not two. But Jesus did not mean that. He is not referring to something God had told Him, but to something God tells you and me. Jesus is speaking about the realm of the witness of the Spirit, and He says that something in our hearts confirms that what we are discovering is true. In fact, it is as if we are discovering something we have always known, only at last someone is making it plain to us. Corrie Ten Boom called the faculty of the witness of the Spirit 'your Knower'. Don't live just by rational pros and cons; rest in what you know from the Father. Jesus said, *"No one can come to Me unless the Father who sent Me draws Him. It is written in the prophets, 'And they shall all be taught by God.' "* [John 6:44-45]. This shows us that the witness in our hearts is not optional, but a vital faculty by which we draw near to God, and by which we learn the things of God. Our 'Knower' is refreshed continually as we listen and obey. If we dismiss the whisper in our hearts, we grow cold and Jesus seems distant. Obey the call of the Father in your heart.

February 16

"When His disciples heard it, they were greatly astonished, saying, 'Who then can be saved?' But Jesus looked at them and said to them, 'With men this is impossible, but with God all things are possible.' " [Matthew 19:25-26]

Notice the connection: the impossibility that we can save ourselves, and the promise of God that He will accomplish this for us. This is God's promise to His people - that He will enable us to do what we formerly found impossible. The difference lies in the coming of the Holy Spirit, and our reliance on Him. What do you find so impossible? Is it some besetting sin? Is it prayer? Is it some characteristic that you don't like about yourself? Is it some habit that you find impossible to overcome? Is it bearing witness to others? By the Spirit and by faith we are able to do all things, and this means things we find impossible, not things we were always able to do anyway! Christ looks on us and declares to us that we will do what we find utterly impossible. Do you feel defeated? Look to Christ and receive the Holy Spirit's ministry and power this day to do the impossible. *"By my God I can leap over a wall"*, said David [Psalm 18:29], and perhaps we dismiss this as being the exuberance of a young man! God will make our tired limbs dance for joy if we will stand up and believe His unfailing word.

February 17

"Call to Me, and I will answer you, and show you great and mighty things, which you do not know."
   [Jeremiah 33:3]

31

The force of this promise is in the fact of our incredible ignorance. How can it be that there are *"great and mighty things"* of which we are completely unaware? Mankind lived for centuries in total ignorance of electricity or nuclear power. We did not invent them - we discovered them. In the same way, Christians are on the verge of great discoveries about God and His kingdom - they are within reach. God has promised to make *"great and mighty things"* known to us. What, then, is the missing ingredient? Quite simply, it is hunger for God. A person who is hungry for God calls out, reaches out, stirs themselves to respond to the promise of God. Our ignorance cannot condemn us, but our indifference can only be described as criminal in the light of promises such as these. Stir yourself, call on the Lord, and let the adventure of discovery begin.

February 18

"...the fruit of the Spirit is love..." [Galatians 5:22]

God cannot create love. That is the startling truth. Love is a crop, God is the farmer, and we are the ground. God cannot snap His fingers and create a harvest of love. That would be like plastic wheat, or wax grapes - nice to look at, but inedible and unreal. God creates the conditions in which love flourishes, and those conditions are summed up by the words 'Holy Spirit'. It is the incredibly fertile Presence of God in us that produces a harvest of love. But it cannot be done without our co-operation. The honour of being a human being is that God has granted us to be His own children, with the image of God in our hearts. This is indeed an honour, but it also requires us to submit our wills joyfully to Him, and be indwelt and constantly filled with His love and holiness. The result is that love buds in our hearts, and we find that there is a further blessing than just *to be loved -* which is to love both God and other people. Truly this is blessedness - to be loved and to love.

February 19

"I counsel you to buy from Me gold..." [Revelation 3:18]

This echoes the cry in Isaiah 55:1 to buy 'wine without money'. This time Jesus is speaking to His Church. What is the currency by which we can transact with God? Clearly, worldly goods do not impress Him. The currency of heaven is the movement of our hearts towards God. This is why Jesus said this Church at

Laodicea was poor - because their hearts were motionless towards Him, neither hot nor cold. They were indifferent. Perhaps this is why Jesus spoke so harshly to them, to evoke a response that would last. For us the challenge is clear: keep your heart moving to God. Don't become passive and indifferent. Stir up your heart to lay hold of God's promises. Here the promise is that we can buy 'gold', which is character, built on genuine faith. Not only is this something money can't buy, it is of untold value. The soul that buys this has made a good investment, for the greatest yields come not in retirement, but in heaven!

February 20

"...that I may test them, whether they will walk in My law or not." [Exodus 16:4]

God is allowed to do what He wills, and He chooses in His divine pleasure to test us, to teach us to know our own hearts, and to lead us to abandon the way of self and unbelief and to follow His will. God has not got some strange plan - He is longing for us to live in a trusting, childlike obedience to Him. His ways are ways of love, and the New Testament teaches that the Spirit of God will lead us to walk in perfect love. Don't explain away the promptings of love in your heart, for God is leading us to know and obey His wonderful love, that can express itself through us as we yield to Him. God has not prepared hoops for us to jump through, but situations where we can be channels to express His love. God is leading us to know His love and to be united with Him in His love. To know the touch of His love and the leading of His love is the greatest blessing we can know. *"If you love Me, keep my commandments"* [John 14:15].

February 21

"But where sin abounded, grace abounded much more."
[Romans 5:20]

This is not the idea that sin makes God gracious - far from it! This is the declaration of the fact that sin's power is terrible and spreads like a rampant weed, but that the cross far exceeds the power of sin. We all know that sin is powerful; in fact it is common to us all that in our experience it is one of the most powerful things in this world. It invaded the world, bringing misery, destruction and death. There is only one thing more powerful than sin, and that is God. So God poured Himself out on the problem of sin and destroyed it in Himself. This act of God was so powerful and so effective, that it cannot really be compared with the power of sin. That is why the emphasis of this verse is *"much more"*. What God has done and has given us is much more than to counteract sin. Christ did not repress or weaken sin - He destroyed it in Himself, so that we might know the power of Him in us. People have been tyrannised so long that they live looking over their shoulders, expecting sin to raise its ugly head. We need a long, steady realisation that the grace of Christ is much more than enough to deliver us.

February 22

"He (the seed of the woman) *shall bruise your head, and you shall bruise His heel."* [Genesis 3:15]

These words were not spoken from some lofty ivory tower. They were spoken in the hour of mankind's greatest calamity. God's heart was breaking with sorrow at the failure of His beloved children. Many, if not all, of us have been hurt or filled with sorrow by the wrong decisions of those we love. We would want to protect them, to shield them from the consequences of their actions, but we cannot. But, through the grief that we experience as part of human existence, we can partake of the greatness of God's character as we learn to respond like Him. In this moment of deepest sorrow, God spoke in poetry - the language of the heart. His words were not condemning; they were promises that He would put all things right again. God's instant reaction was full of the mercy of Calvary. Remember this in your dark moments, either of personal failure, or grief at the failure of others. God will take the centre stage and declare the power of His Son to redeem and save. The cost is great, but God instinctively and instantly reacts with unfathomable love and grace. Let the poetry, the song of love, comfort you and give you hope. God will wipe away all your tears.

February 23

"Melchizedek .... was the priest of God Most High."
[Genesis 14:18]

To meet Melchizedek must have been an awesome experience. He was steeped in the Presence of God. The point here is that he is like Christ in His priesthood. Christ is a man of prayer just like Melchizedek, and that is a statement of the depth to which this man had attained. And, by the indwelling Christ, you have access to the same prayer life. It is yours by gift, not by striving. You have the Spirit of the praying Son of God in you and you are a person with direct, intimate access to God. You do not merely have to aspire to this - you must receive it as a revealed fact and begin to live it. We are all conscious of failure in prayer. Get beyond that. Get beyond the condemnation of falling short, and get into the Spirit of the One who carries you beyond what is humanly possible. You can dwell deep with God, drinking of His peace and love, beholding His face. This is your inheritance. The Lord has sworn and will not change His mind - you are a priest for ever after the order of Jesus Christ.

February 24

"Jesus, knowing that the Father had given all things into His hands..." [John 13:3]

How many of us look at Jesus and really see Him? Most of us generally look at Him through the veil of personal need. We look to Him to provide. We look to Him for comfort. But in this verse John looked at Jesus and perceived His authority and His majesty. We are to get beyond the fact that God identified with us, and to begin identifying with Him. His thoughts are truly not our thoughts, nor His ways our ways. But we are not to take this to mean that we will not change. We are to look at Him with freedom from self and need, and look to see what is in His heart and what He is seeking. If we look, we will know, for He is not inscrutable, nor does He seek to hide Himself. Jesus came to this world to make the Father's heart fully known. All He seeks is a heart that will really take time to search out and steadfastly look to Him, to know Him, and His heart's desire. All those who truly love Him will get to that place. Seek Him, and find that place today.

February 25

"Let Us make man in Our image..." [Genesis 1:26]

Mankind is made in the image of God, which means that there is something about us that is God-like. Clearly, it is not in knowledge or power or wisdom that we are God-like! It is in the fact that we have the capacity to love, the capacity for conscious thought, and the capacity for moral choice. By these we have fellowship with God, and by fellowship with God we discover the reason we are here - to know Him, love Him and serve Him for ever. The key to all these things is the point at which we depend on God, and this aspect of us is very unlike God, for He depends on no-one. We must lean on God, or else all our wonderful human qualities are ruined and distorted. You were made to trust and lean on God, and to be filled with His loving Spirit to make you all that He intends you to be.

February 26

"Enter by the narrow gate..." [Matthew 7:13]

The narrow gate is the cross of Jesus Christ, and the narrow path is the path of discipleship, which means taking up your cross daily. The point is that the narrow gate and path are a filter. The cross is a filter applied to our lives by the Holy Spirit. It is a filter through which we pass, and yet we come through still recognisable, but with the nature of sin removed. The filter removes things and at the same time imparts the love of God. Let your motives be sifted and filtered by the Holy Spirit; let the Holy Spirit's fire purify your motives and your emotions and your will. The result is that you enter into another realm, for the narrow gate is a gate into another world - another kingdom, where different values operate. The result of passing through this gate is liberation. We are freed from all the clutter of a worldly soul, and we find we can freely walk and have like-minded fellowship with the Son of God.

February 27

"What kind of conversation is this that you have one with another as you walk and are sad?" [Luke 24:17]

The risen Lord drew near to the two disciples who were travelling to Emmaus, but He was not recognised by them! His Presence was clouded from their sight by their own sadness and disappointment. They had sorrowful hearts, and had not believed the report of His resurrection. The years separate us from the event, but not from the Presence. It is the sadness or unbelief of our hearts that does that. Recognise Him, for He is risen, and He is near. Throw off the cloak of careless words and worldly atmosphere that stifle faith in your heart. He is able to dispel all the mists of our hearts and bring incredible hope to us.

Dare to take a long look at the One who may have been so long unrecognised in your daily walk. Let Him bless and break the bread with you, and you will recognise Him. Our hearts need revelation, and He is the One who opens our eyes. When He was revealed, He left them, but at the same time He promised them that He was still with them, though invisible. Don't look down; look up and see Him, for He is right there beside you.

February 28

"Hear my voice, O God, in my meditation"
   [Psalm 64:1]

What a test of our prayers! Don't just answer my words Lord, but hear and answer the tone of voice with which I pray! How often do we moan in a self-indulgent way, or sometimes delight with the selfish preoccupation of a child who has got its own way! Lord hear my voice, and let reverence be the spring from which I speak. Let love for God and for others fill my tones. Let strong confidence fill my voice like the trumpet that sounds the victory. Let my voice be filled with confident trust in the faithfulness of God. Truly, God answers a person's voice and not just the words they speak. We can change our words, but to change our voice we must humble ourselves in a radical way. We cannot pretend, for insincerity is revealed in the voice. We must start where we are, and let reality be in our voices from the outset, and mix this reality with the willingness to change our attitude and our ways. God loves to hear your voice - He loves to hear the real 'you' speak. So let Him hear your voice as you pray this day.

February 29

"...I am not worthy that you should enter under my roof."
   [Luke 7:6]

These are the words of one of the greatest men of faith who was alive during the years of Jesus' earthly ministry – the Roman centurion at Capernaum. We can see immediately that humility is the close friend of true faith. This man did not believe in himself, in his riches (and he must have been rich, to build a synagogue for the Jews!) or in any other gift or ability that he had. The healing of his slave was not a reward for anything he had done - it was a gift that was bestowed on him through faith. My hand may receive a gift, but it does not earn it! So, too, faith is the means to receive, not the virtue that earns. Though this man did not believe in himself, it does not mean that he hated himself. He had a balanced and accurate view of himself. A person who is filled with self-loathing is not virtuous and believing! This is a depressed condition, and is neither humble nor balanced. We are to see that we are helpless, but not abandoned; we are unable, but enabled. Faith may operate from terrible circumstances, but it has a joy of wondering confidence that He is good, and cannot fail the person who casts himself on God.

March 1

"Comfort....My people! ....Cry out to her, that her warfare is ended..." [Isaiah 40:1-2]

The Comforter, the Holy Spirit, is the One who cries out to the people of God, declaring the incredible power and victory of the cross. The battle of the ages has been fought, Satan's power has been destroyed, Christ has risen from the dead! The Holy Spirit has come to declare these things, in a way that makes the people of God rise up and enter into their inheritance. Once the Holy Spirit is in us, His work is not to tell us what we need to do. His work is to declare to us what God has done, and has fully completed. At the end of the Second World War, there were some soldiers in jungles or other remote areas, who carried on fighting the war, ignorant that it had finished. At last the news reached them: *'It's all over!'* The Christian can hear in his or her heart the constant cry: *'The battle is won, the victory is secure, Christ has sat down and has been crowned Lord of all'.* Let the Holy Spirit's joy fill you. He not only wells up in our hearts with joy, but He also shows us the reason for that joy, and in that light it is a crime to doubt or be downhearted. The war has ended! Christ has triumphed!

March 2

"...when He sees the blood on the lintel and on the two doorposts, the Lord will pass over the door and not allow the destroyer to come into your houses to strike you."
    [Exodus 12:23]

This is one of the magnificent facts of God's salvation of Israel. He stood in the door, and it was His Presence that kept the destroyer out. When we think of the blood of Christ, we must not think of some superstitious power that keeps us. No, the power is the Person and Presence of God. Satan is terrified of God, and flees His Presence. God sees the blood of Jesus that has washed our hearts, and He comes to us. And there is no power in heaven or hell that can raise its voice against the living God beholding the sacrifice of His Son. If we think superstitiously about the things of God we grow weak, but if we think rightly of His glory and majesty, and of His total identification with us because of Jesus, then we sense the burning fury of God against our enemies. The devil trembles at the mention of the blood, because he knows that God the Father will never forget it, but that He continually looks upon it, and stands over His people defying any power to contradict what Jesus has done.

March 3

"He shall take some of the blood....and sprinkle it with his finger on the mercy seat"
     [Leviticus 16:14-15]

This is one of the most awesome moments of the Jewish calendar - the height of Yom Kippur, the Day of Atonement. The High Priest approached the Most Holy Place, pushed aside the veil and did the unthinkable - he entered God's direct, unveiled, immediate Presence. He had a bowl and he sprinkled blood with his finger onto the place where God's Presence was located. Effectively, he was sprinkling the blood onto God. He would have been trembling as He did so, conscious no doubt of his sins. Hebrews 9:8 tells us that this teaches that the way to God was not yet open. But Christ has come, and has taken His blood into heaven, and there presented it to the Father. He has never retreated from that place, and we follow Him in. On the cross Christ reconciled us perfectly so that we might approach God boldly - not with bravado, but with trembling wonder at the mercy and holiness of Almighty God, who so longs for fellowship with us, that He has gone to these lengths to bring us back to Himself. How can we honour Him? Believe in His blood and come freely to our loving Father, and enter into His welcoming, loving embrace. You are right with God by the blood of His Son, and you cannot only approach His Presence, but you can live there all your days.

March 4

"Walk in the Spirit, and you shall not fulfill the lust of the flesh." [Galatians 5:16]

Here Paul gives the principle by which we overcome 'the flesh'. The first vital point is that it is not by confronting the flesh that we overcome its lusts. We must turn our hearts completely to the Lord, and fix our gaze on Him and on obeying the whisper of the Spirit in our conscience. By walking in the Spirit, we find we are filled with the Holy Spirit. The whole realm of walking in the Spirit is achieved by waiting on God's Presence in our hearts and treasuring the life-giving perfume of His love. As soon as we turn to the Lord, the flesh will lose its power, and all the tyrannising force of carnal desires will evaporate in the face of the pure desires that are the very atmosphere of the Holy Spirit. If we confront the flesh without the Presence of God, we will quickly find ourselves entangled in a battle that we cannot win. The Bible does not suggest several methods to overcome the flesh, and leave us to choose the one that suits us best. The Bible teaches us the one and only method. Overcoming the flesh does not require a strong will, but it does require an **obedient** will. Don't whine about the power of your 'flesh'; turn your back on it, with all the defeats and shame it brings, and walk by faith in inner sensitivity to the Presence of the Lord through the Holy Spirit.

March 5

"...those who are Christ's have crucified the flesh with its passions and desires." [Galatians 6:24]

We do not need to have a hammer and nails in our hands to fulfil this verse, but we do need to have fervency of spirit, and to forsake absolutely a self- and pleasure-centred life, in order to attain the goal of a Christ-centred life. There was no mercy in the act of crucifixion, and the Christian must not deal mercifully with sin, in whatever form it may present itself to us. If we deal uncertainly with temptation, we shall find no mercy in the flesh - it will bite the hand that feeds it. Victory is never far away - it is only a turn away. We must turn our back on sin, forsaking it with all our heart, and receiving that fragrant perfume of Christ. Once His Presence touches us, we are instantly aware that the flesh is totally powerless before Him. Try and face two directions, and the flesh will instantly triumph. The power to walk in the Spirit is given to you, so turn with all your heart and walk. When you walk in the Spirit you may not at first realise that you have instantly overcome the flesh, because God's way is to fill our vision with Himself and cause us to overcome by keeping our eyes on Him, not on our temptations.

March 6

"...Jesus of Nazareth, who was a prophet mighty in deed and word before God and all the people." [Luke 24:19]

The two words *"before God"* are what mark someone out as different. To live before God indicates the right order in life.

What we take as obvious for Jesus must become the foundation of our lives. A person who lives before God may not be easy to explain or to pin down. They will baffle us because they are obeying Another, and are not living to please or impress other people. At the same time, they are extraordinarily uncomplicated, child-like and transparent. To live before God indicates child-like simplicity and trust. This is powerful living because it is rooted in the fear of God. Note that our words and deeds in prayer and righteous living are first powerful before God. They touch Him, and, as He wills, He gives us words and supernatural deeds of power to speak and do before people. Reverse the order and the result is disastrous. If we seek to appear mighty before people, we will constantly be victims of what they think of us, and this will be a breeding ground for hypocrisy and evil. Let your power be in your words and deeds before God first.

March 7

"...that at the name of Jesus every knee should bow..."
    [Philippians 2:10]

It is clear that one day every knee shall bow to Jesus. On that day it will be evident that every human being lives before God, because the resurrection of all - just and unjust - will have taken place. God will then command all the spirits of unbelieving people and devils to bow before Jesus. Whether kicking or screaming, they will all obey. But we must not believe that God does not yet have this power. He does have this power now. When God invites or suggests, we may refuse, but when God commands, whether it be in a whisper or with a voice of thunder, what He says will immediately take place. The commands of God are not mere thoughts or suggestions - they are spiritual events; they create, they form, they seize hold of people. God is the LORD, He alone is God, and there is no other. He alone has authority. See all your enemies under His feet. All is subject to Him, whether willingly or not. For us, we bow with joy, we seek and love His rule and pray with all our hearts: 'Your kingdom come, O Lord!'

March 8

"For God so loved the world that He gave..." [John 3:16]

The tense of this sentence seems wrong when we realise that

42

Jesus spoke these words to Nicodemus three years before the cross. Why then did Jesus use the past tense? He was referring to the explanation of all that He would do and will ever do. Before time began, God gave His Son and offered Him up as the act of grace that is the underlying bedrock of His act of creating the human race. Grace did not begin at the cross. Grace flows from eternity, when God gave His Son and the Son gave Himself up to the Father's will, to be the sacrificial provision for our wholeness as human beings. God saw each one of us from the dawn of time, and loved us, and was full of grace towards us. God so loved that He created the world; God so loved that He called Israel; God so loved that He speaks to us. God so loves, and that is measured by the act that lies at the foundation of the universe. Let the breathtaking love of God be the foundation of all that you are. You are invited to become one with God, by offering yourself up to the Father through the Son. Once this is sealed in your life, all your acts and deeds can flow from that grace and love. Let your offering up of yourself be as total as the offering of Jesus before the foundation of the world, and grace will be the fountain-head from which all your future battles will be fought. You will be able to give because you have been given to. Grace and love can be the tone of your lives because God has so loved you.

March 9

"...Father, glorify Me together with Yourself..."
    [John 17:5]

At first this prayer seems uncharacteristically selfish, since Jesus was praying for His own glory. But we need to understand it in the same way as someone who says to a guest: *"Honour me with your presence."* Jesus' prayer is based on a sense of the Father's greatness and glory. It is full of the fear and love of God. Jesus' prayer is centred on the Being and Person of the Father. This prayer is astoundingly simple; it is really: *"I love you!"* The prayer goes on to develop this passion, asking for the wonder of the indwelling of the Father to be extended to the disciples, and to all those who will believe in Jesus. This is His prayer for Himself and for us: *"Swallow Me up in Yourself, Father, and swallow up these also!"* Echo this prayer. Present yourself and be swallowed up into the Person of God the Father. We swallow the bread and wine in the communion, and this represents what God wants to do with us, as much as what we want to do with Him. In fact the act is mutual - we drink Him and He drinks us

43

in. To be filled with God is God's will for our lives.

March 10

"In the name of Jesus Christ of Nazareth, rise up and walk."
[Acts 3:6]

The key word of Jesus' ministry to need-bound human beings is, *'Rise!'* This is not a command to climb the rungs of the ladder or the steps of the tower that leads to God. Firstly, the distance we would need to climb would be too great. Secondly, we would always fail to reach the top in our own strength. The word 'rise' is the word of resurrection. It is the same word that Jesus used when he commanded the dead to rise [Mark 5:41 and Luke 7:14]. The word of the gospel is that we are to rise out of our fallen and paralysed condition, into the glory of resurrection, and there to walk and live. When God's Presence and blessings seem unattainable, don't be downhearted or discouraged, for they **are** unattainable by our own strength. That is the point. Step out of the narrow world of unbelief, into the wide world of His very life and Person. Grace comes to us every day with the power of resurrection, and in a moment we are there. Rise up and walk!

March 11

"Keep silence before Me, O coastlands, and let the people renew their strength!" [Isaiah 41:1]

We tend, naturally, to be both afraid of silence and yet drawn to it. Silence can bring the dawning realisation that our hearts are empty and dry. The immediate temptation is to fill the void with noise and activity that bear some resemblance to spiritual life. Thus, Christian meetings are filled with music, noise and praises. All these are good things in their right place, but not if they cover up spiritual dryness, since they cannot of themselves satisfy our deep longing for God. In the silence, we must face ourselves as we are, and let our hearts come to calm and peace before God. Every person longs for this calm as the basis for communion, the place of revelation and the creating touch of the Holy Spirit. The Spirit of Christ is always full of great calm and peace. It is the place from which He lived and spoke on earth, without hurry or stress, and with infinite authority. Silence is not an infallible method of renewing our strength, but it is the basis for faith to operate, and for God's touch and word

44

to reach us. Still the constant churning of your mind. Come to silence, look up to Christ, and let Him renew your strength.

March 12

"Now faith is the substance of things hoped for..."
    [Hebrews 11:1]

There is a vital connection between faith and hope. Hope is the seedbed of faith. When hope stirs in our heart, faith will soon come.   Hope is the hand that reaches out to grasp God's extended hand, and faith lays hold of it.   We cannot bypass hope as if it were a lesser thing. It is a God-given stirring of our heart that dares to see things that are not yet seen. You may not be able to believe that someone who is far from God may come to know Him, or that an impossible situation may be solved. But dare to think it - allow the Holy Spirit to make you dream, and see things that are afar off. The Holy Spirit gives dreams and visions, not to tease, but to stir our hearts to co-operate with God in the creation of a new humanity.   God speaks to our hearts, and we must receive His word as the transforming power that it is. God first gives hope, and then, as hope is nourished, faith rises and takes hold of God for that thing. It will happen as surely as a tender plant reaches out to the sun. There are laws in spiritual life, and this is one of them. So nourish your heart in hope, dare to dream and think the impossible, and turn your dreams into prayer before God's throne.

March 13

"So God created man in His own image..."
    [Genesis 1:27]

This is one of the greatest statements about mankind in the Bible. It refers to the origin of mankind. Mankind did not begin in sin, nor did we begin in some primitive form, coming out of the jungles! Mankind in its original state was much more than it is now. We were created to bear the stamp of the divine in our life and character.   In that perfect state, there was no sin or death, no sickness or suffering, no distortion of any kind. The human mind was clear and many times more powerful than it is now. So, what we are now is a shadow of what we were meant to be. The purpose of God has never changed, and though our lives now are limited by our bodily dullness, by a life shortened by death, yet God's purpose for us has never changed.   He

45

intends us to bear the image and stamp of Himself. The redemption of the cross is clearly in two parts - the first in our inner life, to restore us to fellowship with God, and the second in bodily life, to release us from death, with all the sickness and pain associated with it. This second part will only be ours in perfection at our resurrection, and so today we live in the experience of inner release from sin and, by that, with assurance of our full release at Jesus' return. His will is that you be like Him. Embrace it today with faith for the present and hope for the future.

March 14

"So God created man in His own image..." [Genesis 1:27]
"...man became a living being." [Genesis 2:7]

The image of God in our lives means that we have a consciousness, a thought-life, that can have fellowship with God. This unity of consciousness means that when I close my eyes I am conscious of myself and can be conscious of God, and share my life with Him. I can understand Him and know Him. This is because the human soul, though it is limited, is designed to embrace the eternal God. Truly, we are a strange mixture of glory and clay. We know our clay! But we must also know the glory, and that is to entertain God in the house of our inner life. See your life for what it is - a house with an inner room like the Temple or the Tabernacle. That inner room is the key that gives meaning to the whole of the house. If the inner room is neglected, or even misused, then the house is a ruin, but when it is cleaned and used to receive the Presence of the King, the whole house hums with a purpose, and songs of joy echo through the windows. Your mind was designed to think of God, and your soul was designed to be indwelt by God.

March 15

"So God created man in His own image..." [Genesis 1:27]
"...God is love." [1 John 4:8]

Mankind in the image of God means that we are in the image of love. Love is the most powerful thing in the universe, and when Adam and Eve sinned, it became the most distorted and yet still the most powerful thing in the human life. Love twisted into selfishness is the twisting of all that is good into a monster. Anger, lust, envy and covetousness are all manifestations of this twisted monster. We are powerful beings! The Holy Spirit sets us free from the horror of sin, and restores us to the true image of God, to love Him, to love others, and to be free from worry about our own lives and comfort. The greatest joy is to be released to love others, and the greatest power is to be patient when we are wronged, and not to feel resentful. This is God's powerful plan for us - to make a people who can have fellowship with Him and show forth His nature and His glory.

March 16

"So God created man in His own image..." [Genesis 1:27]
"...therefore choose life..." [Deuteronomy 30:19]

God created us with the power of moral choice. There is, of course, great controversy over this conundrum. If God is sovereign, what choice can we really have? The truth is that only God has absolute free will, and for that we can be thankful! However, in His sovereign grace He has shared this divine characteristic with us. He grants us moral choice. True, it is limited, and we cannot choose where and when we are born or we die, nor our eye colour, height, brain size, parents etc. However, we can choose between right and wrong, and we must. Not only do we have the **power** to choose, we have the **obligation** to choose - it is unavoidable. We would all like to sit on the fence, blur all the issues and let them pass us by as if we never fully knew. The priest, the Levite and the good Samaritan did not want to have to make a choice as to whether or not to help their suffering fellow man [Luke 10:30-37]. But when confronted with the facts, to do nothing or something was the greatest moral choice they could make. Opportunities to exercise our free will are frequent. It is a God-given dignity. Use it today for the glory of God.

March 17

"Our Father, in heaven..." [Matthew 6:9]

These words are too familiar to modern Bible readers to convey the audacity of this statement. The concept of God as a loving, caring Father is foreign to most religions, but it is the foundation of the Christian gospel that God invites us to become His sons. This sonship is even more astonishing than God's Fatherhood. God may be considered a Father, but to call Him our actual Father is to claim a kinship, a bond, a likeness. This is Jesus' goal - to bring us to be sons of the Father and enter into all the wonder of sonship. Jesus alone among human beings enjoyed this true Sonship, and He died to make us sons of God, so that we might call God 'Father'. This is not a sentimental form of words. This is to be the fact of our beings as regenerated people, that we are like God in nature, and born of His Spirit, bearing oneness with Him in our hearts. Also, our Father is in heaven. In other words, we have an origin in heaven through new birth. New birth interrupts our life at a point in time, and it plants our lives in eternity with God in heaven. The loving, heavenly Father is MY Father. My soul is linked to God like a kite is drawn to the skies by strong winds. Call Him Father, and do so with the delight and wonder of all that this adoption means to us.

March 18

"Hallowed be Your name." [Matthew 6:9]

The first thing we are to pray for is that the Father's name may be sanctified - set apart for honour and devotion. The German Pentecostal pioneer Jonathan Paul had a remarkable gift of healing. Once, when he prayed for a man, he asked him, *"For whose glory do you want to be healed?"* With this right foundation established, he was enabled to reach out to God and receive the man's healing. This question should undergird all our prayers. For whose glory will the answer to this prayer be? Is my heart fixed on the glory of God or on my own comfort? God's purpose is that His own name be glorified. This is not because God is seeking to be the first in the queue! God knows that we humans are damaged by the intensity of the selfishness of sin. While our needs may be great, our greatest need is to be released from the cycle of selfishness. Our goal must be His glory - to proclaim His goodness, love, and power. Paul prayed that God would be glorified whether by His life or His death [Philippians 1:20]. Paul's prayer was not vague - it was fervent, passionate and clear: *"Hallowed be Your name"*. Once we get hold of this prayer, we are released from all doubt about what we should pray for. Many prayers will wither and die on our lips because they are not for His glory. Once God is glorified, our hearts will swell with triumphant faith, flowing from pure motives.

March 19

"Your kingdom come..." [Matthew 6:10]

This is the second prayer of the believer, and once more it is not for us, it is for God. This prayer is for the rule of God to extend first to the one praying. Submission of all that we are is one of the most Christ-like qualities that we must put on, and it is the foundation of this prayer. God's rule is full of the mercy and goodness of His nature. Where God spreads His kingdom, there too He spreads His direct care. God takes full responsibility for all that He rules. He is a Father over His kingdom, not a chief executive officer. God is the King of Love, and His kingdom is a kingdom of love. As we bow in prayer, God's rule is extended over us and through us, with all the healing and power of the Person of God. God's kingdom is not weighted down with bureaucracy. Every member of the kingdom knows the King and is personally related to Him. To be in this kingdom is to be in righteousness, peace and joy in the fullness of the Holy Spirit. Truly, Your kingdom come, Lord!

March 20

"Your will be done..." [Matthew 6:10]

We are given the grace of playing a role in our destiny through the gift of free will. Whether we like it or not, we have to make choices all the time, and we cannot blame any other will for what we have chosen. Most of the time people are passive and allow choices to be made on their behalf, allowing life to flow over them. Though they may not be aware of it, this is an exercise of their will. Doing nothing is the action of negligence and it is as morally wrong as any misuse of the will. There is only one right use of free will, and that is to return it to the One who gave it. This must be done initially in an act of surrender to the will of God, but it must also be renewed every day, as we surrender to God what is rightfully His. This is not the abdication of our will in order to be passive. It is the engagement of our will to co-operate with and yield to the will of God. Sometimes this is called commitment. Our hearts must be set on obedience to this wonderful will and plan of God. As we surrender to His will, we find the power of a new heart, which includes a new will, flowing into us, working in us to will and to do His good pleasure.

49

March 21

"On earth as it is in heaven." [Matthew 6:10]

This encompasses the whole prayer of the believer. There are states that people live in, which God does not intend for us. By the work of the cross, a door has been opened in Christ for us to partake of the power of the age to come, and this includes enjoyment of the states of heaven in our lives here and now. While we may often hear the voice of caution, that reminds us of our imperfections, yet we also need to meditate on this prayer that Jesus taught us to pray, that heaven would come down. What is the greatest thing about heaven? Quite simply, that God is known, He is unveiled, and His name and nature are declared. On earth there is ignorance about God; even in Churches, sometimes things are said and done in ways that are simply not truly representative of God. Where God is unveiled there is not merely excitement, there is deliverance from all the petty doubts and fears and small-mindedness of earth. Human glory looks like year-old bread in the light of His Presence. Money, whether it is abundant or lacking, becomes a non-issue. God is enough, and we are to know Him and make Him known. This is heaven on earth.

March 22

"Give us this day our daily bread." [Matthew 6:11]

This prayer contains at first sight what seems a needless repetition. *"This day"* and *"daily"* convey in English almost identical thoughts. But Jesus uses a unique word here, which Campbell Morgan translates as the 'bread of existence', or the 'bread that keeps us going on'. Notice that God is providing our sustenance both physically and spiritually in a way that keeps us moving forward, looking to Him. If we have enough to live on for the rest of our lives, we do not need to pray this prayer - in fact we can dispense with God for our physical needs! This thought should strike a chill into our bones - that we could ever live independently of God. God does not want to give us beyond our immediate need, so that we will live in constant dependence on Him. As we do so, we are sure to go on with God. This is the only explanation of why we often go through periods of leanness; since it is only through this that we will lift up our eyes in trust to our Provider God. Rejoice because all that you need today will be provided. Tomorrow's needs can be

50

forgotten till the new day has dawned. Learn to live in child-like abandon and watch the oil of joy flow in as you go on with God.

March 23

"And forgive us our debts, as we forgive our debtors."
[Matthew 6:12]

The Lord here teaches us to pray a prayer that He never prayed. He never needed forgiveness, so it is a sign of His incredible love and identification with us, as if He were saying, *"If I were you, this is what I would pray."* God completely identifies with us in our weakness and understands us. The need that is addressed here is our need to have a clear conscience towards all others. Our joy and walk with God is dimmed if we have unfinished business - hurts we have caused, or foolish words we have spoken, or sins we have committed. The peace of God is for those who will be constantly watchful to ask for forgiveness from God and people, and to dispense it freely and completely to those who have wronged us in any way. It is no use covering bad relationships up as if they will just disappear; we must persist and ensure that relationships are fully healed as much as lies in our power. A letter or a phone call may bring release to someone else, but it will also bring release to us. Jesus is teaching that all of life is two-way flow and that we cannot ignore things we have done to others, nor dare we refuse to forgive anyone who has wronged us. The power of right relationships with others is measured by the boldness it gives us in prayer and the power of a right relationship with God.

March 24

"And do not lead us into temptation, but deliver us from the evil one." [Matthew 6:13]

This is a prayer for deliverance, and as such it is simple and direct. Believers are not slaves of Satan, but how quickly we get entangled in things that bind us to some pattern of thought or feeling. Our lives are complex, and our liberty in Christ is maintained by God's constant deliverance from snares that are in our way. This prayer expresses what believers must constantly be conscious of - that we are able to continue in liberty only by the mercy of God. We do not know ourselves, and we do well not to boast too loudly about how spiritual or holy we are. We need deliverance, and God will provide it for the person who walks with Him. If we yield to temptation then we need deliverance to set us back on the right track. Watch the areas of your own particular weakness, whether it be in imagination or in pride of heart. Watch the things that trip you up, and pray for wisdom and understanding so that you may be delivered from the snares of sin. This prayer shows the true humility of the disciple, praying daily for cleansing so that we may be able to abide in the Presence of Jesus.

March 25

"Your prayer is heard..." [Luke 1:13]

This is an astonishing fact that the angel communicated to Zachariah. He was explaining that events were unfolding because Zachariah had prayed. This is remarkable, because these were probably prayers of the distant past, when Zachariah and Elizabeth had some hope that they would be able to have a child. Now Zachariah had stopped praying and had certainly stopped believing. But this did not hinder his former prayers, spoken in faith, from being answered. Let this be an encouragement to you to persist in prayer. Our prayers are recorded and stored up with God, awaiting the time of their fulfilment. Learn from this story and let your prayers go up before the Lord in abandoned joy and faith. Ask for the impossible - for the barren womb to bring forth even in old age. God is the God of the impossible, and it is the humanly impossible that drives us to prayer. God begins His great works with people who are barren and weak, and it is from the position of such weakness that we pray. And remember, all your prayers have been stored up with God, like seeds that will bring forth harvest in His time.

March 26

"Lord, remember me when you come into your kingdom."
  [Luke 23:42]

Of all the prayers in the Bible, this is one of the greatest. It was spoken in such weakness, it was vague, but it was so powerful in its effect, since it was immediately answered. Christ's answer was to give this sinner an immediate assurance of eternal life. This is the prayer that each of us must obtain an answer to. This is the greatest promise that we can ever receive. What was the key to this answered prayer? The key lies in the attitude of the one praying. He had true fear of God - he believed that he was guilty and without hope apart from the mercy of God. He hardly expected such a mighty answer, but presented his prayer as the cry of his heart. These are the ingredients of effective prayer. When we pray from a place of absolute weakness, casting ourselves only on God's mercy, and crying to Him from our heart, God cannot turn us away. Such prayer must and will be answered with all the personal authority of the Son of God. Throw away your casual attitude in prayer, tear it up, and talk to Him from your heart. He is longing to hear you truly pray.

March 27

"...tell me where you have laid Him, and I will take Him away."
   [John 20:15]

Mary Magdalene had come to Jesus' tomb without a thought of the stone that blocked the entrance. Now that the stone had been rolled away, Mary still sought for His body, with a heart so full of love that she did not consider the difficulty of lifting and handling Jesus' body. Her cry was for Him, even though it was only His outer shell that she could find. Mary loved Jesus, and this moment goes to the heart of all that the gospel is about. There was nothing merely theological or technical, not even religious, in Mary's response. She longed to anoint Jesus' body as a last act of farewell to that matchless Presence, that loving teacher, that commanding voice, that healing hand. The gospel is not an idea - it is a person, it is Jesus. Perhaps the apostles loved Him with the same breaking heart. But something held them back from this abandoned worship that filled Mary's heart. Perhaps it was rational caution. Perhaps it was raw fear for their lives. But Mary was blinded with longing to touch Him with kindness again, and to be drawn close to that wondrous sense that all is well and all will be well, because He is. Salvation is found, not in a doctrinal emphasis, but in a life poured out at the feet of Jesus, to receive His forgiveness and His Lordship over all that I am and shall ever be. Will you take Him today? Will you let your heart be surprised by the fact that He is waiting to take you this day? Don't let caution or the opinions of others hold you back from pouring yourself out in worship before Him.

March 28

"Then Jacob was left alone..." [Genesis 32:24]

Nearly everything that really counts in a person is done alone with God. Moses spent long years contemplating God in the wilderness, and that prepared him for his divine encounter at the burning bush. Moses later received the Law, alone with God on the mountain. Jesus conquered temptation alone with God in the wilderness. Our greatest and most significant battles must be fought alone, when we are not moved by any audience, or by pressure from others. We must face our problems alone with God. The point is that alone with God we are freed from religious pretence. This takes time, since the last thing that we want is to be forced to face up to what we are really like. It might be scary at first, because we know in our hearts that we are in a worse condition than we have ever admitted. We secretly think that we might face something about ourselves that will disqualify us. The truth is that when we get alone with God, it slowly dawns on us that it does not matter how bad we are, since God is there to change us. Alone with God we are able to yield to Him who draws us, without threats, into His loving embrace, where all our awkwardness is absorbed into Him and we are changed for ever. After being alone with God, we will never be the same again.

March 29

"Blessed is the man whose strength is in You, whose heart is set on pilgrimage." [Psalm 84:5]
"And thus you shall eat it (the Passover): *with a belt on your waist, your sandals on your feet, and your staff in your hand."*
[Exodus 12:11]

This instruction from the Lord teaches that the right attitude for heart fellowship with Him is one of being on a pilgrimage - a journey in search of God and His kingdom. Jesus told his apostles that their ministry was a journey and they were to dress for it [Matthew 10:9-10]. It is to be a journey with no return, like the Exodus. The whole deliverance from Egypt was meaningless unless the people immediately departed from Egypt. What use is salvation unless the saved person turns their back on the world and sets out to find the fullness of God in Christ? Salvation was to be the beginning of emigration. They were to leave behind the culture of Egypt, the mentality of slavery and the cruelty of oppression. We must learn the lessons of journeying. First, travel light - being encumbered with the cares of this life will slow down your progress. Second, fix your eyes on the goal - the Promised Land, the promises of God. Our goal is God, not just heaven. Third, to survive the rigours of the wilderness journey, we will need a rugged attitude, and a care for the weak and vulnerable. There will be days when we ourselves will need help, so while we are strong we should seek to help and encourage others on their journey with God. Are you still set on pilgrimage and dressed for the journey, or have you settled down in some quiet spot and forgotten the challenge of the quest? Renew your journeying spirit, and let the Holy Spirit fire you with the anticipation of wonderful things to come for those who really leave the world behind.

March 30

"To you it was shown, that you might know that the Lord Himself is God; there is none other besides Him."
    [Deuteronomy 4:35]

God is God! This is the greatest concept that we can ever think about - a Being Who is dependent on no other person or power. God does not breathe to live - He is. He does not come from any source, since He is the source and origin of all things [Isaiah 43:10, 44:6]. Unbelievers often ask: *"Who made God?"* This question reveals the weakness of the human mind to imagine a Being without source. Revelation 22:1 describes a river flowing from God's throne. Where does the water come from? It is not a trickle but a mighty flood. It waters the whole earth, and beyond this fact is the truth that the whole universe is created and upheld by Almighty God. The river reveals the immensity of the fact of God. He flows with ceaseless supply, with resources that come from within His Being. He can create as much or as little as He wishes. He can create a thousand universes as easily as one, or a million! How big is God? This is impossible to answer; the Bible declares that He is ONE [Deuteronomy 6:4]. His size is irrelevant, since the greatest fact is that He is God. Such a Being is incapable of being reduced to a symbol or image. Idolatry in all its forms - even Christian forms - dishonours God and must be renounced. Pictures of Jesus can never convey a true sense of who He is. Let the Holy Spirit expand your faith so that you may know that Jesus is God.

March 31

"Remember this day in which you went out of Egypt, out of the house of bondage..." [Exodus 13:3]

Do we remember? Yes, there are many things that we would like to change in our lives, but the fact of our deliverance from the power of sin and the condemnation of hell should change our whole approach to life. The person who continually remembers that they are set free from the power of evil feels relief, joy and wonder. The person who forgets may feel all the same small-minded frustrations that characterised their life in bondage. Don't forget; remember the darkness, the loneliness, the heaviness, the despair and lack of hope. Remember the power of sins forgiven and the fresh discovery of the Presence of Christ. God has not changed, but we drift. The devil knows he cannot sink our ship, so he destroys the compass. The compass is the assurance and wonder of our salvation. Pick it up and repair it. Clean the glass, oil the mechanism. Remember, and keep remembering.

April 1

"Your throne, O God, is forever and ever..."
    [Hebrews 1:8]

The greatest thing that can be said about Jesus is that He is God. Thomas was the only one of the disciples to make this confession, when he said at the resurrection appearance of Jesus: *"My Lord and my God!"* [John 20:28]. We often think that Thomas was a doubter. Perhaps he was struggling with the realisation that Jesus must Himself be Almighty God. Perhaps his faith was pressing through to a confession that would take his spiritual life into a wholly new dimension. Sometimes our confession of faith is too routine. Do we truly realise the implications of this confession? Christ is God, and that means He is infinite, eternal, unchangeable and almighty. In the light of Who He is, adjectives like just 'mighty' become totally inappropriate. He is not powerful, He is all-powerful. He is not strong, He is the Creator of heaven and earth. He does not have great authority, He is the eternal judge of all human beings, with the power of life, death and hell, and holds everyone's destiny in His hands. Confess Him as your personal Lord, but at the same time realise that He is Lord of all, and He is God. Worship Him and remember that there is nothing that is kept back from Him. He is everywhere, all-knowing and all-wise. The word 'infinite' is the best adjective to use in order to try to express the absence of boundaries in His life. He is God.

April 2

"...in the days of his flesh, when He [Jesus] *had offered up prayers and supplications, with vehement cries and tears to him who was able to save him from death, and was heard because of his godly fear..."*
    [Hebrews 5:7]

These verses refer to the Garden of Gethsemane, and the conflict of the ages that was battled out there. Jesus' prayer was heard, which indicates that He was not praying in the garden to escape the cross. He was praying that He would be strengthened to overcome the sorrow of His soul, and not die of grief there in the garden. His prayer was heard, and an angel appeared to Him, strengthening Him [Luke 22:43]. What sorrow was this that was threatening to tear the very life out of Him? There can be no doubt that the cross was agony, but there was also unspeakable agony there in the garden, as He prayed through and was made able to bear that cross to the end and be made sin for us. The anguish of God over the state of the human race, is the anguish of love that is torn asunder over our misery and pain. How He longed to do something that would thoroughly heal the human heart. That is what tore Him apart, and that is what Calvary is all about. The victory was won there in Gethsemane as Christ embraced the answer for us, namely that He be made an offering for sin. He did it, and it is finished. Thank Him and embrace Him in His redeeming power to heal you from sin.

April 3

"...exhausted but still in pursuit." [Judges 8:4]

These words capture the greatness of Gideon. He was exhausted, or 'faint' (KJV), and that means that all his body was screaming at him to give in, that he deserved a rest, that he had done enough for one day. But Gideon simply went on, and doubtless risked his life in the process. The final push is the one that we make with our last strength, and it is what we do with our last strength that will decide whether we will have total victory. It is not that Gideon showed us that we must be super-human; he showed us we must be clear in our hearts that there is nothing else but victory that consumes us. Defeat is not an option; allowing little sins to trip us up is not to be entertained. Obstacles serve to exercise us; they are not the barrier to our progress. They are there to 'flex the muscles' of our minds and spirits to push on further. Some people faint when there is absolutely no need. Fainting is then a means of drawing attention to their pain and strain. Gideon despised the pain and stress of his body and soul, and pressed on, not seeking an audience. It is the same with Christ - there is not even the slightest hint of fatigue in His words - He pressed on. Press on, and press home the victory.

April 4

"...whoever of you does not forsake all that he has cannot be my disciple." [Luke 14:33]

Here we see the absoluteness of discipleship. The demands of Christ in discipleship are simple - He expects total, undeviating devotion. This should not be surprising, since it is the very same way that He loves the Father. The declaration of His demands always strikes to the very heart of our priorities, and reveals other things to which we are bound. A fanatic is not devoted to Christ, but to the idea of Christ. Obedience to a cause is always easier than obedience to Christ, since we can plan our approach to promoting a cause. Obedience to Christ, however, is under His Lordship. Disciples know that their heart state must be consistent with their claims of devotion. But His claims are so absolute that they are impossible to attain by human devotion alone. Any reader of the New Testament will quickly conclude that, before Pentecost, the disciples failed in their devotion. Fear and self-preservation gripped them, and they failed. Admission of failure and its causes is the first step in true discipleship. Before we face up to this, we live in a delusion of our own abilities, and we are headed for a fall. God's work is to bring us to be truly disciples, and the first step is to bring us to brokenness and awareness of His power.

April 5

"...they said to him, 'You are not also one of His disciples, are you?' He (Peter) denied it and said, 'I am not!' " [John 18:25]

Peter's words show the impossibility of discipleship. Peter said them only hours after protesting and affirming his devotion to Jesus Christ even to death. But here he spoke the opposite: *"I am not"*. These words echo the great *'I ams'* of Jesus in John's Gospel. Peter 'was not' in terms of spiritual life and the power to love - he lacked being, he needed power to live. God's choice of people is based on their willingness to face themselves in the searching light of the Holy Spirit. Peter faced reality at this point, and he realised his need of a miracle in his being. True disciples have not merely received an anointing that sets them apart. They have been broken, and are aware of their own weakness. This brokenness releases the power of the Holy Spirit, and for this reason our spiritual power is in relation to our brokenness. Peter never again trusted in his own power of devotion. He drew from the total devotion of the Holy Spirit to Jesus. The Holy Spirit loves Jesus, and is the source and power of true discipleship.

April 6

"...you cannot follow Me now, but you shall follow Me afterward." [John 13:36]

Here is the prophetic promise of discipleship. Jesus declares the paradox of spiritual life: *"...you cannot... but you shall"*. Discipleship is not built on human strength and potential, but on a realisation of our own bankruptcy and weakness. There is enormous release when we realise that God wants us to bring our weaknesses and inabilities to Him, so that His strength and power will be manifested in us. This takes the striving, and the sense of failure and guilt out of discipleship. God requires our acknowledgement of weakness, and our faith that He will be in us all that He asks us to be. God is the sustainer of inner life. The key to spiritual life is self-emptying so that we may be filled with the Holy Spirit, who is the power to live. The Holy Spirit does not just give power for miraculous deeds, but power for miraculous living. If the age of miracles were past, then Christianity would have little to offer a weak and helpless humanity! Jesus tells us that we can't pray, we can't love, but that we shall be empowered to do all these things and more. This is the rock and foundation of all we shall ever be.

April 7

"...lo, I am with you always...." [Matthew 28:20]

Once, in Cameroon, I was hopelessly lost in a plantation, looking for a missionary's house. Identical roads criss-crossed the area and the tall palms blocked the view in all directions. At last a local man came along, wheeling his bicycle. He was very eager to explain the way. Waving his arms, he pointed in the right direction, and with loud repetitions emphasised that it was far, far, far inside the plantation. I repeated his complicated explanations with the same loud repetitions and asked him if this was correct. With pride, he nodded, smiling, and breathed a loud, *"Yes sir"*. Sometimes preachers are similarly eager to explain the way to go deeper with God, perhaps shouting to try and make it penetrate our dull brains. However, we either forget the detail, or we don't fully understand in the first place. But Christ does not merely explain; He gets in the car with us, and shows us the way. This is the marvel of this verse - that Christ is not just our teacher; He is our guide and our light on the way. We will never get lost, because He will always be with us to show us the way forward. We may not know what lies a year, a month, a day or even an hour in the future. But it does not matter, for He will always be there, and so we can rest in that sure knowledge.

April 8

"When they had twisted a crown of thorns, they put it on His head...." [Matthew 27:29]

The thorns represent the curse that followed the fall of mankind [Genesis 3:18]. On the cross they represent the nature of the human race - that is the opposite of loving embrace. While some of us have a more prickly nature than others, the nature of sin in the human heart is like a thorn bush. When human beings get to know each other, it fairly quickly becomes obvious that misunderstandings and hurts will arise, and there will be a need for forgiveness in order for meaningful relationships to continue. When Christ hung on the cross, He embraced us in our fallen nature, and it was like embracing a bramble bush and clutching it to His chest. Jesus embraces the thorns of our nature to His heart, and absorbs all that we are into Himself; and then He transforms us by pouring His love into us and making us like Himself. After we have opened our hearts to the cross, our inner life becomes like a great big pillow of love, and we are able to receive others with loving embrace. Rest daily in His love.

April 9

"...the Spirit of grace and supplication..."
    [Zechariah 12:10]

This is one of the rare times that the Bible mentions the Spirit of prayer. It is alluded to in other verses, but here it is given this wonderful title. Ask God for the Spirit of grace and supplication, for it is the prelude to outpourings of the Holy Spirit. The Spirit of prayer is marked by a consciousness of grace - that is, of God's care and compassion, not just His holiness. If God were holy without grace, He would be a Pharisee. But though God is holy, He looks with compassion on failure and sin, longing to save and heal. It is this that is imparted in the Spirit of prayer - the consciousness that the Holy One longs to demonstrate His power to save. This longing rises in God's heart with great intercessions that cannot find easy expression in any language. Christ intercedes; but the Father does not pray - He yearns - and it is this yearning that the Father shares with the Son, and that is imparted to us too. It is a daring thing to pray, but ask God for the Spirit of prayer.

April 10

"You are good, and do good..." [Psalm 119:68]

God's goodness is the basis for our bold approach to Him in prayer. We may not always agree with God's ways, because we do not always understand them. But we can be absolutely certain of His goodness in all that He does. Many people wonder whether it is always God's will to heal the sick. However we may answer this question, one thing is certain - God is always good and He has the best in view for His children. When your heart fails with sorrow at bereavement or difficulties or pain, go to God with faith in His unfailing goodness. He wants to bless and exercise His loving rule over our lives. Here lies the basis for faith in God as we pray. There need be no doubt at all as we pray, for God *will* answer, and all that He does will flow from the everlasting streams of goodness and mercy that flow unceasingly from His Being.

April 11

"But God forbid that I should boast except in the cross of our Lord Jesus Christ...." [Galatians 6:14]

The scope of this desire of Paul was total. It meant that he would not accept any praise for any achievement by his ministry - the praise was entirely due to Jesus. How subtle is the human heart that we are tempted to feel smug and conceited that we have come to such an unselfish frame of mind! It is even possible that someone might declare the cross of Christ with such skill and passion that they receive accolades for their cross-centred preaching! If we claim to boast in the cross alone, then we are not actually seeking anything for ourselves, but only for Him. We are praying not that God will anoint *my* ministry, but *the* ministry. We are praying not that God will bless *my* Church but *His* Church. There is something so liberated about Paul's life, that he was not building a reputation for himself, but for the gospel of Christ and Him crucified. Let go of all your ambitions to be recognised and applauded. You will be applauded anyway (and persecuted!), for it cannot be otherwise that, when Christ is glorified, our faces glow and our lives pulse with joy and purpose. Such people stand out from the crowd, but in their hearts they continually remember that it is not them, it is Christ living in them.

April 12

"...let us go forth to Him, outside the camp..."
[Hebrews 13:13]

This verse is at first puzzling, since the 'camp' is that of the people of God! Does this mean we are always to be leaving God's people? Not at all. All of God's people are given this invitation to seek and know the Lord. We are all to make sure that we have a point of reference in our lives apart from the spiritual atmosphere in our Church. There has to be something in our lives that is set aside entirely for God, by which we maintain our bearings on our pilgrim walk with Him. No matter how good our Church or group is, it cannot replace this place with God, where we draw our strength and purpose. No fellowship with God's people can attain the purity and inspiration that we can only draw from direct face-to-face fellowship with God. If we neglect this place, the atmosphere of our lives and then of the Church will steadily decline; it will attain a purpose and joy that are derived from preferences, not from the will of God Himself. So rise up, and get alone with God this day.

April 13

"And in the daytime He was teaching in the temple, but at night He went out and stayed on the mountain called Olivet."
[Luke 21:37]

The Mount of Olives was a place of olive trees. The inference is clear - Jesus went out to abide in the flow of oil from the throne of grace. Though olive oil itself was not a perfume, yet it was the basis of fragrant anointing oil. There can be no doubt that, when Jesus first came into the world, perfume entered the world. Just as the woman anointed Him with the best, sweet perfume, so He brought the best perfume to the world, to anoint a sinful world. The women brought sweet spices to Jesus' tomb, and there was no smell of death there. The perfume did not mask the smell of death, for Jesus' body did not decay - death was swallowed up by life, and the perfume of life filled the tomb. Jesus comes to us to swallow up the smell of death - the world, the disappointments, the hurts and sins that have caused our garments to smell so badly. We need to learn the rhythm of His life - moving from the 'mountain of grace' to the needs of mankind. As we receive that oil on our lives, so we also have something that will transform the neediest person we will ever meet.

April 14

"...they were all with one accord in one place." [Acts 2:1]

The New Testament believers here were in the place of prayer, and it is in this place that God moves. We are not to 'make many prayers', to build a monument to our own spirituality; we are to find and keep the place of prayer. Where is this place? Jesus describes it in Matthew 6 as the secret place, where Father sees us and pours out His bountiful rewards. It is the place of self-emptying, not self-fulfilment. It is the place of letting go and therefore having capacity to receive. It is the place of absolute confidence in God and a carefree dismissal of trust in our own ability. It is God who moves here, who fills our hearts and stirs us to pray things that we never dreamed of. In the place of prayer, angels ascend and descend Jacob's ladder - it is the gate of heaven, the house of God. We may find it when our pillow is made of stones and sorrow fills our hearts, or we may find it when we hear the gospel preached. But whenever we find it, we must recognise its power and importance, enter into that place, and never never lose it. If you can look back on times of prayer - a place before God you once knew - then ask God to show you how to regain it, whatever the cost.

April 15

"And suddenly there came a sound from heaven...."
    [Acts 2:2]

As sons of God, we must never lose the ability to be completely spontaneous in our reactions to the Holy Spirit. *"The Spirit/ wind blows where it wishes, and you hear the sound of it, but cannot tell where it comes from and where it goes. So is everyone who is born of the Spirit."* [John 3:8]. Notice here that it is not just the Holy Spirit who is unpredictably spontaneous, but also the child of God. Spontaneity is the key to the realm of love and power in the Spirit. No-one ever loved who did not also have spontaneous expressions of that love. Love is moved with compassion at the sight of need and pain, and the Holy Spirit in us commands us to do and say things that are a spontaneous expression of the love of God. If we will flow with the Spirit and obey, there will be a release of power and a revelation of God. On the Day of Pentecost, the Holy Spirit came suddenly, and they were caught up and spoke with other tongues. There is no indication that they lost control of themselves, but there is every indication that they were carried beyond themselves. Catch the whisper of the Spirit as you live this day, and move in quick obedience and faith.

April 16

"But what things were gain to me, these I have counted loss for Christ." [Philippians 3:7]

The balance sheet of loss and gain is something that preoccupies every serious person. No-one likes to waste time or money, let alone life itself. Yet here is the measure by which alone we make up the balance sheet of our lives. The only thing in the end worth living for is to know Him. That alone makes gain. The rest will be loss. Of course, life is made up of many things, and all of us must work in order to live a normal life. But so many people are seeking a kind of life that is full of apparent gain, but not realising the incredible eternal loss they are incurring because they have made no time for Christ. Sacrifice is inevitable, we must all make sacrifices, but are you really prepared to sacrifice Christ in order to gain pleasure and riches? Or will you rather sacrifice things that are of no eternal value, to gain the eternal riches? Don't drift; don't let circumstances or other people make your eternal choices for you. Make them yourself, consciously and deliberately each day.

April 17

"But you, when you pray, go into your room, and when you have shut your door..." [Matthew 6:6]

This is one of the Lord's central teachings on prayer. He affirms to us here that we have an 'inner room'. He is not simply referring to a building and a door of wood. He is referring to our inner life, to our heart, and to the door by which we can close out the clamouring worries of this life, and turn our gaze on Him. We have an inner room - we are not mere matter, we have an eternal spirit. It is this faculty that defines us as being in the image of God. By this inner consciousness we can know God, we can identify with Him, we can feel what He feels and think what He is thinking. The place of prayer is the conscious awareness of Him; it is the great promise that, *"they shall all know Me"* [Jeremiah 31:34]. There may be days when clouds cover His face, but never think that this is your perpetual inheritance. Christ died to give us access to a room called the 'holiest of all', and we are not to be robbed of the knowledge of that holy place, and that holy Presence. It is your inheritance - claim it and enter in!

April 18

"For who has stood in the counsel of the Lord, and has perceived and heard His word? Who has marked His word and heard it?" [Jeremiah 23:18]

The implication of the question is that few have stood in the counsel of the Lord. The words used here open to us the way we are to perceive His word. We are not to seek it like people scanning a newspaper. We are to stand with total attention to the quiet voice that speaks with command and absolute authority. This is a place, and it is also an attitude of heart and mind - a place of complete surrender, and a mind of absolute obedience. It is the attitude, not of a pompous general in the army, but of a devoted servant of the king, who loves to attend on his every wish. When we read the Word of God, or when we pray for guidance, the key is to stand in His counsel and count what He says as like great stone pillars that uphold not only our lives, but the eternal purposes of God. As we stand in His counsel, wisdom and authority flow into our beings. There is incredible authority in the person who waits on God.

April 19

"Father, forgive them, for they do not know what they do."
[Luke 23:34]

This was Jesus' first cry from the cross, addressing the number one need of mankind - *"Father, forgive them"*. Don't rush over this; dwell on it, drink from this cup and let the healing stream flow over you now. Jesus is the Master of the human being, and knows exactly what we need. Jesus knows full well that the deepest need of our beings is to be forgiven. Forgiveness lies at the heart of release and deliverance from so many burdens of our minds and bodies. Tensions in us lead to tearing and heaviness. The answer is forgiveness. Jesus has power to forgive sins; ultimately, He alone has that power. He dissolves guilt's

66

chain from around our necks and it disappears like wax before a flame. Let Jesus minister to you and you will find that He begins here, at the deepest need of the human heart.

April 20

"And when they had prayed, the place where they were assembled together was shaken..." [Acts 4:31]

This was a wonderful and surely unexpected result of the prayers of Peter and John and their fellow believers. The impact must have been to make them aware of the awesome power of God. It is not clear how widespread the earthquake was, but it was not **de**structive, it was **in**structive. From it they realised that God is over all. In a similar way, prayer should lead to an earthquake in our thinking and living - to a radical and powerful change in our perspective and our sense of God's power. Our faith is impacted most of all through prayer, and to the prayerful person, faith is a 'natural' instinct. Pray, pour out your soul to God; do not live in the shadow of things that threaten. Lift up your voice, cry to God and watch the world around you tremble, and things that threaten collapse. The chief priests and elders who had arrested and threatened Peter and John did not disappear, but their threats were ineffective to people whose faith was impacted with the matchless Presence of God.

April 21

"The Lord is risen indeed..." [Luke 24:34]

By the end of the day of Jesus' resurrection, the disciples had come to faith that He really was risen. Their emotions had gone through a roller-coaster, starting with deep despair, then sudden hope, which was confirmed throughout the day with more and more testimonies of the risen Saviour. At last they came to the wonderful conclusion that He **really** was risen! The same is true for us. The resurrection changes everything for ever for those who **really** believe it and grasp the implications. Jesus rose from the dead and created in Himself a new humanity. Although we are not risen with Him in body, yet in spirit we are risen with Him. The resurrection tells us that there is nothing of darkness that can ever stop Him or His people. This is the foundation of joy, and the fountain of eternal security. Let it sink in! Christ is risen, and blessed are they who have not seen and yet have believed.

April 22

"Do not be not afraid, only believe." [Mark 5:36]

This was the word of Jesus to Jairus in the darkest hour of Jairus' life. His daughter had died - the news had been passed to him moments before. It seemed Jesus had come too late and all hope had gone. But God is never too late; it is in the darkest hour that our light arises and hope comes. The temptation at these moments is to give up hope, to give in to despair, and to abandon the foundations of our lives, most of all to doubt God's love. This is the pathway of fear and unbelief that opens to try and swallow us up. The word of Jesus flashes incisive in the darkness, and strikes to the heart of the enemy. The word of Jesus is creative and powerful, and so here an illogical hope was born in Jairus' heart. As he turned to follow the Saviour, he must have known that death, sickness and failure were not in charge. Yes, they threaten us, but they do not have the last word. Jesus rises like the dawning of a never-ending day. Let this illogical but certain hope fill your heart today.

April 23

"He will baptize you with the Holy Spirit and fire."
   [Matthew 3:11]

John's prophecy regarding Jesus is one of the greatest regarding the Messiah. It was made on the eve of its fulfilment. Many prophecies were made with centuries awaiting their fulfilment. But this one was linked with Jesus and also was placed centrally as the identifying mark of His ministry. The plain words of John indicate that Jesus will powerfully change and empower the lives of His followers, and this empowerment will involve refining fire and the Holy Spirit. Jesus' ministry to our hearts is to introduce us to the power of this, His life, and also to maintain this life in us. It is life characterised by the Holy Spirit's indwelling and by fire. Is the mark of your life blazing zeal and love for Jesus, and an inner commitment to remove all things that could hinder that life from ruling in you? That is the mark that proves that Jesus is at work in you. Don't compromise on this; don't settle for anything less.

April 24

"Now give me wisdom and knowledge, that I may go out and come in before this people; for who can judge this great people of Yours?"
[2 Chronicles 1:10]

This is the great prayer that began the golden age of Israel's history. Under Solomon there was unity, peace, prosperity and, at the beginning of his reign, there was spiritual power and the wonderful Presence of God sanctifying the Temple and the nation. It was the counterpart of the book of Acts. So we, too, can pray for wisdom - not just that we might do well, but that God's people may prosper and that God's name may be glorified. How we need wisdom. We need to know how to live each day aright; we need to know how to use our time and our resources. We don't need more things; we need to know how to use what we have. Be definite, see the need of your heart and your life, and pray, ask for wisdom. God has promised to answer this prayer. He will touch our hearts and open our ears to perceive His way and His voice. So pray and God will surely answer, for this is prayer that pleases Him.

April 25

"But indeed, O man, who are you to reply against God?"
[Romans 9:20]

This phrase sums up the arrogance of someone who speaks to God as if they were equal with Him. The sin of pride is not just one in the long list of sins; it is the very core of sin. It gives power to the kingdom of darkness and is the source of blindness; it immunises us against rational thought, while at the same time making us believe it is the embodiment of reason. We must speak to God honestly, but also humbly, about what we think and feel. We may feel that God seems to have made a mistake over some issue, but it is vitally important that we bow before Him and seek understanding. Israel fell because they did not recognise God's sovereign will and right to choose. They believed they were qualified to be accepted on the grounds of their origin and moral superiority. But their acceptance was not traceable back to human virtue, but to God's grace and favour. As soon as we believe we are superior in any point, God will allow us to be tempted on that line, to expose the absolute barrenness of the human heart in spiritual power. Without

God's grace our lives will decay and collapse. We are endowed with many wonderful qualities, but all of them, without exception, flow from God's gracious gift and kindness. The realisation of this produces a wonder and a gentleness in us when we speak to God, and dissolves the arrogance from our hearts. *"For by grace you have been saved through faith, and that not of yourselves; it is the gift of God, not of works, lest anyone should boast."* [Ephesians 2:8-9].

April 26

"When anyone hears the word of the kingdom, and does not understand it, then the wicked one comes and snatches away what was sown in his heart."
      [Matthew 13:19]

The 'word of the kingdom' is not mere information, nor is it merely nice or comforting words. There are many reassuring and beautiful thoughts that bless and edify us. But the word of the kingdom is the word of death and resurrection. As such, it is an all-or-nothing word, since no-one can die and rise again in stages! This seed cannot therefore grow alongside other things, nor can it bear fruit if it lies on the surface of our life. It is a word that must lay hold of the person who hears it. There will be tribulation and persecution for the sake of this word, though there will be little persecution for the sake of beautiful religious thoughts. It is for this reason that we must understand and then nourish this word in our hearts, allowing it to be the principle and power by which we live - namely that we are united with Christ in His death and resurrection as the mainspring of our lives. Bring your life into line daily with the word of the kingdom and see the power of the word fulfil itself in you.

April 27

"...He said to the paralytic, 'Son, your sins are forgiven you.' "
      [Mark 2:5]

This paralysed man had been carried by four eager and expectant friends. They had been so eager that they could not wait for the end of the meeting; they broke up the roof where Jesus was speaking, and let their paralysed friend down. Were they disappointed when Jesus did not immediately heal him? Perhaps, but for the man himself, these words must have been a flood of healing balm. Jesus called him *"Son"*, and this meant

70

more than a religious pat on the head! It meant: *'You are included, you are accepted, you are adopted into the family'.* The phrase *"your sins"* is between the words *"Son"* and *"forgiven"*. The man would have known exactly what sins Jesus was talking about, though they are not detailed. Jesus spared the man public exposure, and released him from the terrible burden of guilt and shame that had doubtless produced, first paralysis of spirit and then of body. The man would have been transported away by the power of forgiveness, into the arms of a loving heavenly Father. Jesus dealt first with the root of the man's problem and then with its symptoms: *"...arise, take up your bed and go..."* Waves of joy came because Jesus had dealt with the man's problems root and branch. He will do the same for us.

April 28

"...He went through the grainfields on the Sabbath; and as they went His disciples began to pluck the heads of grain ... 'The Sabbath was made for man, and not man for the Sabbath.'" [Mark 2:23, 27]

The Pharisees objected to hungry men taking handfuls of grain because it was on the Sabbath. Their error lay in that they began their interpretation of the Law from the point of view that God is both religious and nit-picking. This is a serious error, since all interpretation of God's Word must begin from the basis that God is good and gave His Word to bless us and do us good. If we start from any other place, we misrepresent God. Note God's largeness of heart: He created the Sabbath for mankind. Every day is not made for its own sake, it is not made for the sun that rules the day, nor for the moon and stars that rule the night. No, all these things are made for the delight and blessing of mankind, i.e. YOU! We should not live in craven fear over whether we have upset God because of some little religious observance. God loves us, and when His children are hungry He wants us to be satisfied. The disciples must have felt the sunshine of His love in their hearts, and the delight He felt that their hunger was satisfied. Learn to live under God's smile. Interpret each day in the light of God's joy over you.

April 29

"...you will be mute, and not able to speak until the day these things take place..." [Luke 1:20]

Zachariah was struck deaf (see verse 62) and dumb by the angel as a consequence of his unbelief of the divine message. The result was that Zachariah was unable to communicate his unbelief by word of mouth. God gives utterance to those who have something to communicate, and this is not just a matter of information, it is a matter of the right heart state. When we speak, we communicate our heart state, whether it be in conversation or in preaching. But the angel also struck him deaf, so that he would be shut in to think about the last things that he had heard - those mighty promises, spoken in purest faith by the angel. The last thing that Zachariah heard was the voice of God communicating faith, and in the silence imposed on him, that seed word was producing faith. Just as the army of Israel marched in silence around Jericho for seven days, so Zachariah was for 9 months shut in with God and His prophetic word. At last, Israel shouted and the walls fell flat. Not the loudness of the shout, but the faith in the voice of the people, made the walls fall down. So, too, Zachariah confessed the truth the angel had spoken, by writing it on a tablet, and the result was the loosening of his tongue, and a stream of faith and prophetic utterance flowed from his lips. Let the word of God impart faith to your heart, and if need be, meditate silently before the Lord till faith rises within.

April 30

"And you shall set the showbread on the table before Me always." [Exodus 25:30]

This showbread is a picture of Christ, the bread of life. There are two words used for it in the Old Testament. The first, used here in this verse, means literally, 'the bread of the Presence'. The second word, in Leviticus 24:5, indicates that the bread has been pierced or, literally, 'wounded'. Putting the two words together, we have 'the pierced bread of the Presence'. At its simplest level, this is yet one more proof of God's plan that through the crucifixion of His Son the world should be saved. God caused these hidden details to be written into the weave of Israel's life and history. At its most sublime level, these words indicate that we can nourish ourselves by letting the Presence of Jesus fill our hearts and lives. This is only possible because He was wounded for us. As we approach God, emptying ourselves of pride and independence from Him, we are able to let that precious Presence wash over us, fill us, refresh and heal us. As we abide in that Presence, we abound in health - mental, physical and spiritual. Abiding in His Presence, we worship and are made whole.   God ordered the showbread to be always fresh before Him in the Tabernacle, because this alone can teach the truth that Christ is always fresh and new in mercy and nourishment as we let Him fill us and feed us.

May 1

"...praying always with all prayer..." [Ephesians 6:18]

Paul here sums up a great subject in one sweeping phrase: *"all prayer"*. The phrase indicates that there is a whole discipline to be covered, with many branches. We often think of prayer as a narrow thing, like multiplication tables in relation to mathematics. As essential as these tables may be, no mathematician would ever accept that they are the only area to be mastered when studying the subject of mathematics. In the same way, our little quiet times may be a 10-minute ritual that has become a repeated habit. Prayer is an ocean, and often we have mastered only the most elementary steps. Prayer ranges from deepest quiet in awed silence, to mighty praises that shake and fill our beings with the greatness of God. It ranges from joy unspeakable, to inexpressible sorrow and floods of tears over the lost states of humanity. The range of prayer is as wide as God, and we were made for communion with God. There is something God-shaped about us, and that inner need and impulse can be filled by nothing other than the activity of praying. We are made for God - that is the way it is. Prayer is the sharing of our lives with God, and God sharing His life with us. This is our greatest adventure - to let God in at all times. Pray, then, always with all prayer.

May 2

"You have had pity on the plant... and should I not pity Nineveh...?" [Jonah 4:10-11]

The measure of our love is our reaction to problems, whether our own or someone else's, be they big or small. Jonah lost the plant that had given him shade, and his reaction was extreme irritation. This was the reaction of intense self-love and self-obsession. This is a grievous fault in a preacher such as Jonah, and in his case indicated a return to his former faults which had ruined his life once already. God had changed Jonah by an experience of death and resurrection. But no matter how deep our experience, it never takes away our personal responsibility to maintain the life that God has given us. Jonah exploded with fury and sank into depression at his loss of personal comfort, but had no tears to weep for the eternal destiny of human souls. How we need union with Christ through His death. How we need to abide in His love. The little frustrations of each day are sent by God to teach us the shallowness of our spirituality. If we are truly filled with the love of God, we will not even perceive these minor distractions. We will be too occupied with loving God and those around us, for whom He died. This love is ours, but we must sacrifice self-love, or we will lose it.

May 3

"Therefore, as the Holy Spirit says: 'Today, if you will hear His voice...' " [Hebrews 3:7]

The writer here identifies the voice of Scripture as the voice of the Spirit. When we read our Bibles, we are hearing the voice of the Spirit, if only we will listen. The human soul longs for the voice of God. Unbelief constantly longs for things far off, with a sad despondency that tends to give up the battle. The Holy Spirit, on the contrary, challenges us to forget about tomorrow and realise that He is the God of here and now. The force of this verse is to awaken us to sanity and faith. God is not far off. He has deigned to give the world a book which is God-breathed. He then seeks to remove all barriers between us and Himself. There is no time barrier. There is no geographical barrier. God is within our reach, and will always be so. He is within the reach of every person, and in a form by which every person can be sure of Him and have no doubts. God has spoken, and He has caused His speaking to be put into a book. He is constantly speaking to every person who will take that book up and read it with faith. Let the Spirit of true devotion soften your heart and draw you into immediate fellowship with God, today.

May 4

"Is it right for you to be angry?" [Jonah 4:4]

Anger is a storm that rises to smash and destroy the things that stand in our path. It is essentially a sign of pride and selfishness. Downtrodden, suffering people become incredibly patient. They seem to have no anger because they have lost any sense of having rights. Such people become passive and listless. God does not intend us to be passive and listless, but neither does He intend us to be filled with the blinding anger that characterises so much of the affluent world. The Christian is to know a place of freedom from the storms that shake and destroy the inner life. We are to be carried by a greater passion, but one that heals and does not destroy. Love is the wave that is to carry us to meet

75

life's trials. Love does not notice obstacles in the path of our self-realisation. Love notices others. It sees other people. It takes note of their burdens, their needs, and reacts with careless disregard to self, and a joy in helping others. We are carried either on a storm of frustration or on a wave of love. Self-realisation may seem an attractive goal, but it is a rotten fruit, and brings no joy. Only in laying down our will and loving others can we find true joy. This is the Spirit of Jesus that is to fill our hearts and impassion our minds.

May 5

"...for thou hast created all things, and for thy pleasure they are and were created." [Revelation 4:11, KJV]

At the beginning of the 19th century, surgeons were beginning to understand the complexity of the human body by performing autopsies and examining how the body functions. An anecdote recounts how one atheist boldly claimed that he could demonstrate the function of every part of the human body in purely physical terms. A human being was, he claimed, a physical and mechanical entity - a collection of chemicals and structural parts, and nothing more. A Christian surgeon, on hearing these words, pointed the atheist to a piano and issued the challenge: *'Take it to pieces and tell me when you find the music!'* The point is that the piano was made for the purpose of producing music, but music has no physical substance, even though it is produced by physical means. It begins in the human soul. The piano is meaningless unless there is music. So, too, the physical world, and we ourselves, have no meaning without the Creator's plan and purpose - that we should live a beautiful life before God, full of the music of love and kindness. You were created, like a musical instrument, to produce beauty and bring pleasure to God.

May 6

"Of every tree of the garden you may freely eat; but of the tree of the knowledge of good and evil you shall not eat, for in the day that you eat of it you shall surely die."
    [Genesis 2:16-17]

At the Creation, Adam was placed in the garden and given a moral command, implying he had the power of moral choice. It was not a purely negative command - it was a positive

76

exhortation to enjoy all the fruits of the garden, except for one. Mankind could not escape the demands of moral choice then, and neither can we now. We may wash our hands as Pilate did, but there is no way of escaping our responsibility. This moral stature is an indication of the huge distance between us and the animals. Humanists take a materialistic view of the universe, which claims there is no absolute right and wrong, only opinions about these things. But this is clearly not the truth, since the world is infected with evil, which brings misery and death to millions. We are moral beings. Winston Churchill said:

"Would you rise in the world? You must work while others amuse themselves. Are you desirous of a reputation for courage? You must risk your life. Would you be strong morally or physically? You must resist temptation. All this is paying in advance, that is, prospective finance. Observe the other side of the picture: the bad things are paid for afterwards."

Where there is disobedience, there are results; we must reap the rewards of our sin, in personal misery and shame. To attain moral character and stature, we must deny ourselves. God is the Creator, and we are to read and understand his instruction book for human beings! The rewards are long-term and abundant in unspeakable joy. Invest your all this day for eternity.

May 7

" 'For My thoughts are not your thoughts, nor are your ways My ways', says the LORD. 'For as the heavens are higher than the earth, so are My ways higher than your ways, and My thoughts than your thoughts.' " [Isaiah 55: 8-9]

God is different from us - His ways are higher and nobler, His Being is filled with a majesty and a glory that sets Him apart. His holiness produces godly fear in those who approach Him. As Moses approached the burning bush, he was commanded to remove his sandals, since the ground he stood on was holy; he then covered his face at the sight of God [Exodus 3:5-6]. God's love may make us think that He is one of us since He comes down to our level. But despite His humility, He does not become base like we are - He remains glorious. The disciples became so familiar with Jesus that on occasions they spoke to Him as if He were a mere man; Peter rebuked Jesus in Matthew

16:22. But only a few days later, they were on their faces before Him, blinded by His unspeakable glory [Matthew 17:6]. God demands more than external moral conformity to His law - He requires truth in the inward parts [Psalm 51:6; Matthew 5:8]. God is unapproachable in holiness, as pictured by the innermost room of the Tabernacle. In our sinful state, we cannot have fellowship with God – His holy Presence would mean death to us. The gulf between God and us is so huge that it could only be spanned by Christ's death. [Hebrews 10:19]. Here is the invitation: God is holy, but He has made a way for you to be His friend and to share in fellowship with Him.

May 8

"You are of God, little children, and have overcome them, because He who is in you is greater than he who is in the world." [1 John 4:4]

The great issue of our victory as Christians is not related to our power, but to God's. God cannot be measured by any human means. He is beyond all our attempts to contain or grasp Him. There is no other being that is remotely close to God in His infinite and eternal dimensions. True, we partake of eternity by the gift of God, and angels and fallen angels also partake of eternal existence. But even so, mankind and angels have a beginning - they were created. God has no beginning or end, either in time or space. Thus he is infinitely greater than the devil or all the powers of humanity and demons together. God has more power in a whisper than all the combined powers that oppose Him. In the battle for our souls, it is not a question of how strong we can become, but whether we will be on God's side or the devil's. As soon as we are clear where we stand, the conflict is brought to a conclusion, and the devil is defeated. The devil cannot stand against God in us. You do not need to gain a position of incredible power - you simply need to realise the awesome power of the One who is within you. The measure of our life is not self-realisation, but believing that God is who He says He is, and allowing Him to rule in our lives.

May 9

"Shall not the Judge of all the earth do right?"
[Genesis 18:25]

God judges the world continually. He is in charge. Often

Christians feel that they are serving the God who lives in the Church and is waiting to be active at the end of time. Many secretly believe that He is largely powerless in the affairs of the nations. But the truth is that we often know God only as children know their father - they see him at home, he loves them and cuddles them and plays with them. He is their personal father. But he also has a greater role in society, of which the child knows nothing. My father was a policeman, and once I read in the newspaper about how he had caught a speeding motorist by chasing him in his police car. I normally saw nothing of this side of my father's life, and so it is with Christians. We see little of Father's activity in governing the universe. To really enter into prayer for the nations, we must see our God at work in the nations. We are not praying that He might work, but pleading with Him regarding the way that He will work. God will always decide the future of the nations. He is the one who humbles, punishes, exalts and blesses the nations. Make sure you do not serve a merely 'private' God, but the true and living God of all the earth.

May 10

"...that you put off, concerning your former conduct, the old man which grows corrupt according to the deceitful lusts, and be renewed in the spirit of your mind..." [Ephesians 4:22-23]

A Hindu was sitting in the market square in an Indian village. He observed a man selling live quail. Each quail was attached by a string to a brass ring that was threaded onto a bamboo pole set in the ground. The quail were walking in circles around the pole, pecking at the ground. The Hindu, being a vegetarian, was troubled at the sight of all these birds destined for the pot. He approached the seller and, after a short discussion, he handed over some money and the seller set all the birds free. Imagine, then, the Hindu's dismay when the birds did not fly off to the forest, but continued walking in circles as if they were still bound by invisible bonds. We may chuckle at the thought of this, but it illustrates precisely the problem that Paul is addressing in these verses in Ephesians chapter 4. Christ has set us free by His blood. He has liberated us through a powerful baptism with the Holy Spirit. Now we must break the power of old habits in our minds and our wills. The grooves in our minds and imaginations have been worn deep by long self-indulgence, and now that we are Christ's, we need to break with the habits of a lifetime. As human beings, we love habits, but the power of

79

the Holy Spirit is within us to break them, and to enable us to create new ones. Catch yourself, in your humour, in your habits of speech and of thought that do not honour the Lord, and resolve to crumple them up like old newspapers and throw them away. You will be surprised at the resources that are at your disposal to form the character of Christ in you. Christ has set us free from the power of sin, but we must learn to walk away from it.

May 11

"For in this (body) *we groan..."* [2 Corinthians 5:2]

Paul is describing in this phrase some of the agonies he endured as he laboured for the gospel. He is also describing the sense of weakness, frailty and mortality that is the common experience of all human beings. We may feel we have super-human strength when we are young, but that is a short and passing phase. Our bodies are weak and fragile; as we grow older, the ageing process can produce groans of frustration and longing for a better life. The human race longs for a pain-free world. Paul, who saw so much of God's supernatural power in his ministry, nevertheless also experienced physical weakness and pain. But he calls this process *"our light affliction"* [2 Corinthians 4:17] and rejoices that, while the 'outward man' perishes, there is a constant miracle of renewal going on in the inside. Paul must have longed for miracles to relieve his suffering, and this longing is common to us all, whether we suffer in physical pain or perhaps in the emotional pain of difficult relationships. Paul groaned because God has not promised us a life without challenge here and now. But He **has** promised the inner renewal of our hope by the Holy Spirit. Don't miss out on God's answer for your condition. Receive His matchless ministry to your 'inner man', letting the blemishes be erased from your spirit for ever.

May 12

"I am the God of your father - the God of Abraham, the God of Isaac and the God of Jacob." [Exodus 3:6]

God is the God of Creation, and by His omnipotent power He created the beauty of the universe. But here He declares Himself to be the God of three ordinary individuals who responded in human weakness and frailty to His word. God is the God of individual human beings, and the Bible declares that the most powerful thing in history will be the individual response of ordinary people. Kings and Pharaohs of the ancient world have come and gone and are forgotten, but Abraham, Isaac and Jacob have affected all the families of the earth. The challenge is simple: live out your life within the confines of ordinary circumstances, and God will pick up these very elements and build an eternal kingdom that shall never perish, but shall outlast all the greatness and glories of human kingdoms. The political decisions of earthly rulers shake this world, but the ordinary issues of conscience and personal obedience shake the kingdom of darkness and glorify God. Mortal rulers parade their greatness in front of mortal observers. Christians live out their lives knowing that they are under the watchful eye of the everlasting God. When God observes the little acts of loving devotion in our daily walk, He gathers these things up and shapes the course of nations and of history to declare that He is our God. Walk before Him, and discover the power of walking humbly with God.

May 13

"A little leaven leavens the whole lump." [Galatians 5:9]

What is the leaven? It is human striving. What is the lump? It is my whole Christian experience. It includes my sense of God, my ability to pray and to care for others with abundant love. Paul is teaching that a Christian life based on self-effort will lead to the corruption of the whole plan of salvation in my life. In other words, my Christian life simply won't work! Whether we like it or not, the Christian life is based on God's life in us, not on what we can achieve for the cause of Christ. If only we can find the secret of letting the Holy Spirit be the power of our daily life then we will find the secret of Christ's life. Christ lived in fellowship with the Father, allowing Father to be the power of His life. We are to do the same. We think of ourselves as either good or bad, and try to end each day with a balance on the 'good' side. We need to begin each day with the yieldedness to Christ that allows Him to fill us with power through the Holy Spirit to live a Christ-centred life. No amount of human striving can ever attain this, and Paul here teaches that even a pinch of human virtue will spoil the whole taste of my daily walk with God. Let God fill each moment. Let circumstances be the setting for the revelation of God's provision of power and grace. Imagine being at a performance of Handel's Messiah, and humming, whistling and joining in with all your favourite bits, thinking that it will add to the performance - how long would it take the ushers to come and escort you to the exit!

May 14

"...it pleased God... to reveal His Son in me..."
    [Galatians 1:15-16]

Paul here sums up his experience of salvation. He is explaining that the great purpose of God in every individual is to make our life a setting for Christ. If we keep this perspective, we can understand God's plan in the detail. God is not interested in making me important, famous or great! He is not exalting me - He is using the material of my humanity to fashion a setting for Christ. He is the jewel, and I am the setting. If I think of myself as the jewel, then I must promote myself, and make others realise how full of faith I am. I must parade my achievements, hoping to gain credibility. But if I am merely the setting, then I can put aside all the stress and strain of being the centre of attention, and lift up Christ. This is the key to the poise of Christian living. I do not have to strive to be something, I must simply serve God's purpose and exalt Christ. This immediately removes the hurt of being not noticed or appreciated. It is our joy to glorify the love and grace of God as revealed in the cross of Christ. Our chief joy is when He is praised, when He is thanked, when His touch is ministered. If our lives are a setting for self, then we are heading for frustration and disappointment. But if we truly love the glory of God, then we are filled with a joy that can know no disappointments.

May 15

"...the Spirit of truth, whom the world cannot receive, because it neither sees Him nor knows Him; but you know Him, for He dwells with you and will be in you." [John 14:17]

This verse implies a very small 'distance' between the Spirit being *"with you"* and *"in you"*. Jesus is clearly recognising that the believers are His - they are not worldly - they are distinct and different from 'the world'. But there is a deeper experience of His Presence, in the power of the Holy Spirit, that comes through the entire surrender of their inner beings to Christ. This surrender is something that we give as we become deeply convinced of His love and care. There is such tenderness in

Jesus' teaching on the Holy Spirit. He opens our hearts with that tenderness and love. In fact there is nothing else that deserves our absolute surrender. Do not be robbed of your birthright, but draw near to Jesus in absolute surrender and let Him have your innermost self. There is a door within our hearts that we keep under our firm control. This is right, and no human being has the right to rule over another's heart and thoughts; but as we realise the character and love of our Saviour, we are drawn to yield to Him our deepest beings. This is the last surrender, but it is the most significant. It is the most transforming step, and changes the tone of our lives and words and works. Let Him fill you with His Spirit.

May 16

"The ark of the Lord remained in the house of Obed-Edom the Gittite three months. And the Lord blessed Obed-Edom and all his household." [2 Samuel 6:11]

"And I will pray the Father, and He will give you another Helper, that He may abide with you forever..." [John 14:17]

The ark is the symbol of God's holy Presence. It was a fearful and a wonderful thing to enter that Presence, and only the High Priest could do it. Obed-Edom never saw the ark, because it was always covered when being transported. It was placed in his house, and he must have trembled in the first days and nights after it was placed there. But then he would have noticed that the atmosphere of his home had changed. There were fewer arguments, no tension. The peace of God must have filled every room and every heart. Then there would have been bumper harvests, and the vines would have given sweeter, tastier grapes. And then one day, David appeared, to take the ark to his house! How they must have thanked God that they had been blessed with the Presence of God in that form for those 3 months, and how they must have ached with regret that it had to leave them. But we have a far greater promise: God's Presence with us, and not just to visit, but to stay for ever. What blessings there are that flow from God, but among them all there is none greater than to have Him. Obed-Edom only tasted, but we have the real thing! Obed-Edom had to wave goodbye to the blessed One, but we have that life-giving, transforming Presence for ever.

83

May 17

"So when the Lord saw that he turned aside to look, God called to him from the midst of the bush and said, 'Moses, Moses!' And he said, 'Here I am'." [Exodus 3:4]

The cycle of a move of God always begins when someone touches God and a wave of His Spirit's moving is released. To truly touch God is not something that can be imparted to us by the prayer of another person. It is a lonely place, without human mediation, except for the mediation of the glorified humanity of Jesus Christ. To receive fresh moves of God, we must withdraw to find that touch. For this we must be deeply persuaded that God is able and wants to refresh our lives. We must yield all directly to Him. Nothing else will satisfy either God or us. True baptism with the Spirit is not a passing excitement, but a deep wave from Almighty God that carries us to the shores of His eternal kingdom. We must not look over our shoulders to see who is following, but we must fix our eyes on God and follow Him with undivided gaze and undiluted faith.

May 18

"For He made Him who knew no sin to be sin for us..."
    [2 Corinthians 5:21]

Christ met humanity in all levels of our need during his years of ministry. He ministered to sick, demon-possessed, sinful, and ultimately to dead people. However, on the cross Christ did not merely meet us in our need; He met with the cosmic force of sin in all its horror. In our need, we are conscious of the effects of sin in our lives. In our prayers we focus on our immediate problem: *"Forgive me, wash me, deliver me."* On the cross Christ encountered a force of evil which has touched us all but of which we know almost nothing. We know that this is the evil that lies behind the holocaust, and other unspeakably inhuman acts of cruelty. On the cross Christ encountered sin on a level that not only neutralised it, but also destroyed it and made it possible for human beings to be delivered from its awful power and bondage. Christ is the Lamb of God that takes away the sin of the world. When He had done this, He obtained the power to put us back into right relationship with God and with Himself. Christ is the centre of the universe, both as Lord and Creator, but most importantly as Redeemer. He has penetrated the centre of our fallen world. Christ has entered into the power of sin and broken it. Wonder, worship, believe and enter in also. It is the place where endless night is turned to everlasting day. It is the dawn of the New Creation. It is the place where we go over the crest of a hill, and all our past falls from view, and before us is the vista of a new life and a new future. It is yours to receive by faith.

May 19

"...according to His abundant mercy..." [1 Peter 1.3]

God is abundant. There is nothing stingy or mean about Him. He cannot give in a way that leaves us feeling He has withheld His best. The hindrances to receiving lie in the human mind. So often we are small-minded, and think that there is little blessing coming our way. In other words, it is unbelief that hinders God. Think rightly about God, think rightly about the measure of blessing that is yours. This does not mean that you will have no problems, nor does it mean that you will have no lack. Paul was often hungry, weary and sleepless [2 Corinthians 11:27]. Nevertheless, Paul was filled with abundant joy and hope, full to overflowing with the Holy Spirit. It is this incredible abundance that marks God's dealings with His people. We need to exchange our mean views of God for the accurate view that He will pour out upon us such an abundance of mercy that it will transform our lives into joy-filled ones, constantly full of His love and goodness. God's people are filled with all the fullness that is in Christ. That indicates a fullness of compassion that is constantly expecting God to work. When we touch God, it is like touching a dam behind which a huge pressure of abundant mercy is waiting to be poured out when our faith breaks through, and His mercy is lavished upon us.

May 20

"But we see Jesus, who was made a little lower than the angels, for the suffering of death crowned with glory and honour, that He, by the grace of God, might taste death for everyone." [Hebrews 2:9]

You have probably occasionally tasted something so bad that you have instantly spat it out of your mouth - perhaps something bitter or sour, like an unripe fruit – but it did you no harm. But Christ 'tasted death'. This means that he allowed it into His being in all its deadly force, and, having absorbed it into Himself, He destroyed it there. He did not just taste something unpleasant, like bad fruit. He tasted something that is disgusting both to God and to mankind. What He tasted swarmed with deadly poison, deadly bacteria, sicknesses like cholera and typhoid. It teemed with spiritual parasites that eat away at human hearts. This was not only distasteful, it was the opposite of all that Christ is and loves. Yet he received it because of the great love He had for us. Then He destroyed it. He turned bitter waters sweet and made our lives full of the sweet flavour of His Presence. What wonder and what joy belong to us who love and serve Him.

May 21

"...sin is the transgression of the law." [1 John 3:4, KJV]

We all too easily measure our righteousness, and therefore our rightness, with God by little rules we have kept. We have a well-ordered life without lies or crimes. The danger is that we become satisfied with a life that does not 'transgress' our code of conduct. But sin is not failing in some personal standards; it is failing to meet up to the standards set by God for human conduct. God has set these standards in the Law of Moses, and then shown them lived out perfectly in the Person of His Son. God has put within us a conscience that trembles at the example and lifting up of Jesus, as we realise that we so completely fall short of God's righteousness. We have sinned, and we do well to name it as sin. But the lifting up of Jesus causes us not only to tremble but also to believe, for He is not like the Law. He is not cold, impassive and made of stone. He has brought the righteousness of God within our reach. God in Christ, the perfect man, reaches down not to condemn but to save. Christ is God's righteousness, and He gathers us up and lifts us to Himself, enfolding us in that marvellous strength that washes and empowers. Don't measure your life by some petty rules, but measure yourself by your relationship with Jesus.

May 22

"Give me children, or else I die!" [Genesis 30:1]

Rachel was speaking to Jacob, but in reality she was praying. This prayer was not so much a religious utterance as an overpowering longing of her heart. This is one of the keys to

86

prayer. Prayer is longing directed to God. Sometimes we pray for something that we do not long for. *'Give us revival Lord!'* *'Save my neighbours!'* But all the time our hearts are sadly indifferent to the outcome of our prayers. This is not true prayer. True prayer is being mastered by the yearning for the answer. Rachel longed for children. This is a woman's longing. It went deeper than jealousy and was an expression of her longing to fulfil her womanhood. In the same way, true prayer is the longing of the human soul to fulfil its true calling. But longing is not enough. It must be directed upwards to God. In other words, there must be faith mixed in with the longing heart. What do we do if we do not thirst for God? We must repent and ask God to take away the dullness of soul that robs us of true spiritual progress. We may choose to define our problems as psychological states that we can do nothing about. But the Bible calls these things 'sin'. Turn to God, and he will give you the desires of your heart.

May 23

"And behold a leper came and worshiped Him, saying, 'Lord, if you are willing, you can make me clean.' Then Jesus put out His hand and touched him, saying, 'I am willing; be cleansed.' Immediately his leprosy was cleansed."
[Matthew 8:2-3]

This is not only the prayer of a sick man; it is the passionate prayer of someone who is convicted of sin. It is a great prayer, and goes to the very heart of all that we are as human beings. Don't be slow to pray it. We don't pray this way every day - this kind of prayer is the kind that reaches to the foundations of the hills [Psalm 18:7] and even the foundation of the world [Psalm 18:15]. This kind of prayer is the laying bare of the deepest thoughts of which we are capable. It is a thirst for purity at the deepest level. It is frightening to hear someone pray like this, for they are longing for a change to come in their lives that goes to the roots of their being. Some people might say, *"That kind of thing should have been dealt with early in the Christian life"*. Such a view may be 'correct', but is sadly lacking in spiritual reality. When the Holy Spirit uncovers things about us that we would prefer not to face up to, then we either brush these things aside, or we break, and pray with all our being. God loves to answer this kind of prayer, and He will answer it more than once. When your heart is sick with sin, pray for cleansing - don't justify yourself, just do it. There are things about us that we cannot understand - all we know is that it is not something we can fully explain. Go to God, pray with all your heart, and know that He will answer you with a newness that you only dreamed of before.

May 24

"And it came to pass, when Jacob saw Rachel the daughter of Laban his mother's brother, and the sheep of Laban his mother's brother, that Jacob went near and rolled the stone from the well's mouth, and watered the flock of Laban his mother's brother." [Genesis 29:10]

Jacob loved Rachel at first sight. He *"lifted up his voice and wept"* because of the great love he felt for her! It is a beautiful story, and speaks of Jesus' love for sinners. The focus here is on the well that is blocked by the great stone. The stone could not be moved by Rachel, nor by the sheep, and it blocked the flow of water by which they would have life. Jacob's great strength to roll away the stone came from his love for Rachel. There is only one other stone that was rolled away in the Bible - the stone that the angel rolled away from Jesus' tomb, thus demonstrating that He was risen from the dead. The heavy stone that blocks us from drinking of the Holy Spirit is our past sins, that make us worthy of death, and that bar the way to the tree of life, and to the fountain of living waters. Jesus looked on our helpless state and rolled away the stone. There are many powerful things in the human heart. One is anger - it rises like a fierce storm; but love is by far stronger than any other power, and causes people to do the impossible. Jesus' love for us stirred Him to do the impossible - to remove utterly all our shame and guilt, and declare us worthy before God's throne. Jesus swallowed the power of sin and death and took away the things that disqualified us, and now invites us to eat and drink with Him in His kingdom.

May 25

"...He anointed the eyes of the blind man with the clay." [John 9:6]

True, this clay was made with Jesus' saliva, but it still must have really irritated the blind man's eyes to have mud smeared over them. Our eyes are perhaps the most sensitive part of our body, and feel the tiniest speck of dust as a major irritant. The eye is here used by the Lord to teach us the nature of our soul. The soul is as sensitive inwardly as the eye is physically. We guard our eyes from all intrusions, and rightly so, since if we sustain the tiniest wound we might lose our sight. So, too, if we sustain a wound in our souls we can so quickly lose our sense of God. The truth is that our souls are dull and blind to God because of our sins and uncleanness. We keep our inward souls to ourselves, with our longings and disappointments, that we express in the loneliness of a heart that aches for God. God is the only one who can touch our inner 'eye' and wash us and make us clean. The touch of Jesus is the touch of love, and it is that touch alone that can reach the needs of our soul. We long for the touch of love, and it comes to us as we hear His voice and respond. Open your inner life to Him and be amazed at the floods of light that will fill you and bring healing and refreshing.

May 26

" 'It is not good to take the children's bread and throw it to the little dogs.' And she said, 'Yes Lord...' "i [Matthew 15:26]

This Gentile woman's great quality lay in her entire submission to the Saviour's diagnosis. When He stated that she was not worthy to receive the blessing she craved, she immediately agreed. The wonderful simplicity of faith lies in its estimation of the word and power of the One to whom we pray, and our entire agreement with our own unworthiness. 'Yes', said the woman, 'I am just a little dog, but You love even little dogs and will let us eat the crumbs that fall from Your table'. We modern Christians see ourselves all too easily as the special object of God's grace because of some inherent goodness in us. The truth is that the blessing we receive is all because of Him. That should make us laugh with confidence, because although we have no grounds of appeal in ourselves, yet we have unshakeable grounds of appeal in Him. The Lord's heart leapt for joy at her declaration: "O woman, great is your faith! Let it be to you as you desire." The woman had a deep burden, but at the same time, a careless disregard for self. She cast herself on Him; in the light of His love and mercy, she was confident of His answer. If we approach God in any other way we will end up doubting whether He will hear our prayer with favour. Cast yourself on Him in joyous abandon. If the woman could hope to benefit as a mere dog, how great her surprise to discover that, through the cross, she too was included in the covenant family and could sit at the table and eat the loaf, not just the crumbs.

May 27

"...a sower went out to sow." [Matthew 13:3]

The sower is Jesus, and He distributes little parcels of living power through His word. The word of Jesus lies waiting to explode with life when it is germinated by the Spirit of God. The Christian life is not a building that we keep adding bits to; it is a tree, and it grows by the principle of life that it contains within itself. Christ and His word are one, and He is the life that He imparts to us through His word. The great principle of seed, both in the natural and in the spiritual, is death and resurrection, for this is the DNA of Christ and the secret of spiritual growth. As we lose our lives, so we discover that we have gained. The second great principle of spiritual growth revealed in the parable of the sower, is that life cannot germinate in a divided heart. If there is competition, the seed will not function at all. For the word to germinate, a believer must embrace the word with their whole heart. This is because the word brings us to nothing, and so to life from the dead. If we are pursuing the things of the world, we will not be brought to nothing. If we are worried and careful about many things, we will not be able to focus on the power of the cross. The word that Jesus sows, and that lies in our hearts, is *'all or nothing'*. Go the whole way, yield all, let the word have its way in your heart, and discover the matchless wonder of the explosive power of Christ within to shape your life.

May 28

"You shall not shout or make any noise with your voice, nor shall a word proceed out of your mouth, until the day I shall say to you, 'Shout!' Then you shall shout." [Joshua 6:10]

This command is perhaps one of the hardest, namely to hold our tongues and to walk in quiet obedience until the shout of the Spirit becomes an all-consuming cry of faith. The tongue is one of the means by which faith and victory so easily leak out of the believer's heart. If we can obey God in the use of our tongue, we will come to deeper and greater victories. The key is to keep a quiet heart and a still mind, listening calmly to the voice of the Spirit. The tongue is like a background noise, both in the brain and in the mouth, that drowns out the voice of the Spirit. If only we will be quiet long enough, we will sense that there is another voice speaking inside our hearts on a different level from our chattering minds. We can get caught up in triumphalism, talking up our faith in a kind of self-induced enthusiasm. It takes great faith to realise that the Spirit is not relying on our enthusiasm! He is relying on us hearing His words and His note, which is triumph of a totally different order. When we catch the shout of the Spirit, faith rises instantly. Then something changes in our hearts because we have spoken out not merely what we want to happen, but what the Spirit declares prophetically will happen. Be still, and let the shout build up in your heart as you ponder the triumph of Christ.

May 29

"And Joshua went to Him and said to Him, 'Are you for us, or for our adversaries?' So He said, 'No but as Commander of the army of the LORD have I now come.' " [Joshua 5:13-14]

This was a decisive turning point in Joshua's life and ministry. It is marked by the word *"now"*, indicating that things had changed. Joshua had taken the people in faith past the point of no return, and when this had happened, the Lord appeared to him, to show him that things were to be of a different order. Joshua was to experience a power and a victory over the coming years through God's good pleasure resting on His people. The victory was to be so complete because the Commander of the Lord's army was now personally in the vanguard of His people. In truth it was because the people had taken their place behind Him, not because He had joined them. This is clear from the Commander's answer, that it was the people who had taken God's side, and not God who was on the people's side. This profound change is within our reach, if we will take our place clearly in the will and purpose of God and burn our bridges, going beyond the point of no return. This is not merely our personal victory, this is our participation in His victory, for purposes and plans that have a greater meaning than any of the smaller things that preoccupy us. In the fog of war, the key is to obey the orders that come down from HQ, believing that things that may make little sense to the footsoldier will one day become clear. We give our lives to Him and for Him, not for self-interest but for the greater glory of God.

May 30

"Doesn't your teacher pay the temple (two-drachma) *tax?"* ....
*"...go to the lake and throw out your line. Take the first fish you
catch; open its mouth and you will find a four-drachma coin.
Take it and give it to them for my tax and yours."*
[Matthew 17:24-27, NIV]

Here is brief lifting of the veil to reveal the Lordship of Christ
and the faithfulness of His provision for His children.   The
provision is so precise - the need was for 4 drachmas, and the
fish had precisely that amount in its mouth! The combination of
the provision with incredible Lordship is both arresting and
comforting. How many steps were involved in getting that coin
into that fish's mouth, and then directing that fish to that hook?
A fisherman loses a coin from his pocket, a fish swallows it and
then is caught with the coin still in its mouth. These things show
us that we are not to depend on natural means for our support,
nor can we ever work out how the provision will come. God is
Lord of the details of our lives, and the weave of circumstances
that surround us is woven by the Lord Himself. Your needs,
physical and spiritual, will be met, and met perfectly. Notice
that the provision was only for what was needed. Jesus has
everything at His beck and call. There is no reason to give you
more than you need, since His supply is based on His ability to
draw from an inexhaustible store. Elijah was fed by ravens in
the midst of a famine. Two million Israelites were fed with
water, manna and fresh meat for 40 years. Five thousand were
fed in the desert. What do these things teach us? He will never
leave us or forsake us, and His provision is as sure as His
Lordship.

May 31

"...you have not passed this way before." [Joshua 3:4]

The Holy Spirit leads us in ways that are not merely a repetition
of the pattern of past blessing. If this were not the case, we
would not need Him. The uncertainty and unfamiliarity cause
us to feel our way forward like a child learning to ride a bike, or
a stranger arriving in a foreign city. The effect is humbling and
faith-building.   We must look to God, and not to past
experiences, for the assurance we seek as we move forward.
God will cause our circumstances to change, and if we will not
step out into the unknown with God then we will remain in the

shallows of predictability - nothing can ever happen that will disturb our calm, because we iron it out of our lives. The result is spiritual deadness. This is a challenge to all who have responsibility for others. The Church must go through new challenges, and if we do not rise to meet them, then we will become a people with a good past but a static present. Joshua had to face obstacles, battles, and situations for which no past experience could prepare him. All the riches of our experience with God cannot replace the need to walk with Him now through the challenging new things we will face if we will dare to follow the leading of the Holy Spirit. God is the God of endless newness, and one of the marks of the Holy Spirit is that He rarely repeats Himself, while never contradicting Himself. Reach out, obey, believe and discover the wonder of the infilling of life in the Spirit.

June 1

"Assuredly, I say to you, whatever you bind on earth will be bound in heaven; and whatever you loose on earth will be loosed in heaven. Again I say to you that if two of you agree on earth concerning anything that they ask, it will be done for them by My Father in heaven. For where two or three are gathered together in My name, I am there in the midst of them." [Matthew 18:18-20]

These words indicate that, where there is unity between believers, there will be great spiritual power. When humanity was building the tower of Babel, God declared that, because of their great unity through one language, they were on the verge of enormous discoveries. God said that: *"nothing that they propose to do will be withheld from them"* [Genesis 11:6]. This is true in the merely human sense of linguistic unity. It has proved to be true in that the English language has united the world's scholars and enabled humanity to make great strides forward in science and technology. But if it is true in a natural sense, it is much truer in a spiritual sense. The Church must not allow the devil to divide and conquer. If brother can be divided against brother, then the prayer life of the Church will be paralysed. If a Church can walk in unity and love, then the Lord will take its prayer life into wonderful union with the throne room on high. Resolve to restore any wrong relationships. Perhaps you have blamed others, but is there anything you have done wrong that you should confess? If you restore and heal broken relationships, you will come into a new dimension of power in prayer.

June 2

"And when the Philistine looked about and saw David, he disdained him; for he was only a youth..." [1 Samuel 17:42]

It would not have made any difference to the outcome if David had been a toddler. David set out against the champion of the Philistines, who was well-armed, experienced in battle and extremely strong. Behind Goliath stood the armies of the Philistines, ready to attack. They looked on a mere youth, unarmed and inexperienced in battle. If only they could have seen the Invisible One, they would have trembled and fled. We may be tempted to look on the hosts of darkness, but we need instead simply to hold the hand of the Creator/Redeemer Jesus, and then we stand invincible, whatever our age. The outcome seemed clear to the Philistines, and the outcome will seem clear to a person of the world. The Church may seem weak and irrelevant, and sometimes may look as if it is about to be swept away by the tides of evil flowing in the rocky riverbed of history. The Church is like an army of helpless children, fighting against the sophisticated armies of earth. But the army of children will win, because they walk with Jesus. How blessed to be aware of the inevitable victory of Christ. All fear and dread disappear and are replaced with eager anticipation of how He shall make His people triumph. The details are different in every battle, but the outcome is the same. We are more than overcomers through Christ.

June 3

"For the promise is to you and to your children, and to all who are afar off, as many as the Lord our God will call."
    [Acts 2:39]

Perhaps the most important truth concerning the Holy Spirit is that He is as active and present in the world today as in the days of the Acts of the Apostles. In fact Acts is one of the few books in the Bible that does not end with the word 'Amen' - indicating that it is not yet a finished history! True, the inspired account is complete. But the inspired account deliberately gives us the faith that God will be the same with all subsequent generations. Church history is full of miracles, prophecies and other manifestations of the outpouring of the Holy Spirit. The Bible is our infallible guide and is all-sufficient in all matters relating to spiritual life. But we are not merely intellectual Christians, and it is not an all-sufficient Bible that we worship, it is the All-Sufficient Christ, to Whom the Bible leads us. He baptises with the Holy Spirit, heals, reveals and works wonderful things in His people and through His people. Christ ministers the Holy Spirit to His people and by this brings them into a dimension of life and power that is more than we could ever have dreamed of.

June 4

"If anyone thirsts, let him come to Me and drink. He who believes in Me, as the Scripture has said, out of his heart will flow rivers of living water." [John 7:37-38]

Faith is a key that allows the kingdom to come in power into our hearts. We must examine ourselves to ask how much we believe and expect God to really pour out His Spirit and form Churches that are like the one found in Acts 2. This kind of faith is matched by strong desire and determination to see God work. Jesus said that there is a deep work of the Holy Spirit that makes us one with God through the death of His Son. This work is the foundation of the Church because it makes believers into a community of love. It takes the sin and awkwardness out of us and makes us bear with one another and wash each other's feet. Do you believe this work is real? Do you believe that God can do this deep work in your heart? Can you ask in faith, believing that God will do it for you? Faith sometimes involves hanging on when all seems dark, but at other times it is a great open-hearted reception of all that God has promised. Jesus is not here describing a state of life that is merely hanging on, but one that has launched out in joyous abandonment into the greatness of His abundant salvation.

June 5

"Receive the Holy Spirit." [John 20:22]

Mankind is sinful, and unworthy to receive the Holy Spirit. This is a legal barrier that makes it wrong for God to pour out His Spirit on sinners without a sacrifice for sin. But there is also the barrier of guilt in the human heart, as every sinner knows that they are unworthy to receive such a gift from God. However, justification is the declaration that God has accepted the sacrifice of Jesus. By this sacrifice He has made us legally acceptable before God. This legal acceptance is the meaning of the word 'justified'. However, it is not just a deliverance from the negative; it is also the imputing of the positive. Imagine someone who is a debtor. They owe a million dollars. Christ, through His blood, has not only cancelled the debt, but in its place He has filled the account with a million dollars credit! Christ has forgiven our sins **and** imputed to us His virtues. Thus, we are not just free from the guilt of past sins, we are positively worthy through Christ to receive the Holy Spirit. [Colossians 1:12]. It is as if we had failed an exam, and God not only erases our failure, but gives us a pass with distinction! We are now fully reconciled to God, and it is a righteous act for God to give the Holy Spirit. Our realisation of this is a key since, without it, we will strive endlessly, believing we must earn the gift of the Spirit. There is nothing you can do to earn the gift of the Holy Spirit, or to earn His faithful infilling day by day. All we can do is believe in His justifying grace, and receive.

June 6

"And they were all filled with the Holy Spirit and began to speak with other tongues, as the Spirit gave them utterance."
[Acts 2:4]

The 120 people in the upper room all prayed with tongues in response to the coming of the Holy Spirit. This indicates an inner abandonment to the Spirit's working – they were not filtering everything through their intellect. This kind of abandonment may appeal in a wrong way to those who are inclined to be undisciplined - there is no doubt that it is open to abuse, and some people may make noises and claim that this is the manifestation of the Holy Spirit. Paul clearly teaches that the gift of tongues will produce personal edification, and that it is not primarily for public use, and if used in public, must be accompanied by an interpretation. Also, on the Day of Pentecost, it was not unknown languages but known ones that were released by the Holy Spirit. Nevertheless, the possible dangers should not rob us of the very real blessing in yielding ourselves in entire abandonment to the Holy Spirit. This is a key in the release of the Spirit on a congregation and in the work of the ministry. In other words, the Holy Spirit does not work through mere intellectual exercise. Our intellects should be thoroughly engaged in understanding the truth of God, but in the flow of worship we must let go and allow the Spirit to have free flow through our lives. If He can flow in us through the gift of tongues, then it will not be long before He is flowing through us in prophecy. Yield, with understanding, with faith, to the marvellous flow of the Holy Spirit in you and through you.

June 7

"Confess your trespasses to one another, and pray for one another, that you may be healed. The effective, fervent prayer of a righteous man avails much." [James 5:16]

The Holy Spirit cannot be poured out and mixed with sin. Therefore sin is the most serious obstacle to a true New Testament Church, and to a true outpouring of the Holy Spirit. We must confess and utterly forsake sin. Our hearts must be emptied of all uncleanness. All habits that weaken our hearts must be renounced. We must take time so that our repentance

97

is deep and thorough. If repentance is not taken seriously, there is no reason why God should take us seriously when we pray for an outpouring of His Spirit. The 'religious' person has more to fear than the worldly sinner in this respect. The worldly sinner has nothing to lose.   Everyone knows that he was not a Christian, and did not profess to be one.   However, when the religious person confesses and repents, they have more to lose. They must lay down their reputation. This will be harder the longer a person has claimed to be a 'Christian' and the higher their position in the Church.   God does not want to shame people – that is not the purpose of repentance - but we must have a broken, humble attitude that indicates a readiness to acknowledge mistakes and sins of prayerlessness, pride and spiritual dryness. Sin that we have not repented of is an inner wound that festers and will breed infection. Deal quickly and decisively with all that mars your inner walk with God, and abide in the joy of being right with God.

June 8

"But the Helper, the Holy Spirit, whom the Father will send in My name, He will teach you all things, and bring to your remembrance all things that I said to you. [John 14:26]

The Holy Spirit teaches and guides believers.   He does this through many different means, but the main way is through the 'witness of the Spirit' or the inner 'anointing' by which we know things. John writes that, by this inner anointing, we *"know all things"* [1 John 2:20]. He does not mean that we know Church history or we no longer need to hear preaching and teaching! John is referring to things that not only **are** known by the inner anointing, they **can** only be known by this means. By the inner witness we know we are children of God [Romans 8:16]. By this inner witness believers can sense a deceiving spirit [1 John 2:18-20].   Of course, we use our minds to detect wrong doctrines, but we know wrong spirits by the anointing.   Not everyone who has a strange doctrine is of a wrong spirit, and not everyone who has right doctrine has a right spirit! The witness alone can lead us to make right choices in our lives.   Acts 16:6-10 describes how Paul and Silas discerned the next place for them to preach the gospel. The Holy Spirit communicated His will to them, both directly and through circumstances, including difficulties. But whether life is easy or hard, no-one can know God's will unless they are being taught by the inner witness of the Holy Spirit. Keep a quiet heart; keep listening to the inner promptings and tugging of the Holy Spirit, communicating God's mind and will.

June 9

"...when you pray, go into your room..." [Matthew 6:6]

When Jesus teaches about the *'inner room'* He does not mean our bedroom! While we are wise to choose a quiet spot to pray, many people will not actually find a 'room' with a door to close. In wealthy people's homes this may be easy, but in the homes of the poor it is not, and it was to poor people that Jesus was speaking. When Jesus says, *'Go to your Father in the secret place'*, He is referring to our God-given ability to enter God's direct, living Presence. This is not just a mental attitude or the exercise of our imagination - it is real. The Holy Spirit is the inner place, and we ourselves have within us something that is best described as a 'room'. The Tabernacle, with its outer court, Holy Place and Most Holy Place, is a picture of our outer body, soul, and inner sanctuary of the heart or spirit. Jesus Himself 'tabernacled' among us [John 1:14] - the Greek for *"dwelt"*. Jesus had the 'inner room' that no-one saw or entered while He was on earth. When we enter the secret place, we surrender ourselves to the Holy Spirit, we are filled with God's living Presence, and we begin to pray in the Spirit. It is this act of surrender by faith that is the foundation of Jesus' teaching on the life of prayer. To know God's Presence is to taste the fountain of eternal life, and the effect can be overwhelming, most of all because it frees us from mere pleasure-seeking. God's Presence purifies and ennobles our hearts, freeing us from self and making us true liberated worshippers of God.

June 10

"...pray to your Father..." [Matthew 6:6]

We have free access through grace. Jesus is so simple in the way He describes the wonder of prayer. Although the word 'justification' is absent from the Gospels, yet our Justifier is always present. The cross was still in the future, but God anticipated the justification of sinners even in the Old Testament, and Christ justified sinners in the way He treated them and still treats them. He speaks to sinners in a way that invites them simply to come. We are not justified by a doctrine - we are saved by faith in the justifying welcome of a Person!

God in Christ welcomes us into the holiest of all [Hebrews 10:19]. Christ teaches this same thing here - that we are simply to come to God in prayer, and He will receive us. This truth can baffle a new believer and return to puzzle the oldest saint. We are prone to believe that we must earn God's acceptance. So people who feel they have failed God in some way may simply stop praying because they feel unworthy. On the other hand, some mature Christians pray with pride in their spiritual stature! They will recount the hours they spend in prayer, as if it is through their efforts that people are being saved and healed. The truth is that we can never **earn** acceptance with God - we are unworthy ever to approach Him. But God is full of grace and mercy, and invites us to approach; and it is by this grace alone that we are made BOLD to approach His holy throne. It is by His grace that we have answers to prayer. God will simply grant our request, whether we are able to spend hours praying or just minutes!

June 11

"But you are those who have continued with Me in My trials. And I bestow upon you a kingdom, just as My Father bestowed one upon Me, that you may eat and drink at My table in My kingdom, and sit on thrones judging the twelve tribes of Israel." [Luke 22:28-30]

It was the great quality of perseverance that made Peter the outstanding disciple of the Gospels, to be matched later by the same quality in Paul. They persevered in loving Jesus, although their love was imperfect; they persevered in humbling themselves and seeking forgiveness when they were convicted of sin. Once Peter told Jesus to depart from him [Luke 5:8], indicating that Jesus should give up trying to make him a better man. Jesus had to call Peter from fishing three times before he finally gave it up and trusted Jesus to provide for him [Mark 1:17; Luke 5:10-11; John 21:19]. But Jesus does not give up easily, and it is by His faithfulness that we are saved, not by ours! Peter went through the deep waters of his own fickle heart - denying the Lord in the moment of temptation. But Peter's heart broke, and through the tears of brokenness come great prayers of **surrender**, not commitment. Our great prayers of commitment are matched by great failure! But it is when we are broken that the real test of discipleship comes. Will we refuse to wallow in failure, and instead hand the broken pieces over to God, to remake us as trophies of His amazing grace? Peter's destiny was totally undeserved, but that is what grace does - it takes poor nothings and makes them kings and priests, to sit on thrones with the Son of God.

June 12

"Paul, a bondservant (or bond-slave) *of Jesus Christ..."*
    [Romans 1:1]

Paul does not refer to himself as a disciple anywhere in his writings. His preferred word is 'bond-slave' - indicating that he saw himself as belonging entirely to Jesus Christ. This concept of slavery underlies his whole view of his relationship with Christ. A slave has no rights - he has no free time, he has no right to choose what clothes he wears, or when and where he will go on holiday. The slave has no rights at all, and no wages. The reason is that he is owned by his master. This recognition of the Lord's entire ownership of our lives is the point at which the cross becomes reality in us. *"...you are not your own... For you were bought at a price; therefore glorify God in your body and in your spirit, which are God's."* [1 Corinthians 6:19-20]. Redemption means not only that we were bought in the slave market and made free; it also means a change of ownership. Yet this slavery is perfect freedom, for the slave is the property and the responsibility of his Master. While a slave has no rights, he also has no burden to carry for his own life. His only burden is the Master's will. All his food, clothes and means of transport are provided for by his Master. So he is not anxious about any day or about the future, knowing that his Master has everything under control. The cross is to us perfect liberty as we recognise the wonderful Master who now has the rights over our entire life.

June 13

" 'Follow Me, and I will make you become fishers of men.' They immediately left their nets and followed Him."
    [Mark 1:17-18]

This moment of Peter's call is the starting point of 'The Way', as the Christian gospel was first known (see Acts 9:2). Meeting Jesus Christ means being confronted with a huge choice, on a level we never knew existed before. It means that we become aware that there is a level of life totally different from anything we have ever dreamed of. This call stirs a longing deep in our hearts, awakening us to the awareness of a purpose that fills all of life with meaning. Not to know the call is to live without meaning. To follow this call will cost you everything you have. Peter and his fellow disciples left their nets immediately - there is no indication of any preparation. They were suddenly faced with a spiritual reality that presented itself and then would pass on, with or without them. They answered with an act of renunciation. The call was not to a ministry or to a country - it was to be with a Person who captivated their affections and their will. They were drawn to Jesus. The call is the sense of being drawn to something irresistible - the spiritual, magnetic force of Jesus. It cannot be explained in merely rational terms. People give up fortunes, crowns, the love of their life, just to belong to Someone that they cannot see, nor prove in philosophical logic. Jesus is the focal point of the call of God. God faces us with Jesus again and again. He is presented to us as the key, the explanation, the goal, the destiny. We are called to follow Him wherever it may lead.

June 14

"One who turns away his ear from hearing the law, even his prayer is an abomination." [Proverbs 28:9]

God's Word and God's law are a foundation on which our life of prayer is built. It is no more possible to build a life of prayer without the Word of life, than it is to build anything more than a shack without an architect's plans. God's Word is food for us, gives us the framework to understand God's mind, and is a doorway to His Presence, which refreshes us and gives us faith. Start each time of prayer with the Word. Let it open the conversation between you and God. If you place upon yourself the burden of hearing God every day, but don't open the conversation with His Word, you will crush yourself in defeat and wander in vain agitation or, worse still, into deception. Let God open each day's communion, and let prayer be a conversation. The Bible is a Spirit-breathed, supernatural book, and those who read, meditate and listen will find their hearts overflowing with confidence in prayer, and a flow of things to pray about. Prayer, intercession, praise and worship all flow from the place of heeding God's Word.

102

June 15

"Then Herod, with his men of war, treated Him (Jesus) with contempt...." [Luke 23:11]
"God has chosen... things which are not, to bring to nothing the things that are..." [1 Corinthians 1:28]

It is easy to take for granted that Jesus let go of His life. This verse from Luke describes a moment in the cruel frenzy of mockery and rejection of Christ. He was made nothing, and so let go of His life. The sign that He had let go of His life was that there was no retaliation or inward bitterness. Jesus Christ accepted being made of no reputation, and was brought to nothing. Then God made Him the centre of the ages. God made Christ the Lord and ruler of all. In our lives, God is not seeking to rearrange our character in order to bring out the best in us. He is seeking to bring us to the same absolute surrender that makes us nothing. A person who has become nothing is dead to personal insults, criticism or being overlooked; they are free from bitterness and selfishness. It is on the basis of this inner surrender to the cross that God fills us with the Holy Spirit and moves so powerfully through us. As we become nothing, we will be amazed at what God makes out of us. The cross is the end of human-centred striving that promises so much and delivers so little. It marks the beginning of all that God can create and do in a life that is fully surrendered to Him.

June 16

"Then Jesus, being filled with the Holy Spirit, returned from the Jordan and was led by the Spirit into the wilderness, being tempted for forty days by the devil.... Then Jesus returned in the power of the Spirit to Galilee..."
[Luke 4:1-2, 14]

Jesus received the anointing of the Spirit at Jordan and then spent 40 days being tempted. It was this wilderness experience that released the power of that anointing. The person who resists temptation is the one who will prove the full power of the anointing. Great ministry must pass through severe tests - this pattern can be seen throughout the Bible. What God has imparted through the baptism with the Holy Spirit will leak out if we have a casual attitude to personal holiness. The way of power is simple - we must simply say 'No' to temptation, on whatever level it is presented to us. When we say 'No' we might be in the midst of dreariness or loneliness – i.e. a real wilderness which seems so far removed from 'ministry to people in need'. But really, those lonely moments are critical in our life and ministry. Those moments are the real crossroads of life. To say 'No' to self, pride and the flesh is to take the road that will lead to the healing of the broken-hearted, the deliverance of captives, the opening of blind eyes. It is to proclaim a 'year of grace', because grace does not merely **cover** sin, it gives **victory** over it. It abounds with power to keep us in our personal walk with God, and overflows in reaching out in love and compassion to those who are in need. Stand up, and determine to fight each lonely battle.

June 17

"Remember now your Creator in the days of your youth, before the difficult days come, and the years draw near when you say, 'I have no pleasure in them'." [Ecclesiastes 12:1]

At all stages of our lives, the opportunity to put things off till later is open to us; the danger is that we assume we will still have abundant opportunities in the future. The older we get, the fewer opportunities we will have, but there is a much more serious point here. This earthly life is not the trial run - it is the real thing. There is no such thing as a trial run. Forming godly habits is something that we must begin today. We may feel the pressure of the moment, the temptation to join the crowd, to go with the flow. Resist the flow, swim against the current, form habits that will give you the victory in what seem like far-off days. Someone may read this and say, *"But I am not young!"* The point is that we must not wait for the difficult days to come before we learn to fight. Fight at the time when there is no pressure, when responsibilities are fewer. Love God, attend to His Word, learn the habit of prayer. These habits will carry you and help you to do the right thing when it is ten times harder than it is at this point in your life. God is so good and gives us so much opportunity to learn the lessons of life and be ready for the 'evil day', when sinful people seem to rule and God seems distant. Stand up and do what is right, don't wait for the pressure of difficulty.

June 18

"...take up the whole armor of God, that you may be able to withstand in the evil day, and having done all, to stand. Stand

therefore, having girded your waist with truth, having put on the
breastplate of righteousness, and having shod your feet with the
preparation of the gospel of peace..."
[Ephesians 6:13-15]

Our warfare as believers is not merely against natural
temptations. There are powers that surround us in the spiritual
world, against which we must wage war by these vital elements
of our armour:
Truth: this is biblical truth, but the Greek word covers the whole
realm of 'reality'. In other words, we can wage war only as we
acknowledge our failings, otherwise there will be a spirit of
hypocrisy and spiritual defeat in us. Biblical truth will gird our
minds to live according to what God has said, and not
according to what we see or feel.
Righteousness: while truth is a belt that holds the armour in
place, righteousness is the armour that covers our heart.
Without it, our heart is vulnerable to attack, and a wound to the
heart is fatal. Maintaining righteousness is vital if we are to
continue to have life itself in the Spirit.
Peace: this always follows righteousness, and cannot precede it
[Romans 14:17]. There is no peace for the wicked [Isaiah
57:21]. The gospel is a gospel of peace through reconciliation.
Peace is the mark of the gospel. In the world there is only false
peace, which is short-lived and evaporates in the face of evil
and death. But we have a peace that passes understanding and
gives power to our gospel witness.

Are you ready to resist the attacks that will certainly come
against you?

June 19

"...they (the giants in the land) *are our bread..."*
[Numbers 14:9]
"...take up the whole armor of God, that you may be able to
withstand in the evil day, and having done all, to stand.... above
all, taking the shield of faith with which you will be able to
quench all the fiery darts of the wicked one."
[Ephesians 6:13, 16]

Our warfare is against all things that rise up against God,
whether in our own hearts or from the kingdom of darkness.
When these enemies appear, we must never be faint-hearted.
This warfare is common to all Christians, and we need the spirit

of Joshua and Caleb, who viewed the giants as a good breakfast! They clearly viewed opposition as something by which they would prove God's faithfulness and power. Faith is the opposite of worry and fear. We must not fear the devil or temptation, but hold up the shield of confidence in God, and faith in God's power to defend those who trust in Him. You may not have great faith for great miracles, but you can have great confidence that God is on your side. This faith then extends to the tearing down of strongholds such as Jericho, which is a picture of the fortresses in our minds such as unbelief. The devil constantly taunts us with our little faith and achievements. Somehow we even agree with him and call it humility! But while we know we bring very little to the Kingdom of God, we know also that we serve a great King who is matchless in battle. You don't have to boast in yourself having great faith - boast in the King! Sit down with Him and eat your enemies for breakfast.

June 20

"...take up the whole armor of God, that you may be able to withstand in the evil day, and having done all, to stand.... And take the helmet of salvation, and the sword of the Spirit, which is the word of God; praying always with all prayer and supplication in the Spirit..." [Ephesians 6:13, 17-18]

Battle drives us back to the foundations of why we are living as we are. What is really worth fighting for? Persecution clarifies our minds and focuses us on what is really important. While we may not all be facing persecution, we are constantly facing opposition from the same prince of darkness.

Salvation is the Christian's helmet, covering the realm of mental attacks which come in the form of condemnation from Satan. We must cling to the truth of reconciliation by Jesus' blood. If Satan moves us off this ground, our head is suddenly defenceless against his attacks. We are perfectly right with God through Christ.

The Word of God is the only weapon of attack in our armoury. With it, we attack the enemy's strongholds - we trust the Word of the Spirit to penetrate even the most hardened unbeliever. The Word of God imparts faith to unbelieving hearts, it speaks power into strengthless souls and life into the spiritually dead. The Word is also powerful to counteract the devil's lies, and just as Jesus used it to resist temptation in the wilderness, so we too must ask God to lead us to Scriptures that will enable us to resist the devil on our own lines of weakness.

Prayer - Paul here mentions *"all prayer"*, indicating that there is more than one way of praying. We must learn all the different ways of praying, as the Holy Spirit teaches us. The effect of prayer in the Spirit will be to empower the ministry of the Word preached. Be filled with the Spirit of battle.

June 21

"In the beginning was the Word..." *"No one has seen God at any time. The only begotten Son, who is in the bosom of the Father, He has declared Him."* [John 1:1, 18]

With the words *"In the beginning"*, John here takes us to the earliest point in time that can be conceived. Genesis 1:1 opens with similar words, reaching back to the creation. 1 John 1:1 reaches back only to the incarnation. But here in John 1:1 the 'beginning' is the condition that exists in God beyond time. The beginning, then, is not merely in time, but in position. It is the fountain-head of God and of all that is. To imagine this, we have to imagine a place before all things were. In the beginning there were no cars, no houses, no trees, no stars. Above all, there was no sin, no devil, only God. In the beginning was Christ, alongside and in relationship with His Father. There is in that relationship a profound stillness of being. The seraphim around God's throne were created for this place, and have covered their faces since the day of their creation at the wonder of it. Think of one of them visiting our gatherings - they might rightly wonder if they are servants of the same God! Yet these same creatures, attendant on the man Jesus Christ, would have sensed the unspoilt wonder of eternal life and rest in Him. Christ is in one sense the place itself. He is the Light that shines [John 1:4-5, 8:12] and the Life that sustains [Colossians 1:17]. Whatever else may ever be said about prayer and our relationship with God, it is foundational that our hearts enter into quiet waiting on Him, or we will never truly understand who He is.

June 22

"...I am from above." [John 8:23]

Here is the key to life in the Spirit - dwelling in an unclouded relationship with God. This is Christ's inner life - the Son with the Father [John 1:18]. Christ dwells above with the Father. He has a soaring Spirit, and approaches every situation from the standpoint of the Father's love and of eternity. This perspective can only be attained by living fellowship with God in Christ. It should come as no surprise to us that the Church is given two wings like those of a great eagle [Revelation 12:14], so that she might escape the onslaught of the devil against her. Sadly, the Church has used other means to fight the powers of darkness, and they have proved weak and ineffectual. Philosophy and education may improve the mind, and prosperity may improve our physical living conditions, but only soaring on eagles' wings will keep us from the attacks of the powers of darkness. This, then, is a key for all who would know the secret of victory over sin and darkness. Fellowship with Christ makes us soar. Learn the power of a soaring spirit. Learn the secret of coming at life from above, from the eagle's nest. Rising above has the power to change all of life.

June 23

"In the beginning was the Word..." "That was the true Light which gives light to every man coming into the world."
[John 1:1, 9]

Christ is the Light of the world. Physical sunlight provides nutrition in green plants, and sustains plant life. It produces vitamin D, which is vital for healthy human bodies. Sunlight warms the earth and keeps conditions right for all of life. It brightens our minds and refreshes our hope. All these are mere physical effects. Christ is uncreated Light. He shines through and imparts life to those who receive the Light of His penetrating Presence. He is the Light that releases our hearts as we wait before Him. He awakens hope and washes our beings free from unbelief and all negative things. As we wait on God, we are transformed into His image [2 Corinthians 3:18]. Light indicates an increase of understanding - not understanding that comes just from study, but from the realisation of the Person. Our minds are weak and our understanding clouded until we receive the Light of Christ's Presence. Study, but go to Christ by faith. Receive the ministry of His life-giving Presence. Spiritual darkness includes unbelief, sinful attitudes, depressions and fears. Do not wait to overcome these things by the force of human understanding alone. Go into the Presence of Jesus. Imagine a person in total darkness, pleading for light. What use would it be to tell them to drive away the darkness first, as a condition for bringing in the light! In the same way, Christ does not tell us to make ourselves clear and bright. He bids us come

108

to Him.

June 24

"Blessed is the man who listens to me, watching daily at my gates, waiting at the posts of my doors. For whoever finds me finds life, and obtains favor from the Lord..."
[Proverbs 8:34-35]

Waiting on God is the foundation of life in the Spirit. The human soul must find its poise, its purpose. The humming bird beats its wings rapidly in order to hover and draw nectar from a flower, but there is an ease and a poise in its flight. So, too, we must find the ease of praying, of waiting on God. Pause, let the hurry and strain go out of you. Jesus Christ demonstrates the perfect human soul in fellowship with God, and He longs to form that soul in us. Christ was a listener - it was His natural inclination to listen to His Father. The person who waits on God will be refreshed and empowered to act. Christ kept the poise of quiet inner focus on the Father, and the result was a flood of activity, flowing from the inner fountain of love and healing. Like the humming bird hovering, the level of activity might sometimes appear to be a great strain on us. But with our inner calling in perfect fulfilment, our life is able to maintain an effortless flow. 'Seek first the Kingdom of God.' We seek God's rule with deep inner surrender. Is the result passivity? Never - or it is a deception. Surrender to God in our heart is the poise of perfect flight. Watch, wait, listen and see your wings unfold to perfect flight.

June 25

"Whoever shuts his ears to the cry of the poor will also cry himself and not be heard." [Proverbs 21:13]

How we long for answered prayer! How deeply we need God to work on our behalf. These verses teach us that there is a cycle of life in the Spirit that God watches over with utmost care. If we feel that God's ears are blocked to our prayers, then we are definitely mistaken. We may instead need to look for the cause of the problem in ourselves. Are our ears open to cries for help from others? Have we made it a habit to respond seriously and quickly to cries for help, or have we turned people away so often that they have stopped asking us? If God's ears seem blocked to us, we must attend to our own ears; and if we feel that others are not sensitive to our needs, then we must attend to our own giving. *"Give, and it will be given to you: good measure, pressed down, shaken together, and running over will be put into your bosom. For with the same measure that you use, it will be measured back to you."* [Luke 6:38]. Get in the river and flow. Don't try to dig a trench to divert God's supply to your own patch of ground - it will dry up before it reaches your little spot! Get in the flow, open your ears to hear the cries around you, and you will be amazed at the effect on your fellowship with God.

June 26

"By His Spirit He adorned the heavens; His hand pierced the fleeing serpent. Indeed these are the mere edges of His ways, and how small a whisper we hear of Him! But the thunder of His power who can understand?" [Job 26:13-14]

God is greater than any of us can ever conceive. How glorious is His creative power in speaking the stars into existence! Our minds are brought to speechless wonder at the infinity and beauty of the universe. How great was the demonstration of His power in piercing the fleeing serpent, conquering our enemy at the cross of Calvary. But these demonstrations of His power are the 'mere edges of His ways'. This does not mean 'edges' only in terms of dimensions - it doesn't mean that God will one day create even bigger stars to dazzle us. No, these works of God - one in creation, one in judgment - are in themselves merely the edges of His ways. At the centre of His ways stands the matchless Son of God, with a different order of life and shining glory of personality. The centre of God's ways is an outshining of love that makes mountains and stars seem insignificant, and the victory over Satan like shooing chickens from a back yard. The real 'thunder of His power' is being disclosed by the Spirit as He reveals the power of character that makes God what He is. That character was revealed at Calvary and shall be ever more unfolded to adoring hearts through all eternity. That power was applied to mankind's problems at the cross, but will be seen one day in its own glorious setting, untroubled by enemies, and without the dreadfulness that terrifies sinners. God is dreadful in majesty, and as we are set free from sin, we enter more and more into the wonder of who He really is.

June 27

"And he (Abraham) believed in the Lord, and He accounted it to him for righteousness." [Genesis 15:6]

Abraham believed God. He had no works, not even circumcision, when his justification was pronounced. He was still ignorant of how it would all work out. He was also not yet in full faith; in that soon after this, he took Sarah's maid, Hagar, and had Ishmael through her. In other words, God in no way demanded perfection from Abraham; neither did his mistakes diminish his salvation. The underlying fact that maintained his salvation was that he believed God. All his mistakes were not in direct rebellion against God; they were through smallness of faith, and in the belief that God would need Abraham's help to fulfil all that He had said. Abraham's faith was small at first, but because it was genuine, it grew through all the trials. In the end it was made perfect, and he obtained all that God had promised him. However, Abraham was justified from the moment that he believed God. Note also that *"he believed in the Lord"* means he believed in the character and integrity of God. He did not yet see how it would all work out, but he believed that it would all work out because of who God is. Faith in God is faith in the fact that God is faultless, sinless, true and trustworthy in what He has said and in what He does. So faith is not just a means to obtain something, it is much more. It is the greatest gift we can receive from God. By faith we enter into relationship with God that lasts and develops as faith grows. We walk in the steps of our father Abraham.

June 28

"The law of the Lord is perfect, converting the soul..."
    [Psalm 19:7]

Really, the secrets of spiritual life are few and simple, and here is the most basic: take advantage of one of God's inestimable gifts - His Word. The Bible produces faith in the reader [Romans 10:17]. The Bible teaches that faith comes as we perceive and apply God's Word to ourselves. Faith is therefore a product of the Word working on our hearts and producing living faith, as opposed to merely intellectual assent. The Bible has a perfection that baffles the mind of the sceptic. Rationalists will not accept the Bible as perfect, since to do so would be to recognise its supernatural, miraculous quality. Numerous word studies have been made which show there are patterns in the

Bible text that are themselves an indication of an underlying perfection. Jesus also said that not one jot (the smallest Hebrew letter) or tittle (a minute ornament over a Hebrew letter) would pass from the Law till all of it was fulfilled. This refers to the literal inspiration of the Bible through the writers. Peter affirms that, *"prophecy never came by the will of man, but holy men of God spoke as they were moved by the Holy Spirit"* [2 Peter 1:21]. God has given us a doorway into the unseen world; open it and go through it! John Wesley said:

"I want to know one thing – the way to heaven; how to land safely on that happy shore. God Himself has condescended to teach the way; for this very end He came from heaven. He has written it down in a book. O give me that Book! At any price give me the Book of God!"

June 29

"O Lord, how long shall I cry, and You will not hear? Even cry out to You, 'Violence!' and You will not save."
     [Habakkuk 1:2]

Habakkuk's prayer is defiant, asking God about his lack of action despite much prayer. God did not rebuke Habakkuk for speaking his mind, because he directed his complaints straight to God. We damage ourselves when we complain to ourselves about God, and worst of all to friends and even unbelieving neighbours. It is hard to cover up inner disappointments, and they have a habit of surfacing at embarrassing moments. The answer is to go to God with all your conflicts and confusion, and pour them out to Him. God has the ability to absorb all our frustration, as long as we mix it with submission. Submission means that we must listen to God, for He will answer. Listening is not an easy habit, it involves self-denial and faith, but there are great rewards. Go to God, tell Him your true feelings and then pray that God will change you and touch you. There is nowhere else to go! It is only as we draw near to God that we find an answer to our hurting hearts. The government of the universe is not going to be transferred to us. God will include us in His government, and listen to what we say, but He Himself has the far-seeing eye and the depth of understanding. As we draw near, we not only **have** influence, we **are** influenced! Prayer is effective in changing the world on every level, both in the answers received, and in the effect of God on the person praying.

112

"We who are Jews by nature, and not sinners of the Gentiles." [Galatians 2:15]

This seems a strange verse at first. Paul says that he was a Jew by nature, and not a Gentile sinner. But it is clear that we are all - both Jew and Gentile - born with the nature of sin in our lives. That is changed by the power of new birth and the gift of a new nature. What Paul is referring to here is the 'nature' that is cultivated through upbringing - in other words, the habits of a lifetime. Paul was brought up to know which foods were on the permitted list for Jews; it was second nature for him to refuse to eat pork. The lesson here for us is that we must turn the imparted nature of Christ into the habits of our new life. If we had the habit of always criticising people, then we must cultivate the habit of encouraging them. If we had the habit of sinking into depression every time there was some negative response to us, then we must develop the habit of praise. Christ has imparted to us a new nature, but we must turn that new nature into habits of thought and life through obedience. This is not easy, and it involves a great deal of repentance, as we realise how easily we fall back into old ways. Old habits are strong, and shape our responses, and they must not be allowed to do so, or they will rob us of a consistent testimony. Determine to be a Christian by the power of the Spirit, and make faith, praise, love and obedience the habits of your life.

July 1

"...not by works of righteousness which we have done, but according to His mercy He saved us, through the washing of regeneration and renewing of the Holy Spirit..." [Titus 3:5]

What credit can we take for our salvation? An African story tells how the elephant and the ant teamed up to work together. The ant rode on the elephant's back, staying close to its ear in order to communicate with the elephant. They came to a bridge and the ant said: *"Let's shake the bridge!"* The elephant nodded solemnly and set off across the bridge, and with only the slightest extra effort the bridge began to sway under its pounding feet. People fled from the bridge in fear. When the elephant had crossed the bridge, the ant lifted itself up, stretched its legs and declared: *"We really shook that bridge!"* We are similarly inclined to forget how little we bring to God's kingdom. We boast that it is we who prayed (whispered in the elephant's ear), as if we had also answered the prayer! The worst boast would be for us to claim to have made a significant contribution to our salvation – e.g. *"I left a lucrative career in a casino to follow Christ."* None of our acts of repentance or faith actually contributed to the salvation God bestowed upon us by grace - they just opened the door for Him to do it. It is astonishing humility on God's part that He sees us as co-workers with Him, even as partners. The result is powerful beyond our wildest dreams. Thank God that He works together with you, and there is nothing that you will face today or throughout your life that together you cannot get through!

July 2

"Christ Jesus.... made Himself of no reputation, taking the form of a bondservant, and coming in the likeness of men."
[Philippians 2:5-7]

God's first answer to mankind's problems was to send His Son to become a man. Because all had sinned, there was no-one else good enough to show the human race the way of escape. Jesus shows the sinless life. Jesus was God but, as Paul explains, He became one of us. He took on human form in order to show us how to live and walk with God. Jesus Christ is God's pattern for human beings. We cannot attain His way of life by self-effort, but we are able to attain it through His gift of salvation and the power of the Holy Spirit. By a new birth, we begin a new life,

fe in the manger. We may not have the
ess, but we do have the power to be holy
/ without sin. If we walk with God, we
times in our lives to those that Jesus went
life - through waiting years, temptations,
, agonising prayer, and works of power.
ı; Jesus came first to show us how to live,
is life. We are not to be like the disciples
like Christ and like the disciples in their
ıe book of Acts. God wants you to give
it He can give His Spirit to you and live His
life in you. What a beautifully simple plan!

July 3

*"Then all this assembly shall know that the Lord does not save
with sword and spear; for the battle is the Lord's, and He will
give you into our hands."* [1 Samuel 17:47]

Goliath, the giant Philistine, invaded the territory of Judah and
challenged the armies of Israel. No-one was able to stand
against him. At last David appeared and, dressed as a mere
shepherd, he challenged and attacked Goliath without a sword
in his hand. He beheaded Goliath and led Israel in a
tremendous victory. This is a picture of the cross - it tells us
what the cross looked like in spiritual terms. All the hosts of
darkness were arrayed against the human race, and no human
being was strong enough to fight the devil. But Jesus came and
led the fight, absorbing all the power of evil in Himself and
destroying the devil in His mighty grip, motivated by purest love.
Jesus did not use the weapons of the flesh; He used the power of
love for lost sinners to destroy the devil. The devil's power was
broken - he suffered total defeat at the cross. Now he has no
grounds to work in the human heart, and because of this,
whoever believes in Jesus can experience immediate
deliverance. We as believers need no carnal weapons to
overcome the powers of darkness - we need only to receive the
love of God in Christ. No word of warfare came from Christ's
lips as He hung on the cross, only words of love, except for His
last cry. At the end He cried, *"It is finished"*; this is what the last
standing gladiator would cry in the Roman arena. Christ has
loved us to the end. Put on the garments of love and follow in
this battle.

July 4

"Be holy, for I am holy." [1 Peter 1:16]

Holiness is a uniquely divine quality. It refers to God's 'otherness' - to the huge difference between humanity and the divine. God is holy, pure, and clean in a different dimension. In Isaiah 6 the seraphim cry out, *"Holy, holy, holy"* without ceasing. This cry is not a conscious decision; it is a response of their being to the Presence of God. The astonishing thing is that the seraphim are not sinful. It is entirely to be expected that a sinner should cover his face before God, but angels that have never sinned are not covering their faces from conviction of sin, but from their overwhelming sense of awe at God's Being. God in His holiness is above all that we can imagine Him to be. We become holy only through the work of the **Holy** Spirit. This means that we belong to God and bear His stamp and seal. Holiness means 'set apart for God'. This explains why the Holy Spirit is grieved every time we do or think something that is unworthy of a vessel in which God dwells. We need the Holy Spirit. He has worked in our lives since we were conceived in our mother's womb. He was present throughout our childhood. He was the One who, unknown and unnoticed, worked in us to incline our hearts to receive Christ in salvation. He longs to be known and fully received by us so that He might have full sway and impart His chief characteristic - divine holiness. The Holy Spirit does not make us divine, but He does impart the stamp of God's Being. Receiving the Holy Spirit is a central point of entering into God's plan for our lives. By it we are adjusted to Him and His ways.

July 5

"God is Spirit...." [John 4:24]

Spirit is the dimension of God's Being. God does not have a body as human beings do. This means that God can both indwell and be indwelt. Fallen mankind does not know what 'spirit' is. Our eye rests on flesh and on external things. This means that faith is unnatural to us. When the Spirit of God comes to us, we suddenly become aware of the realm of the supernatural. The Spirit imparts faith immediately, bringing us to life on the inside, making us aware of God and the reality of heaven and angels etc. 'Spirit' also refers to the essence or heart of a person. When we think of God's Spirit, we should think of

God's innermost Being - His heart. When God pours out His Spirit, He pours out His heart. Christians rightly pray for God to pour out His Spirit, but often they do not realise the greatness of this request - that God should pour out and commit His innermost person to the lives of human beings. God rightly waits until our hearts are broken and deeply repentant before He will commit His precious inner self in this way. The outpouring of God's Spirit must be met by a similar act in us. Do it, pour out your spirit, and see how God responds.

July 6

"We have not so much as heard whether there is a Holy Spirit." [Acts 19:2]

The Holy Spirit is content to be invisible, as He loves the glory of Jesus. Even some believers do not notice Him! He cannot be known by carnal mankind, since there is no sensitivity to the Spirit of God in sinful people. Sinners can easily relate to the concept of God as Father and as Son, but they have no concept of what or who the Holy Spirit is. Most new Christians may think of Him as a power, like electricity. But the Bible reveals that He is not a power but a Person, with feelings and sensitivity. Stephen said in Acts 7:51 that the Jewish leaders were *"stiff-necked and uncircumcised in heart and ears"*. This was a grave insult, especially to a Jew! Nevertheless, it is true of the whole human race. The human heart is hardened and our ears are covered with a thick layer of 'flesh' that makes us totally unaware of God. Many people's conversion takes place when they suddenly become aware of the Presence of God through the Holy Spirit. What a sad thing to live with such a companion, and ignore Him - not wilfully, but by sheer ignorance or misinformation, or rank unbelief. God loves you and has provided 'another Comforter' who will dwell with you for ever. Believe in Him, open your heart to Him and receive Him.

July 7

"If you then, being evil, know how to give good gifts to your children, how much more will your heavenly Father give the Holy Spirit to those who ask Him!" [Luke 11:13]

The Bible bids us pray that we might receive the Holy Spirit. But prayer is not merely speaking religiously to God. The key to prayer is an inner longing that is directed up in faith to God. Some people pray for revival but do not long for it. A mother may not be very 'good at prayer', but will groan all day with longing for her son to be saved. She may not realise that she has been praying all day, but her inner longing is heard by God. Jesus said that He would give the Holy Spirit to those who thirst and come to Him and ask. It is not like asking for a cup of coffee! It is more like a man asking for a woman's hand in marriage. It is a deeper step in an eternal partnership. When a young man asks a girl to marry him, he will prepare the moment as well as possible. If he truly loves the girl, he will wait for the answer with bated breath and beating heart! The Bible portrays God as a young man in love in the Song of Solomon. The most common picture of the Church is the Bride of Christ, making herself ready for her wedding day [Revelation 19:7-9]. God is inviting us to share eternity with Him. God has promised to hear our prayer if we ask with all our heart [Jeremiah 29:12-13]. Ask in faith, believing in God's unswerving faithfulness to His promise.

July 8

"...while He prayed, the heaven was opened. And the Holy Spirit descended..." [Luke 3:21-22]

The first time we see Jesus praying is in the waters of Jordan, and the Holy Spirit is descending upon Him. This already should teach us the wonder of praying in the power of the Holy Spirit. By our praying, we too can open heaven if our hearts are right with God. The heart of all ministry is to pray and see the Holy Spirit descend on those we minister to, revealing God and doing the works of God. This pattern was to continue as Jesus preached and worked miracles. He was in touch with Father, and so great works were done through Him. Often the 'anointing' is seen as an impersonal power, but in reality the power of Jesus' ministry was in the simple fact that He had a clear, unbroken relationship with the Father, hearing His voice, and knowing that His prayers were heard. Jesus did not have to withdraw for hours every time He needed to do a miracle. He prayed in the midst of the crowds; nothing was ever allowed to disturb His communion with the Father. It is right to be suspicious of everything that depersonalises the power of God. Jesus was a delight to His Father, and that is what made His life so simple. He lived to please the Father, and the result was an open heaven and an outpouring of the Holy Spirit. Many great

118

things we seek remain out of reach because we are seeking the wrong thing. Look up and love the Father and, whether you realise it or not, heaven will be wide open over you and His blessing will be flowing all around you.

July 9

"We have much to say about this, but it is hard to explain because you are slow to learn." [Hebrews 5:11, NIV]

The Bible never censures intellectual weakness; it would be unjust and pointless to do so, since none of us can change our brain's capacity! The writer here is not suggesting that his readers should try harder by concentrating more. The Greek here for *"slow to learn"* is a word meaning 'without push'. The writer is saying what all preachers know: when there is spiritual hunger in a congregation, it draws revelation from the preacher, and he finds an ease in preaching. God has great things to tell us, but He waits for us to be eager enough to want to receive them. We can know as much as we really want to. We are as holy and as prayerful as we really want to be. God is not chiding our intellectual capacity; He is appealing to the capacity of our hearts, which is directly linked to the way we order our lives. If we hunger for the world, we will have little grasp of eternal things. If we hunger for God, God will move heaven and earth to satisfy that hunger. He will send prophets and apostles into our lives, by books, by encounters, by apparently random events. If we have no room in our hearts, then we might sit in the very presence of the Son of God, and yet find ourselves bored. The hungry person will gather up every crumb, and God will make sure that they are satisfied. Give attention to your heart. If you heart has become dull, empty it of the rivals to the Presence of God, and watch Him fill you with good things.

July 10

"Nor do they put new wine into old wineskins, or else the wineskins break, the wine is spoiled, and the wineskins are ruined. But they put new wine into new wineskins, and both are preserved." [Matthew 9:17]

This parable of the wineskins was given in answer to the question of why Jesus did not teach his disciples to fast. Jesus was teaching that there is a difference in order of life, between

119

His life and that of even the greatest man of the old dispensation of law. John the Baptist was a great man, but he did not know the power of the indwelling Christ and all the riches of life that come from the New Covenant. The parable is disarmingly simple, and hidden in it is a great jewel - the human heart cannot bear the glory of the life of Christ. The standards of Christ are too high and would cause deadly strain if imposed upon people without the power of the Holy Spirit. So, how is the problem solved? A new wineskin must be procured. In natural terms, this involved killing an animal and searing its skin in the fire to remove all traces of flesh. Then, while the skin was supple, it would be sewn up and filled with the new wine. The implications are simple. For the Holy Spirit to have free reign in us, He does not require great commitment, or even great openness to new things. He requires that I yield to God's knife - the cross - and God's fire - the Holy Spirit - to bring self and strain to an end, so that I will not spoil the Holy Spirit's work. John the Baptist was great, but he would have spoilt the Spirit's work. The New Covenant releases us from self-centred striving, to the wonderful ease of a Christ-centred life. Yield to the Holy Spirit, and let Him impart the life of Christ.

July 11

"For I have no one like-minded, who will sincerely care for your state. For all seek their own, not the things which are of Christ Jesus." [Philippians 2:20-21]

It is astonishing that Paul had no other friend like Timothy, who had cultivated an unselfish nature. Timothy genuinely cared for others. When we are born again we receive the gift of a new nature, but we must form new habits by constantly obeying the promptings of the Holy Spirit. Paul tells us that this was rare among the thousands of people that He knew. There were doubtless others who had cultivated their preaching ministry, their business, their career or their family life. Timothy had cultivated the ministry of caring for others, and of leaving obsessive attention to himself. Spiritual qualities and spiritual men and women are rare. This is not to discourage us, but to challenge us to strike out against the stream. Floating downstream is easy as long as we know how to stay afloat! Wading or swimming against the tide is exhausting. We must refuse to be conformed to the flow of cynicism, unbelief and selfishness that we meet on every side. If we do, the reward will be an unselfish life; the most blessed person is one like Timothy.

ırk 5:41]

Jairus' daughter He took the three key
ᵉs and John, to witness the event. What did
ʳ witnessed the incredible power of God to
doubt some measure of faith was imparted to
them, a₃ ᵘ'⁻ʲ   ᵥ Him exercise His absolute and effortless
authority.   Jesus did not raise His voice or make any wild
gestures. He took the little girl by the hand and said 'Little lamb,
arise'.   He exercised power in gentleness. The human soul
needs gentleness and quietness. We do not open to loudness or
brashness; we tend to close up and hide when we meet such
people. The depths of the human soul can only be reached by
the love of God. The surgeon handles the sharpest knife with
skill. Sharper still is the voice of Jesus, and He always speaks
with love. Love alone can heal our hearts. Love is the most
powerful force in the universe. Love has absolute authority.
Love is enthroned on high and heals us without boasting or
manipulating. Open to His love and be healed. Trust in His love
as you help others and show them the incredible power of a
meek, quiet and loving life.

July 13

*"Then Jesus said to them plainly, 'Lazarus is dead. And I am glad
for your sakes that I was not there...' "* [John 11:14-15]

These are arresting words - Jesus was glad that He had not been
with Lazarus to prevent his death. This baffled Martha and
Mary, and at first seems baffling to us. If Jesus teaches His
disciples anything, it is how to die. We human beings tend to
cling to our life, and cry for help to survive. But there are times
when God wants things to get a whole lot worse before He will
step in. If Lazarus had not been allowed to die, he would never
have experienced the wonder of resurrection. What happened
to Lazarus teaches us many lessons. On the physical level, it
shows, as Jesus persistently taught the disciples, that physical
death is sleep, and nothing to be afraid of. On the spiritual
level, it teaches us that God has a radical solution to our human
condition. He has radical surgery to offer, that can only be

121

received by the person who is willing to let go of self, die with Christ, and experience the wonder of a complete transformation of their life. Christ led the way in death and resurrection; when we let go of sin, self, the world and the flesh, and embrace death by faith, then we truly please God. Then He is able to bring us into alignment with Himself in His Son. Nothing else can truly satisfy us, either. Let nothing make you panic. God is in control - learn His ways.

July 14

"Believe on the Lord Jesus Christ, and you will be saved, you and your household." [Acts 16:31]

Paul declared to the Philippian jailer the liberating truth that, if he would believe, the effect on him and his family would be immediate and life-transforming. Paul obviously spoke with passion, but passion is not enough - he spoke by the Holy Spirit, and his words were received into believing hearts. What Paul spoke was creative - it came into being. The man believed it, and it became to him a prophecy of his future. Let God's truth move from being information to being personal prophecy, for that is the right way to receive it. Don't wish you had been there to hear Paul say those words. You have been placed where you are in time. Paul's words to the jailer are as much addressed to you as they were to him. God has caused His Word to be written in such a perfect way that it will liberate whoever reads it with a believing heart. The force of these simple words is the same today as when they were first spoken. If we believe in Jesus Christ, His power will change us and affect our families, including generations to come. The miracle of a believing heart is to release the almighty power of God's Word and realise that the Bible is a Spirit-breathed book of prophecy, not just a textbook!

July 15

"Walk while you have the light, lest darkness overtake you; ... While you have the light, believe in the light, that you may become sons of light." [John 12:35-36]

We so readily assume that opportunities will always be at hand for us, but they may not always be. There are moments of great understanding and spiritual clarity, but these are passing moments. If we seize the opportunity, we will make 'the light' our home. It is like a train pulling into a station - we must board the train in the brief moments before it moves on. We may resent this fact, we may even resist it, but that will not change it. When opportunities do arise, the way we choose to react to them will determine the direction we move in. We may wish we had more time, or that we could live two parallel lives, but we cannot. *"Walk while you have the light."* Board the train of God's truth, and let the power of it carry you away. What does it mean to walk in the light? It means putting things that are doubtful or negative out of my life. It means surrender to the Holy Spirit, especially on the line of things He touches in my life. It means making radical choices about the kind of person I will become. Putting off the decision is risking missing the train. Doing nothing is a decision with the same dire consequences as rebellion. Whatever God puts His finger on, deal with it quickly, while you have the light.

July 16

"And I heard the sound of harpists playing their harps. They sang as it were a new song..." [Revelation 14:2-3]

In our hearts there is something like a musical instrument; the Bible likens it to a harp. But it is totally silent and unused until God touches it. Like an old instrument with broken strings which is covered in dust and dirt, it cannot fulfil the purpose for which it was made. The unregenerate human heart is in a state of appalling ruin. A traveller through the desert might see a mound which in former years was a bustling, vibrant city. Similarly, the human heart is an empty ruin until touched by God's hand. When we first hear the gospel, the hand of God brushes across the strings of our heart, producing beautiful music that echoes through our minds and our souls. We are to spend our lives allowing God to play the strings of our hearts, and learning to produce this music ourselves. Our hearts become the sum and excellence of all beauty when in the hands of God. The beautiful sound is His love, and the result is praise to His name. No-one can find the meaning of life and the true meaning of joy until they have surrendered their life into the hands of the Master.

July 17

"Then Hilkiah the high priest said to Shaphan the scribe, 'I have found the Book of the Law in the house of the Lord.'"
[2 Kings 22:8]

The Temple had been locked up and neglected throughout the long 52 years of Manasseh's reign. Decay and vermin had damaged the treasure of the nation to the brink of no return. Then King Josiah commanded the priests to cleanse the Temple and, as they carefully sifted through the rubbish, there they found the ancient copy of the Law, probably the book of Deuteronomy. There are treasures hidden in people's hearts, buried through years of sin, disobedience and prayerlessness. They neglect reading the Bible, but most serious of all, their inner faculty of knowing God is dead and buried. But God commands the cleansing of the temple of our hearts, and the full restoring of the treasures before they are lost for ever. How do we cleanse and refresh our hearts? Put away doubtful habits. Light up your heart with praise, and wait quietly on God. As our eyes become accustomed to the different light that shines from God's Presence, we see our hearts in a fresh light for the first time. It is by the inner faculty of the heart that we know God. 'Sweep' your heart each day; expose yourself to the light of His Presence, and read His Word so that you come to know the God who reveals Himself through His Son.

July 18

"Moreover he kissed all his brothers and wept over them, and after that his brothers talked with him." [Genesis 45:15]

Joseph embraced Benjamin, his younger brother, who had not been party to his betrayal. Then he turned to his half-brothers, who had bullied him and abandoned him to a life of slavery. Some of these men were cruel and immoral - Reuben had committed incest [Genesis 35:22], Simeon and Levi had senselessly crippled an ox [Genesis 49:5-6]. Joseph had been deeply hurt by them. This was a shattered family. The clock could not be turned back then, any more than it can now. Joseph demonstrates the power of grace and love to forgive past hurts. He reached out and gave the kiss of brotherly affection and reconciliation, and broke the blockage that was in their hearts. Joseph's kiss released these men's tongues to speak, and probably their first words were expressions of sorrow over their past actions. They knew they were unworthy. They had been frozen with guilt and shame. It was forgiveness, love and grace that started them on the path of recovery from their pitiable state. The lesson is clear - it is only if we have grace in our hearts that we can reach out to those whose hearts are locked. The just will always have to lay down their lives for the unjust, the loving for the unloving, the gracious for the ungracious. Where do you stand? Receive Jesus' loving embrace to your heart each day, and pass it on to the frozen world all around you.

July 19

"Let us know, let us pursue the knowledge of the Lord. His going forth is established as the morning; He will come to us like the rain, like the latter and former rain to the earth."
    [Hosea 6:3]

This verse describes the beautiful grace of God that refreshes the one who seeks Him. When we begin to seek God, we start our journey in dry, weary places. We may be so parched that we falter as we begin. This is why the Bible is full of exhortations to rise and seek the Lord. God promises to come like a perfect morning in spring. His Spirit is like fresh rain on dry fields. Life springs forth - God causes spiritual life to appear in us. Note the step of faith: *"pursue the knowledge of the Lord"*. Spend time quietly talking with Jesus, as with a closest friend. Note the promised response of God: *"He will come to us like the rain"* - as inner refreshing. A refreshed soul is not always elated, but is calmly fixed in settled trust in God and His promises. How blessed we are to know not the mere words of God, but the ways of God. Rise up and pursue Him. He will not disappoint those who seek Him. He delights to draw us, and delights when He is able to pour out His grace and kindness in our lives. God is real, He is the living God. Always remember, salvation is a Person, not a thing. We are saved by a right relationship with God. Pursue Him - that is the only way to live as a child of God.

July 20

"Bless the Lord, O my soul; and all that is within me, bless His holy name!" [Psalm 103:1]

David was here encouraging himself! This unique power is

given to believers - to look on ourselves with the eye of faith, and apply God's truth to our lives. Don't wait for someone to come along and give you a word of encouragement. Look on yourself with discernment (after all, you should know yourself pretty well by now) and speak to yourself. David wrote to himself a note, a song, a word of encouragement. Perhaps he wrote it on a good day, and he wanted to draw a line in the sand so that he would never go back from it. Have you drawn your line in the sand? It will be an exhortation that goes right down into the secret keys of your character. It will make you smile because it is so true and apt for you. It will make you return to joyous, triumphant faith. Step out and you will find that you have the ability to prophesy to yourself. The effort of putting the exhortation into words will mean that sooner or later you will meet someone you can encourage with helpful insight. These things should not surprise us because the Holy Spirit is the supreme exhorter, and He constantly urges us to speak faith to ourselves. It is from within that help rises, from our inner well of living water. When others speak to us, they can only trigger the inner well to flow - they can never replace it. So stand up, and command yourself to bless and praise the Lord!

July 21

"...the kingdom of God is not eating and drinking, but righteousness and peace and joy in the Holy Spirit."
    [Romans 14:17]

The Kingdom of God is not run on similar lines to other governments. It is a kingdom of love, and its citizens are righteous through faith. Righteousness is the first great mark of this kingdom, and the foundation of all the other marks of the kingdom. Once righteousness is established in our hearts by repentance and faith, the evidence is peace - peace with God and with mankind. Our sins are forgiven, and we have forgiven all those who have wronged us. Peace is the atmosphere of the kingdom. It is the air in which prayer, worship and faith flourish. The heart that prays without peace is running round and round in circles, and achieves nothing. Peace is the central focus of the heart that would walk with God and believe Him for great things. Once we come to peace through faith, we are sure that God is over all and will answer our heart's cry. The mark of a man or woman of prayer is peace. They live in the assurance that they are watched over and protected from all harm. Some see prayer as the great battle to seize control of a

126

world spinning into chaos. But when we approach the throne of God, we are settled and assured that our Father is in control, and in the midst of chaos we are utterly secure and safe.

July 22

"You come to me with a sword, with a spear, and with a javelin. But I come to you in the name of the Lord of hosts, the God of the armies of Israel, whom you have defied."
[1 Samuel 17:45]

David had never seen the heavenly hosts of angels. He had known the lonely work of a shepherd in the hills of Judea. He had never used formidable weapons like the sword and the spear. David was overwhelmingly outclassed in terms of his weaponry, but he did not look on Goliath's weapons, but on the greatness of God. To David, Goliath seemed small and powerless. If Goliath could have seen God, he would have immediately turned and fled! The problems we face are real, and the spirit of the enemy is mocking and defiant, but we must get the right perspective. There is no enemy that can ultimately overcome the person who trusts in God. With God on our side, the most awful of enemies must ultimately fall at the name of Jesus. If all the nuclear arsenals of the most powerful nations were directed at the Church, they would fail, because God is with His people. Sometimes, compared with the apparent strength of our enemy, the name of Jesus may seem to us as powerless as a slip of paper or a whisper on the breeze. Therein lies the paradox: He holds the universe in the palm of His hands, and all His enemies will bow before Him at even the whisper of His name.

July 23

"But one thing is needed, and Mary has chosen that good part, which will not be taken away from her." [Luke 10:42]

Our supreme need is to sit at Jesus' feet and to hear His word. All other 'needs' are not in themselves true problems - they are effects, not causes. This is why Jesus did not give medical knowledge to His disciples, or start food programmes (these would be necessary later - see Acts 6). Our supreme need is to have the word of God, to quieten ourselves and listen to God. This requires patience, and a steady application to His written Word, and to the inner witness of the Holy Spirit. Mary chose to hear His word, and so she was a worshipper, delighting herself in Him, loving Him and expressing that love by carefully listening. Mary made this choice, and so taught us that this is a matter of exercising our will, to respond to the longing of His heart for a people who will hear Him and love His word. Mary clearly did not do this for fame, money or position. She did not sit at His feet in order to avoid work. She chose Him without ulterior motive, but with a deep realisation that He was more delighted in her attitude than in any food she might have prepared for Him. Jesus gives a great promise to those whose attitude leads them to make such a choice - it will be preserved for them for the whole of their life. He will not allow any power to rob us of this attitude. He will fiercely defend those who love Him.

July 24

"She (Martha) said to Him, 'Yes, Lord, I believe that You are the Christ, the Son of God, who is to come into the world.' "
[John 11:27]

Martha was the first woman to confess that Jesus was the Christ, just as Peter was the first man. Martha was a practical person, not one who loved to be quiet and sit for hours in prayer. The Bible here wonderfully teaches that, for true spiritual health, we need to be both prayerful and incredibly practical. When Lazarus died, Mary had a deeper crisis than Martha did. Mary had developed a sense of Jesus' personal love and commitment to her, but she had not developed the practical 'get up and go' that is needed when events baffle and disappoint us. Martha got up as soon as Jesus came, and went to meet Him, to welcome Him back. It was Martha who first welcomed Jesus into her home [Luke 10:38]. It was Martha who served Him dinner (and it was probably a very special meal)! It was probably Martha who had prepared Lazarus for burial, and it was Martha who pointed out to Jesus that Lazarus wouldn't smell very nice! Our spiritual life needs to be rooted in a deep devotion to Him and, at the same time, a healthy practical attitude of getting on with life until God intervenes. If we lack the spiritual side of life, we will be efficient and organised but dry and uninspired. If we lack the practical side, we may be morbid and introspective when God is silent or when things seem to go wrong. Worship, wait on God, then get up and go and meet Jesus in the ordinary things of life. He will appear when He is ready, and will do more than we expected.

July 25

"And He said to them, 'Let us cross over to the other side of the lake.' And they launched out. But as they sailed He fell asleep. And a windstorm came down on the lake..."
[Luke 8:22-23]

This is the experience of all disciples at some time. We launch out in confident obedience, and then everything seems to go wrong, and worst of all, God seems unconcerned about our plight. The truth is that we are often so concerned with getting through the immediate activities of life, that we forget to believe in God. We serve our ministry, our ordered circumstances, our predictable and safe course through life. When He disappears from our view, we don't notice how much we were living without Him until the crisis comes. Then we are forced to ask who or what we are really serving. All disciples must renounce everything, including the hold our Christian service has on our lives. We must trust Him - when things work out and when they don't, when we feel His closeness, and when we feel abandoned. He is near, and He is our foundation even when all else moves beneath our feet, and we lose the sense of where we are headed. Abraham went out not knowing where he was going. This terrifying uncertainty is meant to keep us looking at the glorious certainty. Are you looking at the storm, or at Him?

July 26

"Behold, I send you out as sheep in the midst of wolves."
[Matthew 10:16]

Our prayer is often that God will place us in nice circumstances among nice people. Being safe and happy is our expectation of what God means when He promises to protect us. But Jesus has, in fact, promised the opposite. He has promised to send us out into hostile and difficult circumstances. Don't wolves eat sheep? Yes, they do, and Paul said, *"For your sake we are killed all day long; we are accounted as sheep for the slaughter."* [Romans 8:36]. But almost in the same breath Paul also says that, *"all things work together for good"* [Romans 8:28]. God's power is not manifested in providing us with a refuge far from the trials and dangers of life; it is manifested in keeping us from the wolves when they surround us, full of hatred and longing to destroy us. We cannot protect ourselves. It has been said that the safest place to be is right in the centre of

God's will. If we plan our own safety, all we shall do is miss God's miracles. Daniel must at least have had an adrenaline rush when he was thrown to the lions! But how he must have rejoiced to see God's mighty hand protecting him. We must stop complaining about the hostile conditions we find ourselves in, and start looking for God's miracles in the midst of difficult people and circumstances. Perhaps the greatest miracle is manifested when we show to the world a lack of selfish care for our own dignity and safety, and that we have the nature of the Lamb, not the wolf.

July 27

"If we confess our sins, He is faithful and just to forgive us our sins and to cleanse us from all unrighteousness."
     [1 John 1:9]

The story is told of an aged Chinese emperor who had no heir to succeed him. He issued an invitation to any young man who wished to be emperor, to come to the palace on a certain day to undergo a certain trial. About 200 young men came. The emperor came out, carrying a large basket full of seed. He gave them this challenge: each man was to take a seed and promise to return in 6 months' time to show what he had cultivated. The condition was that, no matter what happened, each one must return to the palace in 6 months' time. One young man named Yan Nan took a seed and carefully sowed it in a plant pot. But after one week there were no green shoots. He realised that the seed must be dead, and dreaded the day when he must return to the palace. The day came and the palace was filled with young men bearing pots with beautiful plants. The emperor inspected each man's offering, including Yan Nan's empty pot. At last the emperor announced, to everyone's shock, that Yan Nan was the winner. The emperor explained that, unbeknown to anyone else, he had baked the seeds in an oven till he was sure that they were all dead! All those who had beautiful plants were liars! The truth is that God pours out rivers of grace on the humble, and passes by the fake displays of false spirituality. The Christian life is not a life of pretence - it is a life of incredible honesty and humility. The wonder is that there is no need to pretend, since God is able to make us abound with fullness of life.

July 28

"Create in me a clean heart, O God...." [Psalm 51:10]

This is about the most radical prayer a human being can ask God. It goes to the root of what we are. Our reaction to prayers like this is often, *"Oh, I prayed that when I was converted"* or, *"David must have been a really evil man to have needed that!"* We must not analyse too closely the theological correctness of our prayers. Our spiritual history may be outstanding, but our spiritual need may be staring everyone in the face. It is a great climb-down to pray a prayer like this, and involves readiness to let God deal with us at a very basic level. We are asking God to change us at the deep, unconscious level of our beings. We may be only dimly conscious of what is going wrong, but we must bare our soul to God and let Him change us. This is the radical kind of prayer that will mark out true disciples - it is not praying theologically correct prayers that take us deeper with God. This does not mean that we pray this prayer every day, but it does mean that we turn to God when we are conscious of a deep lack in our ability to love others, or to conquer besetting sins. Our lives may be marred by impatience and irritability, but these are signs of a deep malaise that God has the power to deal with. No-one is born with the character of Jesus; it must be imparted by God's grace. It is only our natural virtues, combined with pride, that will ultimately stop us going deeper with God. We don't have to parade our need before people, but we must cease from being defensive in our estimation of ourselves.

July 29

"Most assuredly, I say to you, the Son can do nothing of Himself, but what He sees the Father do; for whatever He does, the Son also does in like manner." [John 5:19]

Christ's life is one of complete surrender to the Father's will. In this verse He speaks of His surrender in the area of personal initiative. This is not passivity - passivity is, at best, a mixed blessing. A lazy person will delight in the idea of a totally passive will, but this is not what Jesus is speaking of. He is describing the complete focus of His will in surrender to the Father. Jesus is ablaze with love and devotion, but they are not directed at acting according to natural desires or enthusiasm. They are directed at stilling all other powers, for the sole purpose of enthroning the Father's will. In one way, this is perfect activity, since it is the focusing of our whole being on the true purpose of our existence, which is God. Our will is not a faculty in isolation - it is the use we make of our powers. When we direct our lives to the pursuit of selfish pleasure, we are engaging our wills. Christ focused His mind into complete concentration and the application of His whole being to the Father's will. He claimed that He saw the Father do things, and that He heard the Father speak [John 5:30]. This is the fruit of waiting on God – Christ's inner eye and ear were opened to perceive God. This was the basis of His 'faith ministry' that saw maimed limbs restored and the decomposing body of Lazarus brought to life. It was also the basis of the life that stood before the Sanhedrin, Pilate, the baying crowds, and finally before His executioners, and saw not the hand of man but the hand of God.

July 30

"...they saw Jesus walking on the sea...." [John 6:19]

Christ walks on water. He walks through the storm and against the wind; He walks over a sea that is raging with ceaseless turmoil. The point is not that we should also literally walk on water, but that we should walk through the far worse turmoil of life, and the attacks of the wicked one. The surface on which we walk through life is not solid ground! It moves beneath our feet. There are several references to Christ being in a boat in a storm. Mark 4:37 describes a sea in which it would have been impossible for a normal person to lie still, let alone sleep! The waves were so violent that they would have left the disciples battered by the frequent knocks against the side of the boat. But through it all, Christ slept on a pillow. Truly, He is from above. The vital point here is that He invites us to partake of the same life and faith that is rooted in a peace that passes understanding: *"Why are you so fearful? How is it that you have no faith?"* [Mark 4:40]. Though Peter failed when he attempted to walk on the water, it also taught him how to stand - he did not perish, but was caught and sustained by the matchless Son of God [Matthew 14:30-31]. Two artists were once asked to draw a picture depicting peace. One drew a peaceful country view, with fields and a quietly flowing river. The other drew a cliff face on a dark stormy night, with huge waves beating against it. In the side of the cliff he drew a nest, where a mother bird covered her young with her wings - that is a better picture of our peace. We are in the midst of the storm, but we have One who covers us and keeps our hearts in perfect peace.

July 31

"And on the Sabbath day we went out of the city to the riverside, where prayer was customarily made... Now it happened, as we went to prayer, that a certain slave girl possessed with a spirit of divination met us." [Acts 16:13,16]

The contrast in these verses is between a beautiful place of quiet calm where the apostles prayed, and the evil confusion in the mind of the girl. This was the beginning of an attack by Satan on the apostles, which ended in cruel beatings and imprisonment, followed by God's direct intervention. These events show us where the cutting edge of conflict in our lives will be located. Satan is the enemy of those who discover the place of quietness in prayer. Such a place is powerful beyond description, and is the source of all that God does, since it is found in the depths of His own Being. It is in that place that peace reigns - the peace of knowing that God is over all, and that all things are subject to His will. Our challenge is to find that place and to drink deeply of its peace until we come to total rest before God's throne. That is the source of the faith that makes crooked things straight and rough places smooth; faith that takes authority over Satan and brings God's order to lives and circumstances. It is no surprise that the devil opposes the quiet of God's Presence in us. In that quietness we hear the truth that contradicts all the evil and misery caused by Satan. Dwell in quietness with God, and treasure that quiet place. Don't be surprised when things come along to disturb and challenge that place. Stand fast, and realise that this is the cutting edge of spiritual warfare.

August 1

"In the beginning God created the heavens and the earth."
[Genesis 1:1]
*"The Lord God planted a garden eastward in Eden, and there He
put the man whom He had formed."*   [Genesis 2:8]

Perspective is everything. In the first account of creation, in
Genesis 1, the Bible takes us to a platform in outer space from
where we see the vast sweep of the universe. In the second
account, in Genesis 2, the Bible takes us down to earth to see
God's care for His crowning creation - the human race. In order
to have right perspective on ourselves, on life and eternity, we
need God to position us. Above all, we need to see that the
physical universe was not there in the beginning, but was
created by God, who has no physical form and is Himself
uncreated. If we miss this we will believe that the physical
universe is first and last. But the physical world is subject to the
spiritual. God is before all things, both in time and in power. It
is only as we get this perspective that we understand the
overwhelming sense of meaning and purpose that fills our lives
and our destiny. The all-wise, all-powerful God created us with
the purpose that we should be lifted out of the narrowness of the
mere physical world, and know him.   The two accounts of
creation assure us that God has a magnificent plan that spans
the universe, and a personal one for our individual lives, and we
have a part in both.   Beware of the lie that explains human
existence in merely scientific terms. For the evolutionist, all life
is ultimately robbed of meaning. Unbelief leads to moral chaos
and confusion because it misses the wonderful truth - our life is
part of a great design, and not only part, but a central part, in
the Creator's loving heart.

August 2

*"Then, six days before the Passover, Jesus came to Bethany,
where Lazarus was who had been dead, whom He had raised
from the dead. There they made Him a supper; ... but Lazarus
was one of those who sat at the table with Him."*
[John 12:1-2]

When a person grows old and approaches death, it is often the
case that their wisdom will sharpen and increase in the face of
eternity.   Christians certainly have this advantage even before
growing old, because we live in the light of eternity. But our

advantages are of a much greater order. Lazarus not only lived in the light of eternity, but died and passed beyond the veil into the unspeakable joy of heaven. And, more than that, he was raised from the dead to live again with the wisdom he had obtained. Yet even more than this, the Christian has the companionship of the One who died and rose again to live for evermore. Lazarus sat at an ordinary table as one who had experienced resurrection. How this must have changed his perspective for ever, and made him a great optimist! Once we have experienced death and resurrection by faith, we pass into eternal companionship with the Son of God, and eat and drink at His table in His kingdom. We are to rejoice and let the glory of the resurrection inspire and define our lives at every moment of every day. Resurrection life is not a slogan; it is a transformed way of thinking about life, before and after death. Eternal life is not something that begins after physical death - it begins when we die by faith and begin to taste eternity, and see the bright lights of earth fade in comparison with the glory of God.

August 3

"There they made Him a supper; and Martha served, but Lazarus was one of those who sat at the table with Him. Then Mary took a pound of very costly oil of spikenard, anointed the feet of Jesus, and wiped His feet with her hair. And the house was filled with the fragrance of the oil."
[John 12:2-3]

This scene is at the same time both homely and sublime. It encompasses the wonder of a miraculous life, and practical care for the physical needs of this life. Martha served Jesus Christ by cooking him a dinner, and the aroma of that meal must have filled the room. Lazarus sat with Jesus as one alive from the dead, and the aroma of life, that makes death an irrelevant point in time, also filled the room. Then there was the worship of Mary, who poured out the entire contents of her bottle of perfume. The room was filled with the aroma of life, loving service and loving worship. How this must have pleased God and comforted Jesus as He approached His death and resurrection. This scene encompasses the range of the Christian's devotion. Our focus is not on big and important occasions that feed our ego; it is on transforming daily moments into acts of worship to the King. Joy is not found in exciting things - it is found in discovering the wonder of Jesus, who sits serene and victorious in the midst of this home. The victories of

Christ risen from the dead are indeed vast and marvellous, and yet their greatest impact is to lift the ordinary life of the believer to a world of purity and devotion where the smallest act is an act of worship, and all of life is filled with glorious meaning.

August 4

"But Gideon said to them, 'I will not rule over you, nor shall my son rule over you; the Lord shall rule over you.'"
    [Judges 8:23]

This declaration by Gideon goes to the heart of the Kingdom of God. Among human beings there is competition to occupy the place of power - there are elections, revolutions and other forms of power struggle. But this is not so in the Kingdom of God. God's throne is never vacant, and none of the positions in His kingdom are open to volunteers. The great beings that surround His throne are given their position by the will and authority of God alone. This should fill all of us, God's servants, with a deep sense of rest about ourselves and our work for Him. All we need to do as servants of God is to find our God-appointed place and rest our hearts there. There we find all the resources and authority we need to fulfil our work. There we also see the futility of politics among God's people. We must utterly forsake the desire to be important, or our hearts will never be at rest. No amount of striving can change the fact of God's rule, nor can it improve our own career in the kingdom! The answer is to bow and worship, and delight in the will of Him who rules over all. This is not a resigned acceptance of the inevitable. When the veil is lifted and we see beyond it, we see a world of millions of glorious beings worshipping and serving. A glimpse into that world makes this world's conflicts fade into irrelevance. There is more power in the little finger of God than in all the combined powers of the human race. It is exciting and fulfilling to find our place in His kingdom, and we will never lose that place - it is ours for ever.

August 5

"He was led as a lamb to the slaughter, and as a sheep before its shearers is silent, so He opened not His mouth."
    [Isaiah 53:7]

Jesus Christ was shorn of His glory by an act of self-emptying when He became a man. He laid aside his omniscience, and

136

lived trusting His Father and not knowing the future. When He was arrested and tried He was deprived of justice, as the Sanhedrin conducted an illegal trial. It was against their Talmudic traditions: (1) to hold a trial by night; (2) to fulfil a death sentence within 30 days and thus not allow for other witnesses to come forward; and (3) to make the accused witness against Himself. Pilate further deprived Him of justice by condemning Him against the evidence. Jesus was then shorn of human dignity by His terrible treatment at the hands of the soldiers, who mocked Him, plucked out His beard, and mercilessly beat Him. Finally, His humiliation was complete when He was nailed to the cross, which combined inhuman torture with execution. Jesus was shorn of all outward dignity, and then cut to the deepest level of His Being by the cross. The marvel of this whole process is that, the more He was cut down, the more brightly the glory of His love shone. Nothing that He suffered reduced the inner glory of His love; it only made His love shine ever more brightly. Never has God been so clearly revealed for all to see than when Jesus died in meek, forgiving love on Calvary. When we take up our cross to follow our Lord, it is to embrace the same life - to be made love as He is love, and to be one with Christ so that His glory is revealed.

August 6

"Watch and pray, lest you enter into temptation. The spirit indeed is willing, but the flesh is weak." [Mark 14:38]

The hardest discipline of all for us is to persist into the unknown realm of prayer when our own flesh seems to drag us down like a swimmer enveloped in heavy winter clothes, or a marathon runner carrying heavy suitcases. Our flesh draws us back, producing heaviness. Nothing we face in life equips us for the challenge of persevering when our natural minds protest that nothing is being achieved. No schoolteacher, no military training, nothing can prepare us for the conflict that awaits us when we pray. The only power that can make us persevere is naked faith in the Lord Jesus Christ. He has commanded us to do this, and has invited us to partake of some of the deepest, most intimate thoughts of His heart. To enter in, we must simply persist in prayer. Jesus continually taught His disciples of the need to persist. The warning of this verse is also a promise. He warned the disciples that they must persist or else enter into temptation that could otherwise be avoided. The implied promise is that if we will go deeper with Christ in the school of prayer, there will be many temptations that we will avoid and of which we will never be aware. Let nothing hinder your flow of prayer - whether it is like wading through mud, or like flying on eagles' wings - and the rewards will be immeasurable.

August 7

"Now when they saw the boldness of Peter and John, and perceived that they were uneducated and untrained men, they marveled. And they realized that they had been with Jesus." [Acts 4:13]

Peter and John were amateurs in the eyes of the Sanhedrin. They were unqualified to speak with authority on matters such as the nature of God, prayer, the law and the resurrection from the dead. It is so easy for us to feel unqualified, and very common for us to feel that our contribution is insignificant alongside the great achievements of the apostles and other great servants of God. The truth is that, in the realm of the Spirit, all of God's children are amateurs. But then, so are all children. No child goes to school to learn to be a child! We must feel our way forward, overcoming all sense of disqualification, and steadily come to realise that we are as effective and significant as every other believer. There will never come a point when God will give us a badge or a certificate to show that we have qualified! We must simply go to God with all our frailty and sense of inadequacy, and realise that that is how it is. Expertise in the Kingdom of God is a contradiction. Who can ever feel equal with Jesus? Such a feeling would be a blind deception in itself. When the weakest believer talks to God, the scene is set for them to make spiritual progress. When the weakest believer quietens his or her heart to approach God, all heaven holds its breath. For God has chosen this setting as the means by which He will channel His power and kingdom into the world. If we are with Jesus, we are in the most qualified place of all.

August 8

"But the fruit of the Spirit is love, joy, peace, longsuffering, kindness, goodness, faithfulness, gentleness, self-control. Against such there is no law." [Galatians 5:22-23]

Love is the fruit of the Spirit. The Christian life cannot be likened to identical, mass-produced goods. Mankind uses methods to produce goods – this requires machinery, investment, manpower etc. Some Churches and Christian movements seem to operate on this kind of principle! But the truth is that all our efforts cannot alter the motivation of the human heart, nor produce a single atom of love. If there is no love in my heart, then all my striving and tears and pleading will not change my state. Love is a fruit, and therefore two things are required to produce it - seed, and the right conditions for growth. If I am to grow in the life of the Spirit, then I must receive living seed from God, and keep my heart in the right condition for that seed to flourish and grow. This is consistent with Jesus's teaching in the parable of the sower and other parables, where the power of growth lies in the seed itself, and growth comes of itself, in a way that the receiver does not understand. We cannot hurry it - we can only patiently nourish and cherish that precious seed. The Christian life, then, is like a plant that grows. It cannot be transplanted as a ready-grown plant. Growth may sometimes be imitated, perhaps through intensive Bible courses or Bible schools. But though these things have their place, they are not a substitute for true spiritual growth. What then is the seed? It is Christ Himself, by the Spirit - we must receive Him into our life and as our life. It is not enough for us to 'make a decision' to follow Christ or to 'seek to follow' His teaching; we must receive Christ deep into our being as our life, so that we say, with the apostle, *"Christ, who is our life ..."* [Colossians 3:4].

August 9

"For all the law is fulfilled in one word, even in this: 'You shall love your neighbor as yourself.' " [Galatians 5:14]

This is a definition of a truly spiritual person, i.e. one who truly loves. Love is not an attribute of God, for God *is* love. All of God's attributes are attributes of love. Similarly, love is not to be an attribute of our life or work - it is to be the ceaseless spring from which all of our life flows. Without love, no-one is a Christian; without love, a Church is not a Church. A Christian without love is a monster - a lamb with the heart of a wolf; at best an image in stone, with a vague suggestion of something beautiful but no direct experience of it. Love is without hurt or harm; it produces an inner calm in which other lives are welcome and held in warmth and tenderness. Love dispels fears, reassures doubts, and spreads kindness and joy in everyone it meets. Love is not a work, though countless works flow from it. It colours every action, and makes everything a manifestation of that most perfect life – Jesus, the Son of God. Some wander from this path and think of life in the Spirit as a life of power, focusing on what we achieve for God, and measuring our value to God and others by statistics of how many meetings held, how many people won, how much fasting and prayer. All of these things are wonderful, but not in themselves the life. The greatest power in the realm of the Spirit is the power of love. People give up - even the most determined and heroic - but love goes on for ever. Love carries within itself the power of self-renewal, for it never runs out. As it is poured out, the greater the flow, the greater the resources seem to be. Love is attractive, seeping into the chinks of the stoutest armour. Love wins hardened cynics, and conquers stubborn rebels. The cry of all who truly seek God's kingdom is, 'Lord, make me love, as God Himself is love!'

August 10

"...she took of its fruit and ate. She also gave to her husband with her, and he ate." [Genesis 3:6]

It has been observed that evil people triumph when good people say and do nothing. This was never more true than when Adam remained silent while Eve disobeyed God. Perhaps he wanted to see what God meant when He said that they would die. He knew definitely that this was what would happen. When Adam saw Eve die spiritually in front of his very eyes, there was something that attracted him, and he also ate. It is at our own great peril that we close our eyes to God's instruction and guidance. There is a comfort in fellowshipping with others in their worldliness. Adam had the opportunity to prevent this disaster, but he did not take it. This wellspring of all sin began with moral passivity in Adam. Evil as we often understand it is in terrible acts of cruelty or moral depravity. But Adam unleashed great monsters of lust and destruction on his own soul and on the human race, by simply doing nothing. Moral challenge will not come from the world, but from the Holy Spirit - from the insistent prompting of the inner voice of God. That prompting is a challenge to set a course that is higher and purer than the acceptable standards of other Christians or even of those closest to us. Ananias and Sapphira agreed to tempt the Holy Spirit [Acts 5:1-11]. They should have risen in fervent exhortation to challenge each other to a higher path of life. It is always hardest to be a disciple when we have to rebuke those we love, whether by word or by our personal obedience. The cutting edge is always, whom do we love most? Adam went down the path of self-fulfilment and broke God's heart. The Holy Spirit is active at the cutting edge of our conscience, and when He speaks, we ignore Him at our peril.

August 11

"Cause me to hear Your lovingkindness in the morning, for in You do I trust." [Psalm 143:8]

The main faculty by which a child receives its parents' love is through the feel of a loving embrace; but in the spirit, the main faculty by which we receive a 'loving embrace' is through our ear. Our hearts are so unused to the ways of the Spirit that we often expect God to put His arms around us in a tangible way. While this is not impossible, it is not the way God has chosen to declare His love to us. God embraces us with His word of love. Love pours into our spirit in the same way that faith does - through hearing. God speaks, and the result is not mere information; it produces a melting of inner hardness. Hurts and resentments are washed from us as God speaks and refreshes our capacity to receive love. Jesus never spent time telling people He loved them, because that would have been merely informative. He talked to people about God and His ways, and as He did so God embraced people by His word, and the result was that people were grounded in God's love. As we listen to God, we hear His word; His tone of voice makes His word liquid love. God can be likened to a fountain of life, to living water, and the liquid element is love. God pours through our spiritual senses, and we are washed and refreshed. God's love washes our feet from our tired contact with a dry and dusty world. His love washes our minds from cynical reasoning. The result is a heart with a spring of unspeakable joy.

August 12

"If the whole body were an eye, where would be the hearing?" ... *"Are all apostles? Are all prophets? Are all teachers? Are all workers of miracles? Do all have gifts of healings? Do all speak with tongues? Do all interpret?"*
     [1 Corinthians 12:17,29-30]

There is a huge temptation for Christians to confuse unity with uniformity. The temptation for a pastor is to want all his Church members to act the same. He may even exhort them all to make

141

identical responses, such as lifting up hands at the same moment. Church members may find safety in knowing exactly what to do and when to do it. But it is in the variety of our lives that God is truly glorified. Just as the beauty of nature is in the blend of a thousand different shades of colour, so too the beauty of the Church is in discovering the wonder of Christ through the uniqueness of each person's relationship with Him. It is for this reason that it is dangerous for Christians to be taught by only one Bible teacher. Paul said, *"we know in part"* [1 Corinthians 13:9]. It is only through the many different expressions of the discovery of Christ that we can do justice to His greatness. So, in practical terms, love Him and discover Him for yourself. While each one's relationship with God is built on forgiveness, purity and the power of the Spirit, yet each of us will by our unique character shed light on a different aspect of the character and love of Jesus. Together, we are like a stained glass window. The light pouring through is the same, but each different part highlights some different and wonderful aspect of our Saviour.

August 13

"Then many came to Him and said, 'John performed no sign, but all the things that John spoke about this Man were true.' And many believed in Him there." [John 10:41-42]

John the Baptist had one of the most powerful ministries described in the Bible. He turned the whole nation of Israel back to God; his life and witness stood as a sign that impacted thousands of people. In this verse, the people are analysing John's ministry and are amazed that he did no miracles. This was technically accurate, since John did not heal the sick and did not have a deliverance ministry. The people nevertheless recognised that his ministry was true and powerful. The truth is that John did not perform signs, because he was himself a sign. It is possible for Christians to get so obsessed with miracles and signs that they live a life of quiet disappointment in themselves, and by inference in God. John the Baptist heard from God and walked in his calling. The result was that many were convicted of sin and turned back to God. Who can doubt that many were healed as a secondary result of this repentance? (Stomach ulcers and heart disease, for instance, can often be traced back to the sin of worry!) Demonic powers were surely broken as people destroyed their idols and addictions. John the Baptist knew his calling was to prepare the way for Messiah, and to leave the rest to God. Our calling is to love and exalt Jesus, and

142

to believe Him to do the miracles. John the Baptist may have been tempted to be jealous of Jesus when people compared their ministry. Resist the temptation to compare yourself with others. God will often keep from our eyes how much He does through us, so that we will keep speaking true things about Him, and not think and talk too much about ourselves!

August 14

"Now there was a famine in the land, and Abram went down to Egypt to dwell there, for the famine was severe in the land." [Genesis 12:10]

Abram received visitations and wonderful revelations from God at many points in his walk with God. But at the moments when he needed guidance, God was strangely silent. Our hearts yearn for guidance, and for understanding of each step we take. But God does not satisfy this thirst for signs and supernatural assurance that we are on the right track in all our decisions. This is because they do not actually help us in our spiritual growth. Abram did not need instruction in what decision to make - he needed to set aside his fears and trust God. We make mistakes when we are gripped with panic, but God's response is not to tell us what to do, for that will not change us. God leaves us to consider the implications of past lessons. It is inconceivable that God will lead us halfway and then abandon us. As God has been with us in the past, He will be with us in the future. Panic blinds our hearts to God's faithfulness and provision. Fear and worry re-interpret our circumstances, and nothing good will come until we lay our fears aside. A settled, trusting heart will walk in God's will. Abram blundered down into Egypt, only to discover that God was still with him even when he got it wrong. God is with us for the long haul, not for the occasional need. He will prove Himself faithful when we get it wrong. The solution is to stop lusting for words and guidance. Those things don't make us people of faith. Settled trust in God pleases Him, and will produce a child-like indifference to our ups and downs.

August 15

"My soul is exceedingly sorrowful, even to death. Stay here and watch." [Mark 14:34]
"...that I may know Him, and the power of His resurrection, and the fellowship of His sufferings, being conformed to His death." [Philippians 3:10]

143

Of all the privileges of the sons of God, this is the greatest - to enter into the love of God in its highest expression at Gethsemane. For this, we have to allow God's love to wean us away from having the mentality of beggars, into the mentality of supreme generosity. While suffering is in itself a negative factor, in the hands of God it has become a tool to fashion our warped and twisted souls back into His image. There are needless sufferings that are bottomless pits of sheer human loss and tragedy. These are the sufferings of those who turn their backs on God, and the worst form is the blackness of despair that engulfs lonely people. But as soon as we fellowship with God, we become aware of a triumph and a victory that comes to us in suffering. Rather than crush us, these things then lift us and ennoble us. We are never to 'enjoy' sufferings, but we are to trust God, love God, and fellowship with Him in the midst of them. We will then see that Christ carried burdens of suffering that were free from the misery of self, and full of the liberty of love. We are set free from everything negative as we look up in trust throughout the trials of our faith. The tragedy of the world is the loss of meaning. The wonder of faith is to know that the love of God is in control.

August 16

"And His name, through faith in His name, has made this man strong, whom you see and know. Yes, the faith which comes through Him has given him this perfect soundness in the presence of you all." [Acts 3:16]

Peter here reminded the crowd that they knew the weakness and helplessness of the man who had been suddenly and unexpectedly healed. He did this to emphasise that the healing came from God. He then further emphasised that it was faith that came from God, not the apostles, that had healed this man. If we exalt our faith as something we have achieved, we are trusting in a weak thread that will snap at the slightest strain. There is a faith that comes from human striving or imagination but it is weak and ineffective. Imagine a man drowning in the midst of a stormy sea. The search-and-rescue helicopter locates him and lets down a rope, with the simple instruction: *"Hold tight to the rope, and we will lift you up over the rocks and the cliffs, and set you down in about 20 minutes."* The man looks at the slippery wet rope, considers for a moment his exhausted, weak arms, and then chooses to try his luck with the storm rather than risk falling onto the rocks. But then a strong member of the crew climbs down a rope-ladder, reaches down with both hands and instructs the man, *"Lift your hands up to me so that I can grip you."* The man lifts up his weak hands, and feels the iron grip close around his forearms. In the same way, we reach out to Christ in weak response, and find to our amazement that we are filled with a confidence and strength that are not our own. Thank God for the faith that comes to us from God as we reach out to Him.

August 17

"...faith comes by hearing..." [Romans 10:17]
"...looking unto Jesus, the author and finisher of our faith..."
    [Hebrews 12:2]

The human heart and mind cannot generate the kind of faith God requires - only God can produce that faith. We tend to long for something we can do to produce faith - as soon as we suspect that there is an activity that aids the process, we busy ourselves on that line. Some people think that faith comes through confessing something with our mouths. Others think that loud or long praying, or generous giving will produce faith. The Bible reveals that faith cannot originate in us, and it is a first step in obtaining faith to realise how powerless we are to produce it. Far from generating faith, our hearts generate presumption, and that is sin! Faith enters our heart through the ear, not the mouth. Faith enters quietly into the listening heart, not with the noise of our inventive minds. Faith is a surprise, a gift, a present wrapped for us by God's loving heart. The more we try to dictate what kind of present it will be, the more we turn it from being a gift into a reward for our straining. Faith comes to the listening, resting heart that looks away from self and up to God. Listening to God is the attitude that pleases God. The whole process of faith is the right relating of ourselves to God, and that alone can please Him. It means leaning on Him, looking up to Him, depending on Him. He will not fail us or let us fall. So look up to Him, and let God reshape the very vessel you offer up to be filled.

August 18

"When You did awesome things for which we did not look, You came down, the mountains shook at Your presence. For since the beginning of the world men have not heard nor perceived by

the ear, nor has the eye seen any God besides You, who acts for the one who waits for Him." [Isaiah 64:3-4]

God is awesome in majesty, and He does not bless and work according to how much we seek Him. He does things that no-one could ever guess or imagine He would do. It is true that God waits for some response from our hearts, but His working is far above what we could ever ask or think. How slow we are to realise that, when we pray for something, it is not our earnestness that is the powerful force that makes God work. The majesty of the God of Isaiah creates a peace in the heart of the reader of these words. God will attend to our situation, and very thoroughly. When the disciples on the Emmaus road returned to Jerusalem, the apostles announced, *"The Lord is risen indeed."* [Luke 24:34]. Even when they realised that He was risen, they were still amazed and added the little word 'indeed' – i.e. He really has done what He said He would do! The same is true for us. God has made huge promises to deliver us from the guilt and power of sin, and fill us with the Holy Spirit. The day must come when we realise that God's word is going to have its perfect way, and really accomplish these wonderful things. Sin really will disappear from our heart. Old, entrenched habits will disappear. Sometimes we have a sneaking suspicion that some things are so ingrained in us that God won't really be able to set us free from them. Here Isaiah declares that God will do that and more. He does not work according to what we can really believe, or He would do very little! He takes our faith and does awesome things, so that later we stand back and wonder that it has really happened to us.

August 19

"Thus says the Lord, who makes a way in the sea and a path through the mighty waters... Behold, I will do a new thing, now it will spring forth; shall you not know it? I will even make a road in the wilderness and rivers in the desert."
    [Isaiah 43:16,19]

How we long for guidance in our life's journey. The way ahead often seems long, and sometimes full of obstacles, confusion, and impossible barriers. God understands our longing to be informed, to understand and to have everything mapped out. So often we pray for guidance, whether for small decisions or big ones. Here in these verses of Isaiah, God encourages His precious people to be aware that He will make a path against impossible odds. The future of Israel was bleak at this point, and the nation trod a long and weary path into exile, from which it only really returned in 1948. But God said that He would make a path for His people straight through the churning, destructive waters, and through the scorching heat of the desert. God does a new thing. He does not guide us as we imagined and even perhaps hoped. He does something far better than we could ever have devised. He makes His people calm and nourished in the midst of the most awful turmoil of nations. God bids us take a step of faith each day - faith that we will find Him in His sufficient love and care. As we do so, we find this to be not merely survival by the skin of our teeth, but abundance far out of proportion to the context we live in. We pray for guidance to blessed circumstances, and we have often already decided what they will be. God says, walk into the dull and dreary day with Me, and it will open up into a walk along beautiful fertile river banks. Look, the river of life is flowing all around you and even in you.

August 20

"If you seek Him, He will let you find Him... But in their distress they turned to the Lord God of Israel, and they sought Him and He let them find Him."
    [2 Chronicles 15:2,4, NASB]

These verses reveal God's mercy in allowing us to find Him. When a father plays hide and seek with his children, he may leave obvious clues around so that the children do not get distressed or tired in seeking him. God has a much grander plan than the fun and games that are the human father's motive! God leaves clues around so that sinners may turn to Him and find forgiveness and mercy. God is only known to those who love Him, and part of that process is that we must seek Him. God's Being and character are hidden to the selfish person, not because God is playing games, but because even if He spoke and revealed Himself, only those who love Him would discern His voice and loving personality. The same is true of the Scriptures. Many misinterpret the Word of God because they are deaf and blind to His wonderful character. God leaves evidence of Himself all around; His aim is not to be hidden, but to be found. If this were not so, we could never find Him. So, seek the Lord, knowing that it is His good pleasure to lead you right to Himself.

147

August 21

"And when the dew fell on the camp in the night, the manna fell on it." [Numbers 11:9]

There were no fanfares to announce the delivery of thousands of tons of food in the camp of Israel. The miracle was accomplished every day, unnoticed, silently and effortlessly. God's people slept while God did His work unaided and in total rest. First the dew formed in perfect silence; there was no thunderous tropical downpour to water the desert floor. Then, on the cool refreshed earth and rock, God laid the grains of manna. We, in turn, must quieten ourselves from worry, fear and striving in order to wait silently before God. Many people try to measure God's work by noise and bustle, but as we quieten ourselves we perceive His hand at work, and perceive that we have often missed His working. While we wait on God, He imparts a grace and power, the flavour of His character, and our hearts are fed with the knowledge of God and His ways. We are strengthened with patience. The result is refreshment and sustenance, and how strong this sustenance is, for it is the living Presence of Christ Himself.

August 22

"And so it was, when Jesus had ended these sayings, that the people were astonished at His teaching, for He taught them as one having authority, and not as the scribes."
[Matthew 7:28-29]

It is easy to read the words of Jesus as the words of an ordinary man, but a moment's reflection will reveal the quiet thunder of His authority. His authority was magnified by the quietness of His Spirit. Yes, He was quiet, but He spoke promises that no mere man would dare to utter. He spoke of things to come in a way that would determine the eternal future of all human beings. He said that all blasphemy would be forgiven us, even blasphemy against Him, but not blasphemy against the Holy Spirit, not now nor in the age to come. He has eyes to see the coming age, as He also saw the moment of creation. Jesus Christ did not tell mere stories - He explained the reason behind all of life, and the principles of eternal judgment. People trembled at the whim of tyrants like Stalin and Hitler, and breathed a sigh of relief when they were dead. But Jesus is full of love and has no cruel whims or unloving thoughts. Yet we should tremble before Him, at the fearful power of His authority and His comprehensive knowledge of all things past, present and future, both of all creation and of our personal lives. There is fearful wonder in Him, and we do well to bow in loving surrender.

August 23

"Look! ... I see four men loose, walking in the midst of the fire; and they are not hurt, and the form of the fourth is like the Son of God." [Daniel 3:25]

King Nebuchadnezzar was here describing what he saw - that the three men he had thrown, bound with ropes, into the fiery furnace were now free and unharmed and in the presence of God's Son. Later, when the men came out of the fire, there was not even the smell of smoke on them nor was their hair singed! The same fire that had burnt the ropes that bound them had not harmed them at all. The lesson is clear: when we pass through fires of temptation or trial, those fires will deliver us from all kinds of bondage, and yet will not damage our inner character. We pray for deliverance and the activity of God's Spirit upon us, but we little realise that God's answer may be to allow us to enter into fires. When pain, suffering, imprisonment or other trials afflict us, we often forget the troublesome areas of our lives that so preoccupied us. But as we come through the trial, we realise later that we are no longer as negative as we were, nor so prone to depression or unbelief. Sometimes it is downright lustful thoughts that have been purged from us while we were in the midst of the flames. Cords of bondage are burnt up, and at the same time we enter into the greatest gift of all that comes through our trials - we are more conscious than ever of Jesus, and through Him we are more whole than we could ever have imagined possible. Trust God to bless and keep you through the worst of circumstances. He is working more than you know.

August 24

"So Samuel grew, and the Lord was with him and let none of his words fall to the ground. And all Israel from Dan to Beersheba knew that Samuel had been established as a prophet of the Lord." [1 Samuel 3:19-20]

Samuel was called by God, and he followed the call. Imagine a room with a sign over it saying 'For great men of God only; for prophets of the Lord'. At first we perceive the sign as a barrier, excluding us from entrance. But Samuel, like Elijah, was a man with a nature like ours [James 5:17]. God's call is to all His people [2 Timothy 1:9]. We do not have to be great men of God to enter into this calling. No, it is as we enter it that we become partakers of that high calling to be intimate friends of God. The believer who enters into this holy place will find that they have stepped out of time, out of the ordinary, into the extraordinary Presence of God. We think too meanly of ourselves, believing that we are destined to be dull and unremarkable. But God has a place for us, that lifts our minds and hearts to think pure and noble thoughts. Samuel was established as a prophet because he walked with God. We may not be called to be prophets in the same way that Samuel was, but we are called to partake of a calling that sets us apart for God, and by it we partake of the calling to be God's true sons. We are all made noble by the call of God in our lives, and it is a high and holy calling.

August 25

"Blessed are you who sow beside all waters, who send out freely the feet of the ox and the donkey." [Isaiah 32:20]
"Cast your bread upon the waters, for you will find it after many days." [Ecclesiastes 11:1]

These promises may seem small but, like many small things, they reveal the heart of the person, and here they reveal the heart of God. Human beings can be so fussy about the people they associate with, but God is a risk-taker - He causes His rain to fall on the just and the unjust. Christ entered Jericho. He was the sinless, holy Son of God, walking in majesty, divine authority and confidence. As He passed through, it was a renowned liar and cheat who caught His eye. Within a few moments of their meeting, Zacchaeus' heart had been forever changed. If we check to see who is worthy of our grace, we may find that we ourselves have become unworthy Pharisees! God loves cheerful givers, because that is what He is. How wasteful and extravagant, how open to abuse! Certainly, and that is how God lives. Watch for the careful, mean attitude of a heart of unbelief, and begin to receive all who cross your path with the openness and delight with which God received you. An open hand and open face disarm people of their hardness and their defences. The world is expecting Christians to look down on them with mistrust and even disdain. Sadhu Sundar Singh dressed like an Indian holy man. There were many so-called 'holy men' in Indian society who claimed to be very spiritual, but they were often dirty and dishevelled wild beggars, and children fled from them. But when Sadhu entered a village, children ran out to greet this clean, smiling, loving man. Lavish your joy and love on everyone you meet. You will be surprised that you will receive the same attitude from others in return.

August 26

"Worthy is the Lamb who was slain to receive power and riches and wisdom, and strength and honor and glory and blessing!" [Revelation 5:12]

Everything that we have is to be poured out upon God and upon the Lamb. This is the right thing to do, but it is also the best thing to do. Whatever is given to God is never lost - it is multiplied a thousand-fold. In fact, what is given to God never ceases to increase. Whatever is not poured out upon God festers and rots and brings no increase - it is body without spirit, it is dead. God is like a fountain that multiplies whatever is poured in. When we pour our intellectual power and wisdom into knowing God and following His ways, we may seem like dunces to the academics; but wait a little - nothing that is poured out on God is lost, and soon it will be plain that divine clarity and wisdom is coursing through the mind that we have yielded to God. So, too, if we give up property and wealth, lands and houses for God's sake, He will not allow us to lose out in any way - the last shall be first. God fills every vessel that is yielded to Him, just like the woman who was told to bring every pot and pan in her house [2 Kings 4:3]. There may be vessels we have never thought of; if we yield everything to God, we will flourish with an abundance and vigour that others only dream of. More than this, our growth will be exponential. The principles we will see at work during this earthly life are just a foretaste of the amazing reward we will get just from loving and serving God and His Lamb.

August 27

"If they do not speak according to this word, it is because there is no light in them." [Isaiah 8:20]

The Bible, the Word of God, is the compass of the human race. To lose the Bible through neglect is as serious for an individual or a generation as for a ship to lose its charts and compass.

When the weather is good, the ship is still in danger from unseen reefs, but when the storms come, the ship is in a perilous state, with no source of help. All believers will agree that the Bible is important, but it is vital to realise that the Bible is all-important. If a person speaks or lives from their own mind and wisdom, then they live without light. Beware the drift in your mind into worldly thinking. Immediately after we have read any book, the process of 'leakage' begins and we are unable to remember all the details. We forget people's names, dates, historical facts, and it is exactly the same with our knowledge of the Bible. The Bible is our map and compass, and we need to consult it afresh each day, or there will be no light within us. God has chosen to reveal Himself through His Word. This means that it is the way best suited to refresh us each day in our knowledge of Him. Switch on the light, drink in the Word. It is God's will for us, and it is within our reach.

August 28

"Finally, brethren, whatever things are true, whatever things are noble, whatever things are just, whatever things are pure, whatever things are lovely, whatever things are of good report, if there is any virtue and if there is anything praiseworthy – meditate on these things." [Philippians 4:8]

A thought is a seed. Once the seed has taken hold, it is as good as an action. This is why Jesus warned that wrong thoughts were equal to wrong actions. The only difference is the level of growth. The battle is always fought in our minds first. If we cross a line in our minds, it will only be a matter of time before we are doing what we have thought. This is a fearful truth, and should make us refuse to entertain even the smallest fantasy that is going in the wrong direction, whether it be a critical or bitter thought, or a lustful one. But this truth also has a wonderfully positive dimension. If we give ourselves to godly thoughts - about ourselves, God and others - then it will not be long before we are reaping a tremendous harvest in our actions and relationships. We are free to meditate on lovely and pure things, and soon we will find ourselves doing lovely and pure things. Our meditation will provide the tracks which will determine the direction in which the locomotive of our hearts moves forward. The human heart is a powerful engine, and can be directed by right thoughts, aided by the Holy Spirit, to manifest the glory of God in our lives.

August 29

"And when I saw Him, I fell at His feet as dead."
[Revelation 1:17]

John had walked with Jesus for the years of His earthly ministry. He had seen Him glorified on the mountain of transfiguration; he had seen Him in the glory of the resurrection; and he had seen Him by the indwelling Spirit on the Day of Pentecost. John had walked with Jesus for some 60 years by the time he was on Patmos, and yet when he saw Jesus unveiled, he fell at His feet as though dead. God reveals His Son to us in stages, because He knows that we cannot bear the full revelation of the glory of God in the face of Jesus Christ. Jesus is more than we will ever know or grasp, and while we know much about Him, there will always be a huge dimension of His Being about which we know so little. This truth should make us seek Him for further revelation of the Son of God. He is the unique One, the matchless One. He is not just more powerful and more loving than any other person we have ever met; He is unique in His essence. There is an 'otherness' about Him. He has come down to our level, but that should not deceive us into thinking He is merely one of us. He is of a different order of Being, and the wonder is that, as we gaze on Him, He lifts us to partake of His life. We were created to be lifted from one degree of glory, life and love to another. God reveals His Son by degrees; look at Jesus, and be lifted to fellowship with the Glorious One.

August 30

"O my dove, in the clefts of the rock, in the secret places of the cliff, let me see your face, let me hear your voice; for your voice is sweet, and your face is lovely."
[Song of Solomon 2:14]

Low self-esteem is a common affliction. Most of us are secretly afraid that we will be rejected or laughed at. It is for this reason that many people are afraid to speak or be seen in any public context. But Jesus thinks we are wonderful. He is like a gardener looking at a flower in full bloom, with joy and wonder filling Him. Sometimes we are far from in full bloom! We might be more like a rough and wrinkled tuber in His hands, that would be unnoticed on a rubbish heap. But He doesn't see the external scars and blemishes. He looks deep into the tuber and knows that it holds a secret treasure, if only He can coax it out. The tuber only needs water, and it will produce breathtaking beauty. We need the reassurance of His love. He longs for us to lift our faces to Him in faith. He longs for us to lift our voices in praise and worship. For Him there is no more beautiful sight than you. You are wonderful and beautiful beyond compare. You are His priceless treasure. One look or word from you, and His heart dances for joy. There is within you a beauty that is breathtaking, and a seed of life that has the power to make multitudes of angels worship God. God looks at us and is delighted at the wonder of what He has made. A look of love, a song of worship - these are the shimmering glories that God has made, and they are in you. They **are** you. You are wonderful, and He loves you.

August 31

"For whoever desires to save his life will lose it, but whoever loses his life for My sake and the gospel's will save it."
   [Mark 8:35]

When we follow the way of self-fulfilment and self-realisation, of satisfying our desire for pleasure and comfort, we are 'sowing to the flesh' - building up a debt to the flesh [Galatians 6:8]. Self-indulgence has a price, and we will have to pay a high price for many years. But if we 'lose' our lives, and give up our rights and our pleasures, then we will 'sow to the Spirit', and we will cultivate something that will bring abundant returns. The spiritual person loses out in the short term, but when the rewards start coming, they multiply and never stop. The habit of losing our life will result in the multiplying of our spiritual resources. While others are embarrassed by their spiritual weakness, we will be overwhelmed by the goodness of God poured into our lives. Those who take a short-cut will pay for it dearly; those who follow God's ways will rejoice in the grace and favour that are heaped upon them. Don't be tricked by quick and easy solutions. They will leave you shallow and empty for years. Follow the ways of Jesus, and wait confidently for the rewards of faith - life eternal and joy unspeakable.

September 1

"Therefore I say to you, do not worry about your life, what you will eat or what you will drink; nor about your body, what you will put on. Is not life more than food and the body more than clothing? Look at the birds of the air, for they neither sow nor reap nor gather into barns; yet your heavenly Father feeds them. Are you not of more value than they?" [Matthew 6:25-26]

Enemies of prayer I: Worry

Worry is a key enemy of prayer because it is in effect the opposite - it enthrones the negative, anticipates disaster, and is empowered by fear. Faith lays hold of God for His provision and miraculous intervention; worry builds a barrier against God, diverting His power and welcoming in the forces of darkness. We might be horrified to realise what we are really doing when we worry; but the question is, how do we overcome worry? The first and most important act is to repent - we must confess worry and forsake it, as a sin as grievous as any. Repentance requires a change of mind and attitude; and it is in our minds that all battles are fought and victory begins. The second act is to 'consider the birds'. The birds neither sow nor reap - but this certainly does not mean that we shouldn't go to work each day! No, the comparison is made so that we might imitate their carefree abandon about the context in which we live. The birds find their food each day; they don't think about where the next meal is coming from. They live in the consciousness of each moment, not in planning their future. Faith is essentially the art of looking up in complete trust about everything - realising that absolutely nothing can ever come our way that is greater than Jesus. We are not birds, and we do have responsibilities that birds don't have. But we are to enjoy our daily lives, not fret over what may be around the corner. The result is unhindered freedom to pray, anticipating His provision.

September 2

"And when you pray, you shall not be like the hypocrites." [Matthew 6:5]

Enemies of prayer II: Insincerity

Insincerity in prayer is a deadly poison. It is odd that many people suddenly become very serious when they pray - their voices become 'religious', their heads are bowed and their hands folded. But all this is comical unless it is genuine. When

155

we pray we should not be heavy with a sense of doom, but carried heavenwards by a sense of the imminent arrival of God in the situation. This is not to say that there is never a crushing burden in the heart of one who prays, but the dominant note in the praying life is one of the releasing companionship of Jesus Christ. Jesus raises our hopes, causes us to laugh at our own seriousness about ourselves. The person who prays has a sense of delight at the centre of their being - a sense of the reality of Christ and His power and provision. When Jesus was asked to pray for Jairus' daughter, He was astonished at the mourners, because their wailing was so clearly insincere. If He were to appear in many of our prayer meetings, He would be astonished at our incredible sense of religious self-importance. The answer to insincerity is to talk to Jesus in a normal voice, to address Him as you would a friend or a loving counsellor. Tell Him how you really feel. If there is a matter about which you are asked to pray, and about which you feel no burden then, above all, do not pretend! This will poison faith in your heart and in those who hear you pray. Tell Him exactly how you see things. Start from where you are. Prayer is letting God have access into our lives, and that means letting Him into our spiritual weakness. As soon as we do this, the adventure of prayer begins.

September 3

"No one can serve two masters; for either he will hate the one and love the other, or else he will be loyal to the one and despise the other. You cannot serve God and mammon."
[Matthew 6:24]

Enemies of prayer III: Worldliness
Worldliness hinders prayer because it is the attempt to back two horses to win a race! Praying to God while pursuing worldly pleasures will result in failure in both realms. Some people have just enough Christianity not to enjoy the world any more, but not enough to really enjoy God. The tragedy is that pursuit of empty pleasures robs us of ever tasting the bliss of God's Presence. Prayer is not a goal in itself - it is the Presence of God that is the goal. But this goal cannot be attained unless we pursue it with all our hearts. The great fact of spiritual life is that it only works on the basis of 'all or nothing'. Moses 'forsook' the pleasures of Egypt [Hebrews 11:27] - he broke irrevocably with that line of things in his heart and life. It takes the power of God to get 'Egypt' out of our hearts and appetites. But God can only do that when once we have made up our minds where we

really belong. The alluring attraction of the world lies in the sense of safety and comfort that it affords. Money is like a cushion that shields us from harm. It provides food, health care, pleasure and security. Worldliness is a substitute for God or, to put it bluntly, idol worship. The tragedy of idol worship is that it ends in tears, because idols fail to deliver. They neither speak, hear nor move. They give no companionship or friendship. All the while God is longing to satisfy our thirst for friendship and love. He will provide for all our physical needs. He will protect and keep us, and all He asks is that we put Him first. Whoever backs the right horse cannot lose, and for those who have eyes to see, it is a one-horse race.

September 4

"If I regard iniquity in my heart, the Lord will not hear."
  [Psalm 66:18]

Enemies of prayer IV: Sin
Spiritual life is a life of contrasts. Holiness is being close to God; sin is getting as far away from Him as possible. Sin is the opposite of all that is good, and as such it is the opposite of love, faith, peace and joy. Some weird individuals spend hours devising computer viruses that will wreak havoc via the internet, and vast sums of money are spent trying to protect computer systems from their harmful effects. Sin is the spiritual virus that makes everything dysfunctional. It makes our hearts deaf to God, and blocks out contact between God and us. Sin means pushing God away, cancelling His promises, weakening His influence, robbing His Word of power. Prayer is the open door in our lives to God and His life-giving Spirit; sin is an open door to darkness and all the gloom that Satan spreads. To pray while harbouring secret sins is the greatest folly of all. Sin, of course, takes many forms, and the worst form is pride and selfishness. The proud person does not admit to needing God; the selfish person will take all the help they can get, as long as they get what they want! The only answer to sin is to confess it. This does not mean merely accepting that we are sinners, but humbling ourselves before God and seeking His mercy and grace. As sin has blocked God out, so the repentant heart will not be satisfied until the channels of communication are open once more. Sin is a wrong attitude to God; prayer is the development of an inner attitude that pleases God. No matter how long it takes to form, there is no greater joy in life than finding the place of prayer. No matter how many tears we may

157

shed over sin, there is no comparison with the depths of joy known to the person who finds God.

September 5

"Whoever shuts his ears to the cry of the poor will also cry himself and not be heard." [Proverbs 21:13]

Enemies of prayer V: Hardness of heart
The cry of the poor may seem distant. In western nations it is 'a problem in far-off countries'. In pleasant middle-class suburbs it is 'a problem on the other side of the tracks'. But however far away the cry of the poor is, it reaches all our ears. If this were not so then God could never ask us to get involved. The question is not whether we are aware of the poor, but what we have done about it. Everyone has a responsibility before God to keep a compassionate heart. It is all too easy to dismiss the cry of the poor. We might say, *"They should do more to help themselves"*, or, *"If we give to organisations that collect for the poor, only a small amount will actually get to them"*. There may well be some truth in this, but if it leads us to inaction then we will have become guilty of hardening our hearts. The result is that God will do the same to us. God sees the human race as a family; He can see the way one member of the family is disadvantaged. We might see the matter very differently – perhaps as the fault of big business or bad government. But God is not asking us to solve the world's problems; He is asking us to attend to the state of our hearts. He is asking us to have compassion for the poor. We might not solve the world's problems, but we will certainly open up our hearts to God's influence in our lives. Once that influence is flowing, it is surprising how God widens the flow, and where we once felt negative about the whole process of giving to the poor, we now see God's hand opening a door for us to be involved in His work. Part of that work will be the sense that God's heart and ears are open to our prayers, and there is nothing more wonderful than to feel that we have caught God's attention.

September 6

"Lord, I knew you to be a hard man, reaping where you have not sown, and gathering where you have not scattered seed."
[Matthew 25:24]

Enemies to prayer VI: A wrong view of God

Perhaps the worst thing we could ever think about God is that He is not good. If God is not good then the foundations of the universe are buckled, and all hope is lost. God *is* good, and that does not mean that He is generally good, if a bit distant. No, it means that He is actively and energetically good. He is not only willing to do us good, He is actively working everything in our circumstances to bless and prosper us. People sometimes speak of a 'conspiracy theory' - that the world is being controlled by a small group of people for evil purposes. But the true 'conspiracy' is that God is conspiring behind the scenes to do us good. He is actively pursuing our blessing, and it is a vital part of faith that we believe that God intends and longs to do us good and to answer our prayers. If someone views their life as cursed and forgotten, their problem is their philosophy of life. Our view of the world is governed by our view of God. The person who thinks God doesn't care will give up praying and will bury their faith in a dark corner of their heart. The strange fact is that the same God is open to all and blesses all who call upon Him. Praying is the one activity which is assured of a positive answer. It does not mean that God gives me everything I want, but it does mean that if I find the place of fellowship with God, I find also the secret plan that fills me with boundless hope. God is good and is actively involved to bless. Prayer is opening the window on the true and living God, who is actively involved in our world.

September 7

"Now as they went down the road, they came to some water. And the eunuch said, 'See, here is water. What hinders me from being baptized?' " [Acts 8:36]

Philip and the eunuch were travelling together through the desert, south towards Ethiopia; as the conversation turned towards baptism, they came across some water. God's coincidences are more frequent than we realise. Once I was going on a mission trip to Africa, and randomly grabbed a book from the shelf as I was leaving the house. It was entitled 'The

Cambridge Seven' and was about seven missionaries from Cambridge University. The flight left London on time but there was a 12-hour delay in the rather sparse airport of Addis Ababa (coincidentally, the capital of Ethiopia)! The man next to me was bored and obviously had nothing to read, so I offered him the book I had grabbed. He was not interested in spiritual things, but he was a tutor from Cambridge University, and so he found the book really interesting. Our lives are made up of divine guidance and divine coincidences. The question is: are our eyes open to notice the beautiful weave that God is working into our lives and circumstances? Some types of cloth are monotone, but others have subtle weaves that add a blend of colour to a grey. God is in the weave of our lives. He has placed us in the circumstances we are in now. Our jobs, neighbours, and 'random' encounters are all part of His will and purpose. We pray for guidance, for God to show us what His will is, and to place us where He can use us. The truth is, we are already there. Lift up your eyes to discover God in your present circumstances.

September 8

"Master, carest thou not that we perish?" [Mark 4:38, KJV]
"Why troublest thou the Master any further?"
    [Mark 5:35, KJV]

Who is your master? The master of the disciples in the midst of the storm was their fear of death. Often we find ourselves controlled and driven by another master than the One we confess with our lips. The truth is that Jesus wishes to master our lives in every way and to displace every other power and influence over them. The mastering element in any life is that aspect of our character that paralyses us and causes us to fall in surrender to the dread influence. The indecisive person will make a decision and then be mastered by the fear of making a mistake. The pessimist will be driven by the dread of the worst that can befall them. The depressive person will be under a cloud no matter how bright their circumstances. The unbelieving person will never cease to question the evidence that stares them in the face. In every case, our reaction is to turn back to our old master and acknowledge him to be greater than Jesus. But fear, indecision, depression and unbelief are hard masters, and they have no reward or joy to share with us. When you are tempted to panic and despair, pause and remember that Jesus is never the author of such things. We must not be

160

prisoners of our own personalities, nor must we bow to any influence other than Jesus. Face the worst, and then bow down before Jesus, and there discover the truth that He is Master, not just of your soul, but of the storm, of life and death, of everything that could ever come across your path. Confess Him as Lord, and Lord alone, for there is no other. Every knee will one day bow to Him, so get it over with now, and bow. His mastery is joy unspeakable, and will fill you with a sense of hope in the most impossible circumstances.

September 9

"And He took them (the children) *up in His arms, laid His hands on them, and blessed them."* [Mark 10:16]

The human heart is like a bell that cannot be struck by any hammer other than the Spirit of God. Pleasures are like weeds that creep around and smother the bell; philosophies are like rust and corrosion that pit the surface of the bell; but none of these things cause the bell to ring. But once the Lord's voice resounds within our hearts, the weeds lose their grip and the covering of rust is removed. A traveller in Africa will often see old rusting machines and vehicles, lying in some field or yard, waiting for a spare part that never came. They may be so collapsed in a corroded heap that hardly anyone even remembers what purpose they once served. The human heart quickly forgets what it was created for, and sinks into spiritual indolence and haziness. But when Jesus strikes our hearts with His love, there is an immediate sense of purpose and everything starts to fall into place - the machine that looked so desolate is restored in a moment to its factory newness. It isn't an argument that restores us, nor is it even an explanation of how things went wrong - it is simply the Master's touch. The story is told of an old violin in a jumble sale, that no-one would buy; it seemed so useless and worthless. Then a certain master violinist happened to notice it, and picked it up. After a few seconds of tuning, he laid the old bow on the dusty violin, and everyone stopped in amazement to hear the beautiful music that filled the room. In the same way, Jesus' touch reveals the incalculable value of a human soul. Everywhere Jesus went, He touched something so deep and forgotten in people's hearts that it made tired sinners turn in seconds into eager disciples of holiness. Never underestimate the power and influence of a moment in the hands of the Master.

September 10

"Behold the proud, his soul is not upright in him; but the just shall live by his faith." [Habakkuk 2:4]

This verse sums up the gospel in a brief phrase - faith in God leads to right living, and without faith, no amount of good deeds can ever make us right with God. It is wrong to think of faith in terms of a few things that we believe about God. Faith is best understood by the word 'trust'. The human heart is twisted by the lack of an anchor and the absence of a plumb line to align the mind with the heart. The knots and tangles of our minds are only released through God's power. The only way in which we can touch God is through faith. We cannot touch or see Him physically. Once we realise this, we give up striving for some sign that will give us assurance. We must reach out in faith and touch the Rock which is God. As soon as we believe God, the strength of the Rock is communicated to us, just as we might steady ourselves by holding on to a wall. The quality of the Rock enters our souls, and our behaviour changes. Faith is the lightning rod by which the power of God enters our life. Our good deeds do not put us in touch with God, nor can they; they always cause us to believe that we have the answer in ourselves. Anyone who does seek to please God through good deeds will soon testify to the emptiness it brings. Good deeds not only cannot put us in touch with God, they leave us dry and empty, and we long for His Presence. But as soon as we believe God, a confidence enters us, and our conduct changes; our minds become strong and full of joy. Before we realise it, even the little things that we do are touched with a lightness and kindness that are not from us, but are from the Rock on which we are building our lives.

September 11

"For those who dwell in Jerusalem, and their rulers, because they did not know Him, nor even the voices of the Prophets which are read every Sabbath, have fulfilled them in condemning Him." [Acts 13:27]

Paul here speaks of hearing the voices of the prophets. He is referring to the majesty and authority that was evident as soon as the prophets spoke. Even though they were rejected and persecuted, yet even their enemies could not escape the sense of God that came through the prophets' voices. It is the same for us who now read the pages of the New Testament. Through them speaks the matchless voice of the Son of God in loving, tender entreaty, and with the underlying note of absolute authority. Reading the Bible is an adventure once we realise that it is not like a flat picture on a wall, but like a window through which breezes blow and music floats. This is because the Author is present with us to make the words come alive with the right tones of voice. Think of reading a book by an author whose voice you know. It might be a preacher or a politician, but as you read, your interest is increased because you can hear the author's voice. The Holy Spirit is not just the author of the Bible, He is ever-present as we read, to make it come alive. This is not our imagination - it is the touch of God that comes in a unique way through the Scripture. We need to read with faith and let the voice of the Scripture strike a note in us. The Lord's voice comes with the impartation of the Holy Spirit, in creative life and power in our hearts. God is closer than we think and His voice is sounding more than we ever realise. If we will only stop listening to the chatter of our own hearts, we will catch the life-giving voice of God speaking every day.

September 12

"If we live in the Spirit, let us also walk in the Spirit."
    [Galatians 5:25]

Travelling throughout this world is fascinating, and there are many people who devote themselves to seeking out its most beautiful sights. But this is all horizontal movement, while all the time there is another world to discover, and to find this we only need to have fellowship with God. The Kingdom of God is in the Spirit. We can step out of this world and into God's Presence, where we can walk, explore, and discover that world's beautiful sights and sounds. The Kingdom of God is at hand and within the reach of anyone who loves God. The sights of earth cause us to wonder at the glory of creation, but the sight of God by faith causes a reaction that is unlike anything we have experienced on earth. Walking in the Spirit causes our hearts to be washed, our character to be renewed, our love to grow and our faith to rise on eagle's wings. One step in the Spirit is more exciting and more fulfilling than a lifetime of travel. The person who walks with God has travelled much further than any explorer - and that is the appropriate word. The explorers who set out years ago to discover the source of the Nile endured dangers, drudgery, pain and hunger, separation from loved ones,

163

and all just to find another bit of the jigsaw puzzle of the map of Africa. Walking in the Spirit involves repentance and setting aside other things in order to attain the goal of knowing God, but the rewards are indescribably great. There is power to live a wholesome life, drawing on the boundless inspiration of the Presence of God.

September 13

"...the kingdom of God is not eating and drinking, but righteousness and peace and joy in the Holy Spirit."
    [Romans 14:17]

The blessings of the Kingdom of God are all interlocking, so that we cannot always distinguish the most important. The order here is important, in that righteousness is the foundation of peace, which then leads to joy. It is also true that, as we keep a peaceful heart, we are able to worship. It is in peace that faith flourishes and we are able to hear the voice of the Spirit in our heart. Joy rises in the midst of peace, and gives us a perspective that overcomes our enemies. The challenge for us is to abide in peace and joy, and so overcome sin and rise above the enemies of our souls. Peace is not the absence of problems; it is the settled focus of a trusting heart on the faithfulness of God. Joy is not happy circumstances; it is the anticipation of God's marvellous future provision based on what He has already done. From prison, Paul kept exhorting believers to have joy - not because he enjoyed prison, but because he anticipated the blessings of heaven. It would have been 'pie in the sky when you die' if Paul had not experienced the foretaste of heaven by a powerful baptism with the Spirit. We have the downpayment of heaven in the gift of the Holy Spirit, and this is what makes us assured of the bliss to come. Keep the settled focus. Remember the blessings received so far. Remember that those are the foretaste of the powers of the age to come. Then let righteousness, peace and joy be the kingdom you live in.

September 14

"Simon Peter said to them, 'I am going fishing.' They said to him, 'We are going with you also.' They went out and immediately got into the boat, and that night they caught nothing.".... *"Then, as soon as they had come to land, they saw a fire of coals there, and fish laid on it, and bread."*
    [John 21:3,9]

Peter had been brooding about something and suddenly reached his decision - he would go and catch some breakfast. He had been struggling with the promise that God would provide for all his needs – but what did that mean in his immediate circumstances? The problem was that Peter was moving outside of trusting fellowship with God. It is not wrong to go out and work for a living! But it is wrong to move out in common-sense when God has promised He will provide. Peter laboured all night and caught nothing. The efforts of common-sense can yield no fruit if they contradict God's declared will and promise. The same God who later told Peter to throw his nets on the right side of the boat [John 21:6] had also kept the fish away from his nets all the night long. When they came to the shore, there was Jesus, in the same humility that He displayed throughout His earthly life. The risen, glorified Son of God had returned to earth to prepare a breakfast for His friends. The event is full of very simple lessons. God will provide for us and be with us in our struggles and in the ordinary daily lives that He has given us. Peter was tired, frustrated and perhaps confused. But when Jesus stepped into the situation, there was refreshment and comfort. All was well. The Lord is indeed risen and glorified, but He has not lost any of His astonishing compassion. He is at home with us, and we should make sure that we do not act as if He didn't care or was too exalted to be involved in our lives. He loves us.

September 15

"The grace of the Lord Jesus Christ, and the love of God, and the communion of the Holy Spirit be with you all. Amen."
    [2 Corinthians 13:14]

The *"communion of the Holy Spirit"* is a phrase that goes to the heart of our relationship with God. Governments operate by communicating information to allow smooth administration of human society. But God does not seek that level of contact - He seeks communion with His people. Communion implies the mixing of our personality with God's personality. It is the deepest level of friendship. It takes place when we come to rest in our hearts and allow the cloud of His Presence to settle on us and fill our conscious and sub-conscious being. In this process, God imparts Himself, and achieves His primary goal, which is to enjoy our loving friendship. God does not love us only enough to rescue us; He wants to be with us and enjoy our worship and our friendship. We so easily seek places and things, but God seeks **us**. This communion is a greater thing than paradise itself. It can be enjoyed in a prison cell or in the slums and shanty towns of earth's poorest parts. It cannot be purchased with money or attained by human striving. It settles on the heart that thirsts for the living God Himself with no ulterior motives. God draws near to those whose hearts are stirred to love Him and find the fulfilment of their deepest longings in sitting with Him and sharing His life. Let the communion of the Holy Spirit be with you evermore.

September 16

"... let us draw near with a true heart in full assurance of faith, having our hearts sprinkled from an evil conscience and our bodies washed with pure water." [Hebrews 10:22]

There may seem at first to be a contradiction in this verse, for how can anyone draw near to God with a true heart and full assurance if they have an evil conscience? This contradiction illuminates the root problem that we think we must be good before we can come close to God. This would be like a man trapped in a dark room pleading for someone to bring him light, only to be told that he must first drive the darkness out before light could be brought in! We cannot be pure enough by ourselves to approach God - it is in drawing near that His Presence washes and changes us, first in our spirit and then even in our bodies. So what is the *"true heart"* we are to prepare? It is a heart that has realised its need and comes in brokenness and humility. What is the *"full assurance of faith"*? It is the faith that God is calling us and has prepared all things so that we can indeed draw near. There is forgiveness and acceptance with God, no matter how deep the stains on our conscience. The longer we allow guilt and shame to keep us out, the longer they will be our daily bread. We must arise and receive the cleansing Presence of God, that dispels our darkness and transforms our lives. The feeling of being excluded is an illusion, a lie of the devil. God has accepted us, and nothing but doubting His faithfulness can keep us out of His life-transforming grace. Once we have crossed the threshold we will wonder why we ever hesitated, for the welcome there is overwhelming. All heaven is urging us to come, and every barrier has been removed.

September 17

"My soul, wait silently for God alone, for my expectation is from Him." [Psalm 62:5]

The greatest man who ever lived was Jesus Christ. He held within His heart all the secrets of creation, and if He had so desired He could have developed His soul and mind to limitless heights. He could have given mankind any of the discoveries that are so highly acclaimed today. But instead of choosing a life of natural development, He chose the path of developing His inner dependence and attention to the voice of God. The most obvious outworking of this was in His chosen profession. He became a carpenter, and remained so for His entire youth. This involved great spiritual challenge for One so gifted as He. He was faced with issues of self-denial, exercise of patience and humility, of faith and trust, of love and obedience. Following this path equipped Him to fulfil His burning passion, which was to know God, to commune with Him, to plumb the depths of God's compassion and mercy. He chose to wait on God alone. Waiting on God is not primarily a state of mind - that would be to reduce it to psychology. Waiting on God is primarily a moral choice that we must renew daily and continually. It is the constant denial of self in all its forms, positive and negative, in order to choose the knowledge of God. Jesus knew that the only cure for the human condition is the knowledge of God. Christians can help the world in many ways, but the only help that will reach the real problem of the human heart is to discover God and make Him known.

September 18

"For since the beginning of the world men have not heard nor perceived by the ear, nor has the eye seen any God besides You, who acts for the one who waits for Him." [Isaiah 64:4]

"But God has revealed them to us through His Spirit. For the Spirit searches all things, yes, the deep things of God."
[1 Corinthians 2:10]

The work of the Spirit is to minister the knowledge of God to those who wait on Him. Here there is a need for great patience, for God is not like us - He does not aim to give us superficial thrills. We must wait patiently and quietly, stilling the ceaseless stream of thoughts and questions. These will act as a barrier, until they are steadily set aside and we begin to hear and see the wonder of God. It is to the waiting heart that the truths of infinite love and everlasting Being are revealed. Then the true meaning of worship is unfolded. For God does not seek honour as the supreme ruler of the universe; He seeks the worship of loving hearts. He seeks to occupy a deeper position than that of ruler. Loving hearts abandon themselves to God's Being without condition, without reserve and without ulterior motive. Some of us do this quickly, others learn to yield as our stubborn hearts are softened more and more. Some of us have to pass through all the selfish reasons why we need God, until we begin to love God for Himself. God is not worshipped on the basis of need, and so true rest is discovered beyond our need. The Spirit of God leads us to be stripped of all personal plans and ambitions, of all other competing affections, until we are left with nothing but our naked spirit to pour out at His feet in abandoned worship and love.

September 19

"And because you are sons, God has sent forth the Spirit of His Son into your hearts, crying out, 'Abba, Father!' "
      [Galatians 4:6]

We are called primarily to be sons of God, not servants (although every son is also a servant), and certainly not hired servants. The hired servant thinks of his work as something he does in return for his wages. The son works because he delights to do the Father's will, and expects no wages for his labour, knowing that he shares in the Father's entire wealth by inheritance. The person who hears the inner witness of the Spirit knows that their chief calling is to walk as a son, and this motivates them to live tirelessly and unceasingly for the Father. This call fills a person with dignity and peaceful assurance that their life and work are hidden in the Father's hand. The prodigal son wanted to be received back as a hired servant, but he totally misunderstood his father's heart. His father could do nothing but receive him back as his son. The older brother drifted from his calling as a son. When he heard the music and celebration in his father's house, he did not seek fellowship with the father, but with the hired servants. When the father came out to find him, he responded with the cry of someone looking for wages: *"...you never gave me..."* [Luke 15:29]. The father's response was wholly loving: *"Son, you are always with me, and all that I have is yours."* [Luke 15:31]. Stand up in the full realisation of your calling, for there are things to be done in the Kingdom of God that can only be done by sons who are utterly devoted to their Father in heaven.

September 20

"No one has seen God at any time. The only begotten Son, who is in the bosom of the Father, He has declared Him."
[John 1:18]

Jesus was settled in the call of Sonship, which meant that He knew He was loved and eternally held in the Father's heart. This is our call also, and as we follow the witness of the Spirit we will find that it leads us always to the Father's heart. It is in the security of His love that God uses us and spends us for the fulfilment of His will. To be the son of a king means that we partake of His wealth, but in the Kingdom of God it also means that we partake of the Father's sacrificial love. It says in Romans 8:32 that God did not spare His own Son, and this is the realm of the service of sons - to spend and to be spent, to be so sure of Father's love and care that we are willing to be used and even (to our eyes) wasted as He pleases. It is in this offering up of our lives that true sonship is revealed. Service and zeal for Father's house spring from a heart that has followed the call to Father's heart. We must learn and become familiar with our heart's cry to *"Father"* and the warm response, *"You are my beloved son"*. The greatest mysteries are the simplest, and the most blessed states are uncomplicated and pure. As we discover the life of a son of God, we are equipped with the wisdom and power to reveal Him to the world.

September 21

"So also Christ did not glorify Himself to become High Priest, but it was He who said to Him: 'You are My Son, today I have begotten You.' As He also says in another place: 'You are a priest for ever according to the order of Melchizedek'..."
[Hebrews 5:5-6]

As we discover the Spirit's witness in our hearts, there is first the dawning of sonship and then the dawning of an everlasting priesthood. The Holy Spirit continually speaks of this twofold call to be sons and priests. He continually leads us out of seeking worldly pleasures, into fellowship with God and offering ourselves to Him in prayer. God's kingdom functions on the

169

basis of the sweet incense of lives offered up to God in prayer and intercession. Clearly, no offering of ourselves in prayer can ever redeem anyone from sin - only one offering could do that. But it is plain from Scripture that prayer and priesthood lie at the heart of God's kingdom, just as they lay at the heart of the nation of Israel. This prayer life may follow a path that involves loneliness, hunger, pain, worship, seekings, groanings, etc. The heart of prayer is being identified with the Father's deepest longings and will, which will include fellowship with Him in His unspeakable grief over sin, and His boundless joy at the power of Jesus to save. This call to be both a son and a priest will lead us to be people after God's own heart, sharing His joys and sorrows. God's call is persistent and patient, yet never dominating. God rules over His own people by His love. Inference and suggestion are more akin to the Spirit's wooing tones than is shouting. As God cried out in the Temple: *"Whom shall I send, and who will go for Us?"* [Isaiah 6:8], so now God seeks those who will be His true sons and ambassadors.

September 22

"But I said, 'Not so, Lord! For nothing common or unclean has at any time entered my mouth.' " [Acts 11:8]

This verse demonstrates the depth of conflict that arises in someone who is discovering the freedom from sin that flows from a heart full of the Holy Spirit. Peter had never broken the dietary laws of Moses, and this must have been a treasured achievement in his spiritual 'balance sheet'. Yet here God was commanding him to break that law. Obviously, this lesson has its dangers, since many people have the opposite problem, and treat God's law with casual disregard. But Peter was not of that sort, and was here struggling to come to terms with the fact that God will not have His gospel associated with religious do's and don'ts. God was commanding Peter to eat pork, and this troubled him. Yet without this step of faith, Peter could never have brought the gospel to more than a very narrow section of humanity. Not only that, his faith would have been polluted by a sense of personal achievement, that he had never broken the dietary laws. We must learn to distinguish between the moral absolutes that must never be broken, and the religious habits and ideas that are more to do with human pride than with holiness. If we will not break with religious superstition, we will frustrate Christ's joy and liberty from flowing in our hearts. Our power as Christians does not lie in promoting ideas about

170

Sundays, clothing, or food and drink, but in discovering the greatness of the Person of Christ. The chief opponents of Jesus were Pharisees, who felt undermined because their sense of being right with God lay in their religious habits rather than in a real relationship with God through Christ. It is not that we throw ourselves open to carnal self-indulgence, but that we fellowship with Him who is the most free human being who ever lived, and yet the most holy.

September 23

"You...have overcome...because He who is in you is greater than he who is in the world..." [1 John 4:4]
"Flee...youthful lusts..." [2 Timothy 2:22]
"Resist the devil..." [James 4:7]

These verses indicate clearly the different ways in which we must progress in our walk with God. Far too easily we fight with only one of these weapons. So we easily assume the devil is attacking us, when it is simply a question of walking away from a situation in which we are being severely tempted. These verses should comfort us with the realisation that growing in grace can never mean we will be freed from all conflict. On the contrary, growth in grace means that we learn how to handle the conflicts that arise. Overcoming the world by faith means that we are able to set right priorities, and not follow the world's agenda. Fleeing lusts means that our normal appetites can lead us astray if indulged in, but by the Holy Spirit we have the power to walk away. We cannot lose our appetites, or we would become less than human, but we can learn to walk away from situations that stimulate desires that will threaten to overwhelm us. Resisting the devil means there are moments when we are without any blame, but are overcome with irrational feelings of guilt or depression. Those are the moments to resist and throw off such feelings and imaginations. The truth is that God is on our side to win the battles we will fight. He has accepted us in Christ and undertaken to lead us through all the conflicts, right to the final victory when we see Him face-to-face. Stand up and walk in victory each day, for it is God who has promised it to us.

September 24

"...He humbled Himself and became obedient to the point of death, even the death of the cross. Therefore God also has

highly exalted Him and given Him the name which is above every name..." [Philippians 2:8-9]

Many people seek authority and power in different realms, but God seeks out those who are able to bear authority. How God must long to find people who will be of the character and mind that can bear His authority! The only qualification that God seeks is someone who will resist the temptation to advance their own ends or promote their own name. When God finds someone who will resist the temptation to self-advancement, He will confer upon that person gifts and authority that will glorify Him and bless that individual. When seeking God's will, we need to concentrate our focus on fulfilling God's ways in our conduct, and leave it for God to fulfil His will in demonstrating the power of the kingdom. The way up is down; the way of authority is the way of serving and self-denial. God's ways are always bafflingly simple, and we often see mystery where there is none, and forget that the greatest mystery is God's love and mercy in ever choosing weak human beings to display His greatness and splendour. Jesus chose the way of self-emptying; He chose this way every time. We must make our choice, and ✳ we will be put in situations where that choice will be so clear. It is then that we either go the way that leads to the manifestation of the Kingdom of God, or else the glory will be veiled by a brief moment of praise from our fellow human beings. The measure of our life is not in the wine we drink, but the wine we pour out as an offering to God.

September 25

"...choose for yourselves this day whom you will serve..."
[Joshua 24:15]

Human beings have the power of choice; it is this that sets us apart from the animals, who are driven merely by instinct without moral responsibility. The greatest fence-sitter in the Bible was Pontius Pilate, who though he held the office of Roman Procurator and therefore of judge in Jesus' trial, passed on the decision to the crowds and the Pharisees. When he washed his hands of Jesus, refusing to make any choice, he made the worst possible choice of his entire life. The worst choice we ever make is to claim neutrality, to refuse to make a choice when we are faced with a clear moral decision. Choices come in different forms; daily, we choose what to wear, what to eat and drink. The large, defining moral choices come rarely, and often

172

without any planning on our part. Pilate was woken early in the morning and faced with the trial of Jesus. So too, circumstances suddenly arise that require us to make an instant decision - we need time, but there is none, we need more information but it is not available. Our minds scream for mercy from the juggernaut of moral demands. But we cannot escape; we must choose, and we must choose on the spot. If we put it off, we will sink into moral weakness, rather like the physical weakness of someone who hates exercise - they become flabby, and their muscles ache if they are forced to any physical exertion. In a similar way, the man or woman who fends off personal responsibility for moral choices will become weak and withdrawn. We are to be actively involved in the pursuit and furtherance of what is right, in our development of a relationship with God, and in the outworking of that relationship in positive love and holiness.

September 26

"...a viper came out because of the heat, and fastened on his hand.... But he shook off the creature into the fire and suffered no harm." [Acts 28:3,5]

When Paul came out of the shipwreck he must have felt relieved and ready to enjoy a moment of rest and respite from the hardships of the storm. Yet here he is, gathering wood to help build a fire to warm himself and others. Then, in this moment of service, he is once more attacked, this time by a snake - through which he was being assaulted yet again by the devil. The poison of the devil came through the viper's fangs into Paul's bloodstream; and that poison can come through other means into our spirits - sometimes through words, events or thoughts. That these attacks will come is a certainty of life, and we must be spiritually armed and ready to take the necessary action. What should we do when he attacks? The answer is to simply shake the snake off into the fire of destruction. It may sound too simple and easy, but so it is with spiritual warfare. God causes us to tread on serpents and scorpions and on all the power of the enemy, and nothing shall by any means harm us [Luke 10:19]. By a simple act of faith we can shake off the awful power of Satan; his attacks cannot cling to a believing heart. His wounding lies and hurtful words will be utterly destroyed forever in the fire of God's love that destroyed evil on the cross. In a moment, we are free and able to continue in our life of ministry to others. Stand up and shake off the serpent, and enter into the joy that God has prepared for you.

173

September 27

"Silver and gold I do not have, but what I do have I give you..."
  [Acts 3:6]

Here is a divine 'open secret' - that we must receive from God in order to be able to give. Take care of the inflow, and God will take care of the outflow. Peter said that he had no silver or gold, which meant that he had no natural means to help the lame man at the Beautiful Gate of the Temple. Nor did he have any store of spiritual power of holiness or healing by which he could, of his own will, heal the man. The only thing that he did have was a living connection with God through the name of Jesus. He was not offering doctrinal knowledge; he was a conduit for the reality of God's Presence and power. The only thing we have to give the world is what we have in the present moment from our relationship with Jesus. It is only as we draw near and develop an inner attentiveness to Him that we will ever be able to help another person. Peter was evidently in close relationship with Jesus, and this should challenge us to do the same. It should not discourage us from realising that God can use us today, if only we will be in a living relationship with Him.

September 28

"But God forbid that I should boast except in the cross of our Lord Jesus Christ, by whom the world has been crucified to me, and I to the world." [Galatians 6:14]

Paul was consumed with the cross and its effect on his life. It had liberated him from selfish, worldly living, and made him a new creature. It was for this message that he bore the marks of the cross in his body. No, there were no nailprints in his hands and feet, but there were many scars from the beatings; there were doubtless many visible signs of the sufferings and hardships he had gone through. He is not suggesting in this verse that his sufferings had any redemptive value. He is pointing to the effect of the cross in him, enabling him to live with such abandonment of his own life and well-being. Truly Paul was an incarnation of the gospel. He had received God's word deep into his being, and it had taken possession of the whole vessel. Paul was not an incarnation of God - he was still a man, capable of falling, capable of frustrating the grace of God. But by his yieldedness, he had allowed the power of the cross to burn through his whole being. It had burnt away carnality, and made him a blazing witness to the power of the cross. Paul says here that he is nothing in himself, but that in and through the death of Jesus Christ, God has turned his whole life around, filling him with love and good works, flowing from the Holy Spirit within him. God can do it for anyone who is bold enough to take Him at his word.

September 29

"For if we have been united together in the likeness of His death, we also shall be of resurrection." [Romans 6:5, KJV]

Death and resurrection were prophetically written into the fabric of creation in the very beginning, when God created plants and trees bearing seeds that must fall into the ground, die and then bear fruit. Seeds are generally small and unremarkable in colour, and sometimes even wrinkled and ugly. But when the seed passes through death, it is 'raised' to give beautiful flowers and delicious fruit. The same is true of believers. As we look on our own lives, we are discouraged and tempted to despair. But as we yield to the cross and let go of our lives, to be filled with the Spirit, God makes us *"of resurrection"*. Resurrection is not mere resuscitation or restoration. It is transformation from one order of life to another - the two realms are so different that there seems almost no relationship between them. Certainly, resurrection life cannot be taught. It cannot be entered into by small stages. If we will let go of our lives in absolute surrender to the love of God, we will experience not just a measure of hope or a renewal of faith. We will experience a transformation so deep that we will hardly be able to recognise ourselves. Like the sluggish caterpillar that takes to the wing as a butterfly, so our sad, tired hearts soar as they leave behind the heaviness of the 'cocoon' of self-centred flesh. This is hope that never tires and faith that never wavers, for it is the glory of the risen Christ in our hearts.

September 30

"They shall beat their swords into plowshares..." [Isaiah 2:4]
"The lofty looks of man shall be humbled, the haughtiness of men shall be bowed down..." [Isaiah 2:11]

On 20 January 1973 Richard Nixon was sworn in for his second term as US President. His hand rested on a Bible, open at Isaiah chapter 2. He had chosen this chapter because of his policy of ending the war in Vietnam. But his hand rested on the whole chapter, and within a few months not only was the war ended, but Nixon himself was deeply humbled by the scandal of Watergate which was already rumbling in the background as he took his oath of office. All greatness carries with it the danger that we will be blinded to other areas of our lives. We might assume, for instance, that excellence as a preacher might outweigh impatience with bothersome people we meet. Greatness is an illusion if it is a 'head of gold' with 'feet of clay' [Daniel 2:32-35]. True greatness is not excelling in one area that is applauded by others. True greatness is patiently noticing and caring for insignificant people. The great German evangelist Jonathan Paul was once walking along the sidewalk with some friends who were deep in conversation. They suddenly realised he was not with them; looking around, they saw him on the other side of the road, helping a woman who was struggling with heavy bags. That famous man considered himself to be of no consequence, and acted out of a compassion that had opened his eyes to see the woman in the first place.

October 1

"Blessed are the poor in spirit, for theirs is the kingdom of heaven." [Matthew 5:3]

The beatitudes are steps into the Kingdom of God, and they are in the order that will keep us in right relationship with Him. This first one seems perhaps puzzling at first. To be 'poor in spirit' surely means to lack spiritual qualities? There are many in history, from ruthless dictators to lazy drunkards, who have been devoid of spiritual qualities! But Adolf Hitler, for instance, never recognised his need of God, even in the last hours of his life. What Jesus is referring to is that ability to see our emptiness in all its horror, and yet go to God in prayer, believing that He wants to help us. This is a liberating truth - I simply have to acknowledge my total emptiness and come to God for help. Really, the only hindrance to this is pride. Some of us may have difficulty with the idea that we first approach God as paupers - it is an insult to our intelligence and gifts - we are not really poor, are we? It is a shock to meet those who are truly poor in the natural sense. Once, on the borders of Ethiopia, the bus I was travelling in stopped near a market and all around were boys from the famine areas, with legs like matchsticks, and sunken cheeks. Our spiritual condition is like that until we are reconciled with God through Christ. It is not blessed to be in that condition, but the first and unavoidable step into the Kingdom of God is to recognise our need of help. It is frustrating for a capable person to think that they may never be able to use their natural gifts and abilities in the kingdom, but the truth is that we have to learn and acquire other abilities. We don't remain paupers, but we do remain dependent on God. We are servants of a great King, waiting on His will and with pride in Him and His grace. When we acknowledge these things, we have made the first step to incredible blessing.

October 2

"Blessed are those who mourn, for they shall be comforted." [Matthew 5:4]

Mourning is the state of heart of those who grieve. From recognising our poverty of spirit, we move to grieving over the way we have hindered God and His grace through our spiritual ignorance and pride. We mourn as those who go to our own funeral; we lament the way we have lived. Attending our own funeral is always a blessed experience, for it causes us to see things in the right light. It should not lead us to grieve like those whose loss is irrevocable, since this funeral is not the end of our life on earth - it is just the end of the wasted years. And it marks the beginning of the ministry of the Comforter. The word 'comfort' does not only mean a loving touch and an exhortation to be brave - it means the empowering of the Holy Spirit to begin a new life. This mourning is blessed because it leads to the sense of a miserable life ending, and a joyful life beginning. Have you ever woken from a bad dream and realised that what you dreamed never happened? The relief and joy are sometimes so overwhelming that you feel like you have been given a fresh chance at life. This is the comfort that the Holy Spirit gives. We grieve over all the foolish things we have said and done, and wish we could start all over again, and the Holy Spirit draws near to us and enables us to do just that. Our former life of folly and defilement passes away from us like a bad dream, and the amazing joy dawns in our heart that we can truly start life this day without all the baggage of the past.

October 3

"Blessed are the meek, for they shall inherit the earth."
[Matthew 5:5]

Meekness is state of heart that comes to someone who has said goodbye to their old life. It is the attitude of a lamb, and indicates an inner ability to be led by the Holy Spirit. When we lose the aggressive spirit of the world, we might think that we will lose out on all the things that worldly people achieve by their grasping and striving. But God here promises that those who let go of the ownership of their lives and of this world's goods shall find that they will own far more than those who love this present world. God is the One who will distribute the goods of this world. They all belong to Him, and He gives them to whoever He wills. God here declares that the earth and everything in it will one day belong to those who have let go of it. A person who clings to heavy gold when they fall into the sea, will either sink with it, or let it go so that they might be saved. The true disciple of Jesus has let go of this world at the deepest level of their being, and has become a meek lamb who can be led in God's will. Jesus is the Lamb of God - He let go of every right and privilege that was His to claim. The result is that He has been given all things in heaven and in earth. On the divine balance sheet, to grasp, to cling and to demand is to lose everything. To release and let go of our life and of every right is to enter into the lamb-like nature that God anoints with power over all the enemies of mankind, and which will one day rule over the earth itself.

October 4

"Blessed are those who hunger and thirst for righteousness, for they shall be filled." [Matthew 5:6]

The hunger to be filled with the Holy Spirit is a deadly form of idolatry unless it is the hunger to be filled with righteousness. There is often much debate about the different kinds of blessings that can appear in Christian circles - there may be discussion about being 'slain in the spirit', or similar things. But there is no controversy when there is an outbreak of righteousness! This is universally recognisable as the effect of God's hand on a life. When God is moving in a person's life, stolen goods are returned and broken relationships are restored because that person has come to brokenness and humility. This thirst to be righteous is not the same as the thirst to be forgiven; it is the thirst for power to live right. Forgiveness will deal with my guilt and shame, and the forgiveness of Jesus does this thoroughly and effectively. But it cannot satisfy the second need of my heart, which is to have power to live. Whatever blessings I may receive will prove empty unless they lead to an improvement in my lifestyle. Notice, too, that this hunger is only satisfied by being filled - a touch or temporary improvement will actually disappoint in the end. We long for that empowering that radically changes our appetites, and deals with unclean things in our hearts. Jesus here teaches that the precursor of baptism with the Holy Spirit is hunger for right living. Beware passive interpretation of Jesus' words - spiritual hunger is not like being born with blue eyes, where we play no active part in the matter. If we have no spiritual hunger, we are eating the wrong things, and we are morally responsible to change the way we live and to begin to hunger after the things of God.

October 5

"Blessed are the merciful, for they shall obtain mercy."
        [Matthew 5:7]

Mercy is all to do with a forgiving attitude that overlooks the faults of others. It is the opposite of demanding justice. Being

179

merciful to others is part of our own repentance, in that we let all the grudges and injustices fall from our hearts, and we ourselves are suddenly free from bitterness. Bitterness is a cry for revenge, for justice, for a day in court to air my grievances. Mercy lets go of everything and reaches out to those who have sinned against us. Once mercy has touched us we are free, and able to realise how wrong we were in our attitudes. We understand why any other attitude is poisonous, first to ourselves, and then to all others around us. God will not continue to be merciful to someone who will not pass mercy on to others. It is part of the chain of life that connects us with God and those around us. Break a link in the chain, and it collapses altogether. The temptation to withhold mercy will be with us at every step of the way. Small things are often the things that most cause us to stumble, because we feel able to get hold of these situations and rectify the little wrongs that are done to us. Jesus told a parable of a man who was forgiven a billion-dollar debt, and then demanded that he be paid the thousand dollars that was owed him [Matthew 18:23-35]; the king then withdrew his mercy towards the man. Mercy touches hearts and frees situations, and it liberates most of all the person who exercises mercy.

October 6

"Blessed are the pure in heart, for they shall see God."
    [Matthew 5:8]

Peter received a clean, pure heart when he was baptised with the Holy Spirit on the Day of Pentecost [Acts 15:8-9]. This is important, since it is possible to associate God's blessings with superficial things. For example, it would be wrong to associate the gift of tongues with a pure heart, since that would be making something lesser a sign of something greater. A pure heart will confirm that the blessings I am receiving are from God - not the other way round! A pure heart, then, is a gift. It is imparted to one who asks in simple faith. It is a change in the tone of our life, and indicates that purity is now part of everything we think and do, as surely as grapes grow on a vine and thorns on a bramble bush. Purity of heart is not merely the promise that we will one day see God; it is, much more, the ability to see Him now. Purity of heart opens us up to the possibility of deep, real fellowship with God. It is the clear eye of faith. It is the open ear that can hear His voice. It is this inner faculty for which we long and without which no amount of moral standards will satisfy our hearts. Purity of heart means having within us a fountain of thoughts that are beautiful, positive and refreshing. Some have thought that this means we can be perfect. Once, in Spurgeon's Bible School, a student was baptised with the Holy Spirit, and began to exclaim that he felt so clean that he was perfect. This was at breakfast, and Spurgeon calmly picked up a jug of milk, walked behind the student and poured it over his head! The student's reaction quickly made him realise that he was not yet perfect! You may chuckle, but don't miss the greater point: there is a blessing and a power in purity of heart that could make you tempted to think you could be perfect. When were you last tempted to think that?

October 7

"Blessed are the peacemakers, for they shall be called sons of God." [Matthew 5:9]

This is a verse that was misquoted by US President Bill Clinton while trying to obtain peace in the Middle East. (He said: *"Blessed are the peacemakers, for they shall inherit the earth."*) But this verse has less to do with politics and more to do with our attitude to those we rub shoulders with every day, in the home, at work and in the Church. Peace does not just mean the absence of strife, though it obviously includes that. If peace meant only the absence of conflict, then many could call themselves 'peacemakers' by doing nothing at all. But standing on the sidelines is not being a peacemaker. The disciple who has found God's blessing on his or her life will not be content to sit and observe, but will actively promote the positive, loving atmosphere which produces that sense of well-being that the Bible calls peace. The peacemaker holds no truck with the critical and cynical attitude of the world, and will hear no criticism of others unless convinced that there is a clear goal of improvement of the situation. The peacemaker prays and works for peace in the home, and takes unjust treatment graciously and quietly. The peacemaker finds good in every situation, and is able to speak well of every person they meet. The peacemaker brings joy and gladness wherever they go, and they are welcome and loved for the healing balm they bring to all situations. They shun arguments of all kinds - be they political, theological or even about which programme to watch on the television! The peacemaker has an inner loyalty to his or her God and Father, who is proud of His sons and rejoices in the effect of their lives in this troubled world.

October 8

"Blessed are those who are persecuted for righteousness' sake, for theirs is the kingdom of heaven." [Matthew 5:10]

The believer who follows the steps of the beatitudes into the Kingdom of God will always find persecution at some point on their journey. In some countries, Christians are persecuted by imprisonment and death, while in others they meet the hostility of indifference and social rejection. It is easy to think that there are some countries where there is persecution and some where there is none, but the truth is that, wherever there is righteous living, there will be persecution. When we refuse to lie, we expose the lies of others and condemn them. Close friends and relatives may smile and dismiss us with a shrug. But remember that Jesus suffered both kinds of persecution. His own brothers and sisters would not believe in Him, and the village where He grew up was the hardest ground for Him to minister in. He understands the cool rejection that grieves us, and brings the suffering of loneliness. We may feel that our persecution is not worthy of the name, but the truth is that all believers need to know God's promise in this verse that all we lose is but a temporary loss. All who desire to live godly in Christ Jesus will suffer persecution [2 Timothy 3:12], and all will inherit the Kingdom of Heaven.

October 9

"Blessed are you when they revile and persecute you, and say all kinds of evil against you falsely for My sake. Rejoice and be exceedingly glad, for great is your reward in heaven, for so they persecuted the prophets who were before you."
    [Matthew 5:11-12]

There is a prophetic quality about disciples' lives. They are testimonies to another kingdom, and they reveal the evil of people's hearts. The fact that they have renounced secret sin, and are honest and sincere, produces resentment and persecution from those who are unwilling to follow the same pattern of life. If we remain without opposition, then we should question how genuinely our lives have changed. The temptation is to 'go underground' with our faith and try our best not to be offensive. The most endearing example of a witness is that of Naaman's maid [2 Kings 5:2-3]. She must have lost relatives through the Syrians' cruel invasion of Israel, and now she was a captive slave to this enemy General, with no hope of seeing her family and land again. But when she heard that her master was sick with leprosy, she joyfully told him that if only he would go to Israel, he would find a prophet of God who would minister healing to him. There is artless love, with no resentment, in this girl's heart. She demonstrates boldness in speaking of her God without fear of rejection in the midst of a nation that was full of idolatry. Our lives should speak of a world where there are no lies, no shadows, no demons, no fears and no worries. We are prophets of another kingdom, and we show up this world for what it is - hollow and empty. Being persecuted means that our witness will often meet with rejection, but this is not a mark of failure, but a mark of the genuine quality of our lives. We do not pray for persecution, but we do pray for grace to be a prophetic witness of the Kingdom of God.

October 10

"My sheep hear My voice, and I know them, and they follow Me." [John 10:27]

Hearing the voice of God is a very wonderful promise, but it may also be potentially condemning. If we feel that we must hear His voice in order to prove that we are truly His sheep, then the pressure to hear God speak can be intolerable. The truth is that it is rare for a Christian to hear an audible voice, and many never have that blessing. It is also rare to have a prophetic word that tells us the future or gives us some supernatural information to unlock a situation. These things do happen, but they are not commonplace. So what does Jesus mean? He is referring in this verse to the inner faculty which is awakened in us by His Presence. As we fellowship with Him, an inner knowledge distils in our hearts, like dew on flowers. Our hearts are bathed with an inner awareness, and it takes a little time and effort to put into words what we have become aware of. The voice of Jesus in our hearts produces an assurance and consciousness of His love and watchful oversight of our lives. Not all believers receive detailed instructions through an inner voice, but all of us have the inner sense of His Lordship and care for us. This sense of being watched over gives us peace, and it keeps us because, when we hear a different 'voice', we are troubled and aware that it holds dangers for us if we follow it. Jesus is not putting us under pressure with this word, but drawing us closer to Him, to trust Him and follow Him.

183

October 11

"And they continued steadfastly in the apostles' doctrine..."
[Acts 2:42]

The apostles were uneducated fishermen, and that is what makes this statement breathtaking, as it reveals God's daring plan to commit the future of His Church into the hands of such men. These men didn't suddenly start writing theological books, and they certainly didn't suddenly produce a systematic theology! Thousands of books have been written about the apostles' teaching, but none of those books can equal or replace it. Our minds thirst for order and explanations, but these cannot satisfy the thirst of our hearts. The apostles' doctrine is all to do with the communication of God's heartbeat. Hearing God's heartbeat will never make us feel clever, smug or superior - it will melt our hearts to tears of love and compassion. It will heal our wounded character from deep scars. Apostles are close friends of Jesus, who have been taken into His confidence. They know His thoughts and His feelings. This is why apostles are so rare. There are no natural strengths or gifts that can qualify them. Their chief characteristic is a deep and raw thirst for God Himself. The voice of Jesus awakens a thirst for God in men and women, educated and uneducated, rich and poor. This thirst carries them out of their natural limitations and makes them extraordinary people.

October 12

"God has raised this Jesus to life, and we are all witnesses of the fact. Exalted to the right hand of God, he has received from the Father the promised Holy Spirit and has poured out what you now see and hear." [Acts 2:32-33, NIV]

When Jesus was raised from the dead, He was given the place of highest honour in the universe. He was not merely given an honorary position; He was given absolute power over all things. This is the message of the Bible - that the Jesus of the Gospels is now ruling over all things. The Bible presents this as the most comforting truth of all to the human heart. There is also a direct link between exalting Jesus and enjoying the peace of His rule. Our worship does not increase His stature or His authority, but it does establish the connection between us and God, and allows His rule to flow over our lives. Worship is the central place in the discovery of God's will. If worship ceases in our hearts, all life dries up, and we cease to enjoy the outpouring of the Holy Spirit in our hearts. Exalting Jesus is acknowledging what is true and agreeing with God's view of the universe. As we exalt Jesus, life begins to flow and darkness flees. As we exalt Jesus, we are at that very moment back in the centre of God's will.

October 13

"Then Pharaoh called to Moses and said, 'Go serve the Lord; only let your flocks and your herds be kept back. Let your little ones also go with you.' But Moses said, 'You must also give us sacrifices and burnt offerings, that we may sacrifice to the Lord our God. Our livestock also shall go with us; not a hoof shall be left behind.' " [Exodus 10:24-26]

Pharaoh was a clever negotiator, and he knew the art of compromise. He had probably prospered in his dealings with other politicians and ambassadors. But when he met with Moses, he met a man who had no mandate to negotiate. Pharaoh here represents not merely the devil, but the trickish human heart. Human beings squirm and seek to make things fit together by getting each party to give up a little ground. But God is no negotiator. We quickly discover that He will not even enter into window-dressing to compete with the attractions that the world offers. God states things as they are and leaves us to realise that His word and His position is unchangeable and non-negotiable. God expects total surrender to Him, and will not settle for anything less. Pharaoh even admitted he was a sinner [Exodus 9:7] but it was all part of his attempt to get his own way. Because of the absolute nature of things, God demonstrated that the only answer for sinful human beings is to take up their cross and embrace their own death. God is unrelenting in His presentation of the way of discipleship, because He is bringing us to be as full-hearted and absolute in our devotion to Him as He is to us. He gave everything to have us, and He expects us to do the same.

October 14

"Against You, You only, have I sinned, and done this evil in your sight..." [Psalm 51:4]

Psalm 51 was the prayer of repentance that David prayed after his tragic moral failure with Bathsheba. It is the greatest prayer of repentance in the Bible, and as such is a pattern for all true repentance. The tragedy of David is that he only realised how deep his sin was when he fell into immorality. If only he could have prayed this prayer earlier in his life, he would have avoided all the heartache and pain of this sad phase of his life. In this prayer David expresses his sorrow at the pain he caused God. At first sight we may disagree with David, and exclaim that it was not only God he hurt. He hurt Bathsheba, her husband Uriah, Joab - the captain of the army - and all the nation of Israel! But what David saw in this moment of terrible realisation, is that he had frustrated God's will and plan for all these people, and in sinning He had hindered the joy that God would have had in blessing them and making their lives bright and fruitful in Him. God's heart is always broken most whenever there is sin, and it was this realisation that broke David's heart. It is only repentance that can lead to freedom from sin, and God has the skill to deepen it and cause us to turn to Him for cleansing and power to be free.

October 15

"And when they could not come near Him because of the crowd, they uncovered the roof where He was. So when they had broken through, they let down the bed on which the paralytic was lying." [Mark 2:4]

Four men carried their paralysed friend to the crowded house where Jesus was speaking. It is small wonder that He nearly always preached in the open air! This house was in the quiet Galilean backwater of Capernaum in the first century. There were no cars, trains, newspapers or telephones. Life would have proceeded at a leisurely place, like many of the remote rural villages in Africa today. So the normal thing would have been to wait for the meeting to finish and then approach Jesus when the crowd had dispersed. But these four men were in the grip of a desire and an expectancy that could not wait. Their faith led them to break through all the obstacles in their path and bring their suffering friend to the feet of Jesus. Faith, love and the presence of Jesus produce a passion and a zeal that will not rest till we have unburdened our hearts at Jesus' feet. The chief obstacles that hinder us are not physical, they are to be found in our hearts and minds. Angels must gaze in amazement at the indifference of human beings, and shake their heads at the excuses we give. The truth is that there will never be better conditions for faith than the ones we have today. The only question is whether we will tear apart the 'roof tiles' that separate us from Him, or else be swamped by the listless indifference of life. Wherever we are, at whatever time of our lives, God is within our reach. He is closer than an arm's length, even closer than the air we breathe.

October 16

"And where I go you know, and the way you know."
[John 14:4]

When Jesus spoke of His death, He did not speak of it as a goal or as an end of things, but as a door. His destination was to return to Father. When we travel, we may speak of going to the railway station or the airport, but we mention these as incidental to our journey. The destination is the important thing. Jesus was here seeking to instil in His followers the majestic consciousness of eternity. Don't think of death as a big ending. Think of it as a door - life continues right on through it. Of course, we feel the excitement of the unknown - we have never passed this way before. But it is the excitement of the big dipper or the high dive! Many of us may have declined to go on the extreme rides at the fun park. Or perhaps we have stood on the highest diving board and turned away in fear. But death is the beginning of a great adventure for those who believe Jesus Christ, and the correct view of our life is to see it stretching on and on, passing through the various landmarks on the way. Viewing things in the right perspective is the only way to obtain true enjoyment of eternal life now. Eternal life will not begin when we die - it begins the moment we believe in Jesus Christ.

October 17

"The crucible for silver and the furnace for gold, but man is tested by the praise he receives." [Proverbs 27:21, NIV]

Of all the temptations we pass through in life, success is among the strongest and the hardest to resist. When we are praised and congratulated, we are likely to forget how weak we are and how dependent on God. We might even believe that we ourselves are truly great. Success can make us shift the foundation from which we live - we shift it back onto ourselves and away from God. It is for this reason that many people fail after reaching their goal in life. They find, not success, but disappointment. The answer is to realise that nothing can satisfy me except the fellowship with God that empowered me to attain my goals. This is why the Bible warns us that we are not to boast in our human abilities (flesh). We are to boast in the Lord alone. A person who is climbing a mountain has to be disciplined and carry only essential equipment. A person who has arrived at the summit can rest and enjoy his achievement. One of the most remarkable facts about the ministry of the apostle Paul is that he never stayed around for long when he was successful. He always moved on to fresh territory, where he was unknown and where he had to earn the love and respect of people from scratch. Starting from scratch means that your trophies are meaningless to those around you - you are a nobody, and your pride in past achievements is irrelevant to those you meet. In other words, you are forced to be truly yourself, and not any image that people have in their minds. But this is what we are to be at all times and in all places, and blessed is the man or woman who can resist the temptation to glory in the praise they receive, and instead pass it on to the One who truly deserves it.

October 18

"For you know the grace of our Lord Jesus Christ, that though He was rich, yet for your sakes He became poor, that you through His poverty might become rich." [2 Corinthians 8:9]

One of the questions we might ask about Jesus is how rich or poor He was in natural terms. He certainly came from a poor family that could only offer doves for an offering [Luke 2:24]. But are we right in thinking He was poor? A very few preachers have suggested He was well off, well provided for by wealthy individuals [Luke 8:3], as evidenced by His seamless robe, and His rock-hewn tomb. But was He a rich man? The answer is that Jesus was completely indifferent to money and to the accumulation of wealth and goods. This is the mentality neither of a rich man nor a poor man. It is the mentality of a Son. Jesus didn't have stashes of money; He had a Father. When Father said: *"Son, tonight you skip food and sleep under a hedge"*, He was content with that. When Father said: *"Tonight you eat at Martha's table and spend the night under Lazarus' roof in a nice warm bed"*, He was content. The fact of Father in His life meant that He knew He would never lack anything when He needed it. It produced a tranquillity and contentment, knowing that what Father had decreed was not merely good, it was wonderful. Jesus was separated from His Father at the cross – that is grinding poverty. He gives us His Father through His blood and

188

the Spirit of adoption – that is riches untold.

October 19

"...my conscience also bearing me witness in the Holy Spirit, that I have great sorrow and continual grief in my heart."
   [Romans 9:1-2]

The fact of conscience in our hearts is a proof of God's existence. Conscience is the inner awareness of a higher will and order of things, to which we must one day give account. We can ignore its voice, but everyone has heard it. We may harden ourselves against it, but we cannot completely extinguish it. Some people have thoroughly rejected God's voice speaking in their conscience, but they pay a terrible price in the strain on their mind and body. This voice is not subject to our will and control, but stands over us, correcting and directing us. Jean Paul Sartre tells how, as a child, he burnt a rug while playing with matches. He shut himself in the bathroom, where he tried to clean the rug. Suddenly he felt God's eyes on Him, through the faculty of his conscience. He rejected that divine touch, but only succeeded in suppressing it by a flood of cursing and blasphemy. Sartre tells wistfully how he never felt that touch again; and we can detect, throughout his writings, a regret and longing for the refreshment of his ability to be touched by God. Conscience is the most precious possession any person has. It is to our spirit what the lungs are to our body. It is that faculty by which God both communicates corrective touches to us, and also is able to lead us to demonstrate His love to others. God seeks sensitive vessels through which His love can touch people's lives. God's love makes us notice those who are far from Him, and the result is grief. Grief over others is a sign of the positive work of God's love in our conscience. Through obedience, we find our conscience to be, not a negative watchman, but a channel for ministering that precious touch of love that every person longs for.

October 20

"Then John's disciples came and asked him, 'How is that we and the Pharisees fast, but your disciples do not fast?' Jesus answered, 'How can the guests of the bridegroom mourn while he is with them? The time will come when the bridegroom will be taken from them; then they will fast."
   [Matthew 9:14-15, NIV]

Do you miss Him? Jesus here gives a principle in the life of prayer and fasting, but it is an aside, and is phrased in such a way that it is possible to miss its vital importance. He explains that the realm of earnestly seeking God is all to do with the sense of missing His Presence, like friends mourn the absence of a loved one. (Of course, if the friends of the bridegroom mourn His absence, then how much more will His bride mourn it?) The disciples had such a normal relationship with Jesus, that the idea of earnestly fasting and praying would have been irrelevant - He was with them each day. When Jesus taught about prayer, He was not concerned with ideas of building up credit with God, or gaining influence through earnest persuasion. His idea of prayer is to develop a normal, healthy relationship with God, as friends. Put in this context, Jesus' words on fasting show that true spiritual authority belongs to those who are close friends with Him. Jesus did not withdraw to pray and fast when He was faced with demon-possessed people, since He was in the place of friendship with His Father. Are we in that place of friendship? If not, do we miss that friendship? Strength of will and character can make people do amazing things, including going on long fasts and praying for many hours. But none of this has any influence on God. It is love that misses Him that carries us into the place of intimate friendship with God. It crosses every obstacle, and will make any sacrifice to reach that goal.

October 21

"Assuredly, I say to you that this poor widow has put in more than all those who have given to the treasury; for they all put in out of their abundance, but she out of her poverty put in all that she had, her whole livelihood." [Mark 12:43-44]

Jesus sat and watched people giving in the Temple treasury. This is in itself a challenging revelation - that Jesus sits and observes what each one puts into the Kingdom of God! Jesus then said that the poor widow had given more than the rich people, because she had nothing left. This means that the true standard of giving is not what I give, but what I have left! One of the most searching subjects in Jesus' teaching is His attitude to money. There is no pressure in the Bible to give as Jesus gave, but there is an exhortation to the kind of faith that moved Him to live as He did. It requires great faith to live like Jesus, owning nothing and trusting Father for every next supply. Amazingly, God never asks us to give more, since that in itself would be an acknowledgement that some Christians can live giving only a part of what they have. God assumes that we belong entirely to Him, and that as we grow in faith and love we will let go of our lives, casting them into the treasury of His love. God never has His eyes on our money, but on our hearts, knowing that it is the things that we own that possess us. The goal of His teaching is absolute surrender. God could point to any number of things that we own, and ask for them. He has that right, since He is our Lord as well as our Saviour. But God's eyes are not on the things we own, but on us. Sooner or later we will have to realise, as that widow realised, that God wants me, not what I can do for Him or give to Him. There is no greater release from worry, worldliness and unbelief than to stand before the altar of God and give Him myself.

October 22

"The kingdom of heaven is like leaven, which a woman took and hid in three measures of meal till it was all leavened."
    [Matthew 13:33]

Of all the attacks on the Church, those that come from the inside are the most troubling, and of all such attacks, 'leaven' is the worst. The reason is that leaven is not easily distinguishable from the body of the loaf! Leaven gets into the very substance of everything. Paul identifies 'leaven' as legalism in Galatians 5:9, and as immoral behaviour in 1 Corinthians 5:6. Jesus also identifies leaven as hypocrisy [Luke 12:1] and wrong doctrine [Matthew 16:12]. It is easy to identify these things in others but not so easy in ourselves. The answer is to submit ourselves to the scrutiny of God's love and to the purging power of the Holy Spirit. The Holy Spirit has no leaven; He is a burning fire that continually purges out insincerity and doctrine that moves away from the spiritual centre of things. When we allow 'leaven' in, our lives become heavy and cease to receive the refreshing of the Holy Spirit. This is why repentance is a constant ministry of Christ to His Churches. The Holy Spirit is always urging inner separation from sin in all its forms, so that we may have a clear, untroubled relationship with Christ. The Holy Spirit is relentless in His determination to keep us free from sin and self, and He touches our hearts continually with a fire that makes us aware how foolishly we are behaving when we look away from Jesus Christ. Wrong doctrine will always err from the centre of things – it may tell us, for instance, that we need never be ill if we have enough faith, or that the age of miracles is past. If only we could smile at ourselves and drop our rigid attitudes, and believe in Him. He makes us sane and holy.

October 23

"Now when Peter had come to Antioch, I withstood him to his face, because he was to be blamed..."   [Galatians 2:11]
"Do not correct a scoffer, lest he hate you; rebuke a wise man, and he will love you."   [Proverbs 9:8]

In the first verse, two great men met and there was conflict. Conflict is troubling, yet inevitable, and we are wise to have a view of life that includes the possibility of it.   Peter and Paul here both demonstrated greatness in the midst of disagreement. Paul did so by his clear stand for what is right, without self-interest.   Peter showed true stature by being correctible.   We must learn both if we are to become mature in fellowship.   The verse from Proverbs speaks of correcting a wise man and deepening friendship.   Peter received the correction, and later he called Paul's writings *"Scripture"* and Paul, *"our beloved brother"* [2 Peter 3:15-16].   In the world, if someone is corrected they often feel humiliated and form grudges.   In the Kingdom of God, correction is a blessing and keeps us in the way of life.   When a rocket is launched to the moon, it has facilities for continual course correction. Without this continual adjustment, a small error would mean the rocket would completely miss its target.   Paul submitted his preaching to Peter's authority [Galatians 2:2] and it was this humility that must have made Peter able in turn to receive correction from Paul.   Peter was a broken man - he was soft clay in God's hands. An unbroken person is brittle and awkward in fellowship with others.   The way we are in fellowship with others is a sure sign of how we are in fellowship with Jesus.   If we walk with Jesus we will receive constant course correction, sometimes by a rebuke, but most often by continual instruction.   We don't have to come to a place where we are always right, but we do need to come to a place where we always have the right attitude.

October 24

"Jesus spoke these words, lifted up His eyes to heaven, and said: 'Father, the hour has come...'." [John 17:1]

Prayer is a place, not an activity.   It is in the 'Holy of Holies' - a room that was soundproofed by several layers of thick cloth and badger skins. If we really want to know how to pray, we must find that place. It cannot be found by geography, since a holy place is made such by finding God there, and we can find God everywhere. Jesus probably prayed this prayer while walking through Jerusalem on His way to Gethsemane. We find the place of prayer by an attitude of heart that turns from self and our problem-laden world, to the Presence of God. It is obviously true that Jesus knew this place, and yet it would be even more true to say that He **is** the place. Whoever comes to Jesus will find that Presence that is full of incredible hope. In this prayer in John 17, Jesus was facing the most difficult hours of His life, and yet He was full of hope. Why? Because He had His eyes, not on the impending crisis, but on His Father. When we get into the Presence of God, we will never find the word 'impossible' on the lips of Jesus or the Father. In the Presence of Jesus everything is possible, and if we can only find that place, we will find that prayer brings rest, as it did to Jesus. Though Jesus did not mention resurrection in His prayer, He was looking into the future with the certainty that the coming difficult hours were passing, and not eternal. Get into the Presence of Jesus, and let His serenity and peace give you faith for everything that you could ever face.

October 25

"Or do you not know that as many of us as were baptized into Christ Jesus were baptized into His death?" [Romans 6:3]

Back in the 1950s, a Kenyan entered his name into a lottery for the American Green Card (work permit) and, to his amazement, won. He saved his money and bought a passage on a liner that left from Mombasa and docked in New York 3 weeks later. He had very little money, and so was only able to take a little food with him on board, which he quickly finished. He made friends with other passengers, but whenever they went to the restaurant he quickly excused himself and went to his cabin to nurse his hunger alone. As the ship neared New York, one of his new friends was unable to hide his curiosity, and asked him why they had never seen him eat. Being so near New York, he felt free to explain that he had not got enough money to eat, just enough for his passage to America. *"You didn't know?"*, exclaimed his friend. *"Your meals were all covered in the price of the ticket!"* Ignorance can be a terrible tragedy, both in natural and in spiritual life. Thousands of winning lottery tickets go unclaimed, as do legacies and other benefits. But most tragic of all,

193

Christians can live in spiritual poverty, when all the time God has given us the true source of all power in Christ Himself. If God asks us to live like His Son, then He must provide the same resources that Christ Himself enjoyed. God has done even better than that, in that He has given us Christ Himself and, with Him, all the resources and power that are in Him. This includes all the power that He won in the battle of the cross. As Christ conquered, so can we, because His victory is included in the gift of the Holy Spirit. Draw on the limitless resources of Christ, to live for Him today.

October 26

"The Father loves the Son, and has given all things into His hand." [John 3:35]
"If you love Me, keep My commandments. And I will pray the Father, and He will give you another Helper, that He may abide with you forever - the Spirit of truth..." [John 14:15-17]

The key to all spiritual life is to love Jesus, not what He can give. When my wife Vicki was a teenager at school, one of her friends arrived one day in a beautiful classic car. Of course, everyone wanted to know how he had got it. The answer was that he'd had a paper round. After delivering papers one day, he had been invited by a lonely old man to come in and have a cup of tea with him. He had agreed and from that day on he always ended his round by visiting the old man. Over the months and years, they became good friends. Then sadly, one day the old man died. A couple of weeks later, the boy got a letter from a solicitor informing him that the old man had left everything to him in his will - which included a house, some money and a classic car! This event perhaps made dozens of boys think of starting a paper round, and look hopefully at all the lonely old folk they knew. But the truth is that the boy didn't have his eyes on the old man's money - he simply loved him. The Kingdom of God doesn't function on 'things' like power, money or influence – there is no such 'reward' for loving Jesus. The Kingdom of God functions on the simplicity of a loving heart. If a person loves Jesus for anything they can get from Him, then they are attempting the robbery of the ages. It would be like someone marrying for money. It is an offensive concept, and will never make any impact on the Father in heaven. The reward **is** to love Him. Whether or not anything else comes our way is not important. When we have Him, we really do have everything.

October 27

"And they feared exceedingly, and said to one another, 'Who can this be, that even the wind and the sea obey Him!' "
[Mark 4:41]
"Then He got into one of the boats, which was Simon's, and asked him to put out a little from the land."   [Luke 5:3]

Of all the attributes of Jesus Christ, His authority is the most awesome. He commanded the storms to be still; He rebuked a legion of demons (a Roman legion numbered between 2 and 3 thousand).   He sits on the throne of the universe, having conquered Satan, sin and death. He is Lord of all and possesses almighty power. Yet Jesus *"asked"* Simon Peter to put his boat out. This mighty conqueror does not command the human race, but invites us, and even asks our permission. We see in Jesus God's true nature – the union of majestic authority with total humility. There is a deep respect in God's heart for the human will - He will not violate our wills, or dominate us in any bullying way. This is at once both wonderful and fearful, since many people might like Him to overrule their wills.   But this would be taking away the very faculty in us that He seeks to win, not to override. Though Christ is God, yet He seeks our fellowship, not the mere extension of His kingdom.   The Kingdom of God is above all a kingdom of love, and while awesome power and authority are at work to protect this kingdom, yet within it there must be willing submission and surrender to the will of the King. The worst thing a human being could ever get is their own way. But God will still not cancel our own thinking, moral power. We can pretend not to hear God, or simply refuse to do what He has said, but we cannot escape the fact that we are responsible to allow Him to help Himself to our lives and our possessions.

October 28

"Depart from me, for I am a sinful man, O Lord!" [Luke 5:8]

In the 1860s, General Gordon was besieged in Khartoum by the fanatical Mahdi army for over a year.   He kept a journal in which he wrote his meditations.   One of the most surprising thoughts that he penned was about himself. He wrote: *"Nothing shocks me but myself."* On another occasion he wrote, *"If only I could be free from General Gordon."* He was a brave, honest man who had the highest standards of personal conduct, yet something in his heart shocked him. He longed for freedom from himself. It is sad to see a woman married to a selfish, unkind husband, but it is far worse to be that husband. The woman will have a few hours of freedom a day, if only when her husband is asleep! But the husband will poison his own life in every waking moment. Jesus Christ causes us to see ourselves, and the result is shock. The person who takes Jesus seriously will sooner or later come up against the most awful barrier to His kindness and love - the power of self. This is precisely why Jesus Christ came - to release us from the bondage of self and make us free to love and serve Him. As Christians, we might add this amazing thought to those of General Gordon: *"Nothing is sweeter than the cross by which we die to self."* Paul said: *"God forbid that I should boast except in the cross of our Lord Jesus Christ, by whom the world has been crucified to me, and I to the world."* [Galatians 6:14]. Paul was not describing a sentimental appreciation of Jesus' sufferings, but the jubilant cry of someone who has experienced the power of the cross to set us free from self.

October 29

" 'And where I go you know, and the way you know.' Thomas said to Him (Jesus), 'Lord, we do not know where You are going, and how can we know the way?' " [John 14:4-5]

Jesus here told Thomas that he knew something, while Thomas clearly was not aware of this knowledge. Similarly, we may often think we have not heard God's voice over a certain issue, but Jesus says that His sheep can all hear His voice [John 10:27]. The truth is that we know a whole lot more that we are conscious of, and if we will take time to quieten our hearts, we will become conscious of what we already know. A Christian from Cameroon was once visiting England, and wanted to see the orphanage that George Muller had established in Bristol. He arrived at the right address, expecting to see a single building, but could not identify the orphanage among the series of huge buildings that he found there. He asked a passer-by where he could find the orphanage, and was astounded to discover that he was already looking at it - **all** the huge buildings around him were the orphanage. His expectation had simply been blinding his eyes to recognise what was in plain sight. The same is often true of God's communications to our hearts. We pray, *"Speak to me Lord, or give me a sign"*, but God says, *"I have spoken, and if you will quieten your heart you will find that you already know* *my word and my will."* When Jesus rose from the dead, again Thomas knew deep down that it was true, but it was only later, when he saw the Lord, that he blurted out his realisation of what he had already known, when he exclaimed to Jesus, *"My Lord and My God!"* [John 20:28]. It is a breathtaking joy to realise that we are God's children and that He is always speaking to us at a deeper level than we ever thought possible.

October 30

"Jesus, knowing that the Father had given all things into His hands, and that He had come from God and was going to God, rose from supper and laid aside His garments, took a towel and girded Himself." [John 13:3-4]

John does a surprising thing in these verses - he looks at Jesus and knows what He is thinking. John did not have any psychic powers to read someone's mind - he simply looked at Jesus with a heart free from self and full of love. It is surprising how much the human heart reads things into situations. Folk will sit in Church meetings and be so absorbed with themselves and their problems that they will not lift up their hearts in worship, nor listen to the voice of God coming through prayers and preaching. John here demonstrates the attitude that the Holy Spirit forms in the heart of His people - He causes us to forget ourselves and our problems, and see the majesty of Christ. John saw an ordinary man, but he saw also the humility of Christ. He saw a man dressed as a slave, ready to wash people's feet, but he also saw the tremendous authority and power underlying the servant love of Jesus. Blessed is the person who knows what Jesus is thinking - and we cannot get there without a steady, long gaze at Him, resolutely turning our thoughts away from ourselves, to become conscious of Him. The amazing thing is that this is so possible. The Holy Spirit is given to us to communicate the character and thoughts of God. If we will only fix our eyes in faith on Him, then there will be an inflow of power to live, motivated by the greatness of Christ. He will touch every situation, whether in the family or at work, in moments of joy or sorrow, on holiday or in bereavement. It is only through sensing the things that motivate Him that we are given abundant strength to live.

October 31

"Therefore, having been justified by faith, we have peace with God through our Lord Jesus Christ, through whom also we have access by faith into this grace in which we stand, and rejoice in hope of the glory of God." [Romans 5:1-2]

This is the great declaration of the power of the New Covenant. We have been made right with God through an act of God - an act of His supreme sovereign will and grace. We have simply to believe and enter into the good of what He has done for us. Then comes the temptation to turn the blessings of being right with God into conditions! If we have no joy, we doubt whether we are accepted. If we lack any of the wonderful blessings, then we doubt whether we are right with God at that particular moment. The wonder of this act of God in justifying us, is that it does not rest at any time on our virtue. It rests on Him and His faithfulness. It is precisely because of this that we are invited to partake of such a depth of peace, and such an honoured access into fellowship with God. At no time are we qualified by our own righteousness to be partakers. We are qualified by the goodness of God. This qualification is total and absolute. It does not rest on how we feel about ourselves, or even whether we sense that we have done well or badly over the last 24 hours. It rests solely on how God thinks and feels about things. The unchanging God has made His position clear. Because we trust Jesus Christ, God links our life, character and destiny with that of His Son. He ascribes to us all the virtue and matchless character of the Son of God, and undertakes to make us like His Son. The overwhelming blessings of the Kingdom of God **are** blessings, not conditions.

November 1

" 'Did God really say, "You must not eat from any tree in the garden"?' The woman said to the serpent, 'We may eat fruit from the trees in the garden, but God did say, "You must not eat fruit from the tree that is in the middle of the garden, and you must not touch it, or you will die".' " [Genesis 3:1-3]

Temptation comes firstly through speculation, to open the mind; secondly through enticement, to awaken desire; and thirdly through persuasion, to engage the will to act. Eve's mind was opened to think about something she knew was wrong. Once her imagination had been stirred, she was vulnerable to begin to desire the forbidden fruit. Then, through the serpent's lie, she was persuaded that no harm would come; her will was engaged, and she acted. This was a key moment, since Eve's will was not a slave to lust, but was still in control. Eve discarded her liberty to act, and became a slave of sin. Now think about how God can reverse this process, to set us free from sin. We must firstly be open to receive correction of our thinking, and believe that God's Word is true. We must then ask forgiveness for our sins - for living by the tyranny of desire. Then we must act, and give ourselves to God, and become servants of God, free from the tyranny of sin. The way down is the way up. How central is the Word of God! The temptation began when the devil distorted God's Word and maligned God's character. The victory comes when we submit to the Word of God, and honour it as the way of deliverance and power to all who believe its life-giving message.

November 2

"Moses ... said to them: 'Set your hearts on all the words which I testify among you today, which you shall command your children to be careful to observe - all the words of this law. For it is not a futile thing for you, because it is your life, and by this word you shall prolong your days in the land which you cross over the Jordan to possess.' "
[Deuteronomy 32:46-47]

Moses here reminds the people of the vital importance of the Word of God. The temptation for us to neglect the Bible must be one of the most common temptations. It comes in various ways. New believers may be tempted to give up because they find some passages too hard. People who know the Bible well may be tempted to assume that they know it all already. But here God addresses these temptations, and promises us that time spent in His Word is never a waste. Billy Graham was asked what he would do differently if he could live his life over again. He replied without hesitation that he would read his Bible more. The Bible is a book of seeds - the promise or hope of good things; God's Word is a foundation of good things that will spring up in the life of the person who diligently reads it. The Word of God will bring forth faith, hope and love in our hearts. It will produce wisdom for all of life's situations, and will keep us from many temptations. It will affect our health and the length of our life on earth. Here is what Smith Wigglesworth (a famous preacher in the early 20th century) said about it:

"God's Word is: 1. supernatural in origin; 2. eternal in duration; 3. inexpressible in valour; 4. infinite in scope; 5. regenerative in power; 6. infallible in authority; 7. universal in application; 8. inspired in totality. Read it through; write it down; pray it in; work it out; pass it on. The Word of God changes a man until he becomes an epistle of God."

November 3

"Joseph said to them (his brothers) ... 'But as for you, you meant evil against me; but God meant it for good, in order to bring it about as it is this day, to save many people alive.' "
    [Genesis 50:20]

Joseph's most Christ-like quality was his ability to be confident in God's hand in all his circumstances. He was never bitter towards his brothers. He never despaired when he was betrayed and later wrongfully accused. He did not become proud when he was exalted to the most honoured position in the land of Egypt. He kept a calm trust in God's goodness, and saw all that happened to him as part of a great plan to bless him and his loved ones. The greatest mark of a person who walks with God is their ability to see God all around them, and not to indulge in despair when things go badly, or in self-congratulation when things go well. Out of all the trials that Joseph went through, the hardest was probably his elevation to the most favoured place in Pharaoh's government. Joseph was clearly a man of conscience and high moral standards. He must have found much in the court of Pharaoh that grieved him. Yet, like Daniel hundreds of years later, he was able to walk with God in the midst of the world without being of the world. Of all the things we can do to maintain peace in our hearts, the most important is to

200

acknowledge the righteous hand of God that is shaping our circumstances and planning our steps to do us good. This is the cutting edge of faith, and the dynamic heart of worship. When we praise God just the same throughout both the ups and downs of our lives, it is then that we truly bring glory to Him.

November 4

"Then He said to Thomas, 'Reach your finger here, and look at my hands; and reach your hand here, and put it into My side. Do not be unbelieving, but believing.' " [John 20:27]

When the nuclear reactor at Chernobyl (in the former USSR) went into meltdown, and the barriers were destroyed between the reactor core and the world around; the effect was catastrophic. People ran into the presence of that concentrated power to cover it with sand, and then ran out, knowing they would suffer irreparable damage if they remained for more than a couple of minutes. In some respects, we can compare exposure to the heart and life of God with exposure to a nuclear reactor. In this verse, Jesus invited his beloved Thomas to reach in and touch His wounds – it was as if the very centre and heart of God was opened to that disciple. For Thomas, the effect of Jesus' invitation was to destroy unbelief and hardness of heart, and to make him a true man of faith. He cried out in immediate response, *"My Lord and My God!"* It seems as though perhaps he had no need actually to put his hand into Jesus' wounds in order to come to this life-changing realisation. This verse pictures the truth that the wounded side of Jesus is open for anyone to 'reach out their hand and touch Him on the inside'. We, too, may enter into all the explosive power of His life. We may have His love, His faith, His holiness, pulsating through the core of our being in all their creating, life-changing power.

November 5

"Take heed that you do not despise one of these little ones, for I say to you that in heaven their angels always see the face of My Father who is in heaven." [Matthew 18:10]

It is easy to underestimate God's keeping power. Jesus said that nothing could hurt his followers, and here He speaks of the ceaseless vigilance of heaven over all children, let alone those who follow Him. The angels continue vigilantly both to watch over children and to watch the Father's face. Nothing can escape this vigilance, and therein lies our assurance. Young converts in Africa are sometimes mistreated by parents and village elders, who try to maintain their authority through superstition and witchcraft. One young convert was tricked by his mother into visiting a witch. His mother told him they were visiting an aunt, but secretly she had begged the witch to drive Jesus out of her 26 year-old son. As soon as the witch entered the room where he was sitting, she screamed with horror and shouted: *"Get him away! The power in him is stronger than my power!"* God's keeping power is more than enough to keep us from every harmful thing, whether we are old in the faith or new. Note, too, the means by which God keeps us. He has surrounded us with the armies of heaven, and their work is to be a link between the love of God the Father in all its tenderness, and the circumstances in which we find ourselves. The keeping power of God is that of a Father. Even an earthly father will not allow any harm to come near his children; how much more the Father in heaven, who sees the approach of enemies that are invisible to the human eye. Rest secure in the undying vigilance of heaven over you.

November 6

"Do not fear any of those things which you are about to suffer. Indeed, the devil is about to throw some of you into prison, that you may be tested, and you will have tribulation ten days. Be faithful until death, and I will give you the crown of life."
[Revelation 2:10]
"...God is faithful, who will not allow you to be tempted beyond what you are able, but with the temptation will also make the way of escape, that you may be able to bear it."
[1 Corinthians 10:13]

This verse from Revelation must have been a hard prophecy for the believers in Smyrna to receive - that things were going to get worse and they would have to suffer prison and tribulation. The Lord did not offer them any way to avoid this path of suffering, but the consolation He did offer them was twofold. First, there would be a time limit on this time of testing; and God comforts us by assuring us that our sufferings are for a season, and will not last for ever. This is vital to grasp, since when we suffer we quickly forget times when things were easier, and lose hope that they will one day be better again. God has further promised us, in this verse from 1 Corinthians, that we will never be tested beyond what we are able to bear. The second consolation is the

202

promise of the crown of life – that is, the laurel wreath worn by winners in the Olympic Games - the crown of the one who has persevered and won. It is the promise of standing in God's Presence with the unspeakable joy of His approval. God asks one thing - that we are faithful until death, i.e. all through life's journey, and willing ultimately to lay down our lives for Him. A disciple who has looked the possibility of death in the face has no further enemy they can fear. Nothing can truly trouble us once we have found in Jesus the strength to go through every test, trusting firmly in Him.

November 7

"Why did I come forth from the womb to see labor and sorrow, that my days should be consumed with shame?"
        [Jeremiah 20:18]

Jeremiah was a failure in terms of the outward success of his ministry, and he often expressed his sense of failure to God. None of the kings he preached to appreciated or obeyed what he said. He saw his ministry fail to stir the hearts of the people to repentance. He was persecuted in many ways, and despite weeping and praying for the people, he was rejected and saw the nation he loved destroyed. But Jeremiah was far from a failure. God sees success and failure in a completely different way from us - He measures success in tears. Jeremiah loved God and had a heart melted with compassion. He obeyed God when everyone around him, even other priests, were rejecting and criticising his ministry. He heard God's voice and maintained a close relationship with God throughout his ministry. Jeremiah had three great marks of success: love for God and His people, obedience to God's word, and intimacy in prayer. No matter what we achieve in life, if we lack these three things then we have failed. Jeremiah is so like Jesus in many ways, not least that both wept over Jerusalem. Tears cannot be imitated - they are the mark of a heart full of love. Not all of us are quiet souls who find prayer and meditation easy. Not all of us have the gift of healing. Not all of us are good preachers and teachers of the Word. But love is to be our common life, and it is in love that healing and power are found. It is not surprising that some of the people in Jesus' day thought that He was Jeremiah.

November 8

"Then the LORD spoke to Moses that very same day, saying: 'Go up this mountain of the Abarim, Mount Nebo, which is in the land of Moab, across from Jericho; view the land of Canaan, which I give to the children of Israel as a possession; and die on the mountain which you ascend...' "
[Deuteronomy 32:48-50]

Of all the things that Moses did by faith, this is the most extraordinary. Moses was not weak or ill, and did not die of natural causes - he simply died by faith. We might wonder how he did it, whether he lay down and waited! The answer lies in the example of Jesus, who also died by faith. He said that no-one could take His life from Him, but that He had power to lay it down and to take it again [John 10:18]. Jesus died when He committed His Spirit into the hands of Father and breathed His last. As Christians, we can view death as a door to life's greatest adventure. The gospel teaches us to die at the end of our earthly days with triumph and with assurance of what awaits us in Jesus' embrace. But it also teaches us to die daily to sin and self by faith. We do not have to wait for sin to become weak, or self to become frail. We can draw near to God and let go of ourselves in total abandonment to Him. The moment we do this, we find that we are renewed and transformed. We discover the blessed secret that death is an entrance to life. It is not that there is life after death, but rather life after life! There is abundant life after the shadow of life that preceded it. It is a trade-in in which we simply cannot lose. We let go the shabby rags of our own life, and start to discover the glorious robes of His heavenly life. The more we get used to dying daily by faith, the more eagerly we look forward to the time when we trade in our old bodies for new ones!

November 9

"....when a lion or a bear came and took a lamb out of the flock, I went after it and struck it, and delivered the lamb from its mouth..." [1 Samuel 17:34-5]
"As a shepherd takes from the mouth of a lion two legs or a piece of an ear...." [Amos 3:12]

David and Amos were extraordinary shepherds who risked their lives to protect their flocks. David is here, in the quote from 1 Samuel, describing actual events from his experience. Evidently on more than one occasion a lamb had been seized by a lion or a bear and had to be rescued from the very mouth of the creature. Most shepherds would probably have said 'bon appétit' to the lion or the bear and saved the rest of the flock - but not David. He boldly attacked the beasts and rescued his lambs. When someone gets entangled with sin and finds themselves in the clutches of darkness, we must never think that God easily gives up the battle for them, even if they themselves are to blame for their plight. There are many warnings in Scripture not to get entangled with the world and sin, lest we lose our salvation, but we must not think that Jesus lets lambs go easily. There is a fierce battle to keep our hearts and minds secure. Amos talks of saving even a few remnants of the lamb, and that at first sight does not seem worth it. The true significance is that Jesus Christ is able to restore us, from even the shattered fragments of a broken life. Not only is He able to breathe life into us, but the life that is restored is ultimately as perfect as His life. The battle to win us back begins with the communication of the Saviour's persistent love. God's love is the strongest power in the universe and is able to rescue and heal the most damaged soul. As soon as we stretch out our arms of faith to Him, believing His love, the battle is essentially won and our future secure.

November 10

"...for John truly baptized with water, but you shall be baptized with the Holy Spirit not many days from now." [Acts 1:5]

The word 'baptism' in the New Testament is always associated with death and resurrection. It indicates a dying to self by faith. This is not a negative death - it is an entrance into life; it is the death of everything that is negative. The cross is like an operation to remove cancer - the patient may fear the surgeon's knife, but he is also grateful for it. By it, the poison and sickness is removed from his life. So, too, the baptism with the Spirit is an experience of the cross. There is loss and there is gain. This is because God will not mix His Spirit with sinful flesh. In the Old Testament there are examples of sinful people, such as Samson, who received an anointing of power - which is never described as 'the baptism with the Spirit'. From this we can understand that God's Old Testament servants experienced something similar to the baptism with the Spirit, but with the important difference that there was no power of the cross in their experience. God's greatest gift is to impart, not merely the

205

cleansing power of the cross, but also the nature of the One who was crucified. The baptism with the Spirit is not an anointing of a carnal person; it is the transformation of a weak, carnal person into the image of God's Son. The most important aspect of that Son is that He shows the love of God manifested in the cross.

November 11

"Nevertheless I have this against you, that you have left your first love. Remember therefore from where you have fallen; repent and do the first works, or else I will come to you quickly and remove your lampstand from its place - unless you repent." [Revelation 2:4-5]

Jesus' rebuke here reveals His highest priority - that the people of God must abide in love. Love is not just an emphasis, it is the air that God and His children breathe. Love cannot be imitated, nor can it be practised from an insincere heart. Love must flow from a heart that is yielded to God. Love is always spontaneous, and is revealed in the sudden outburst of joy and praise. Love plans a thousand things to surprise and delight her loved ones. These plans are the outflow of a love that dreams and hopes and believes wonderful things. Love is incapable of thinking an evil thought, and so it does not get depressed, though it may be grieved. Love never gives up; so even when things go wrong, love is constantly active to pick up from where things are at any given moment. Jesus tells the believers in Ephesus to do three things: remember, repent, and do. This is astonishingly simple and we must receive this command in all its wisdom and power.
Remember the time when love moved your heart, made you get up early, moved you to do things that others might even consider extreme.
Repent of cold attitudes and respectable Christianity that have threatened to stifle the warm flow of the Holy Spirit in you.
Do again the things you once did; don't wait for feelings before you do them - the feelings will come as you act. We benefit from the wisest counsel in the universe, and we must not neglect it.

November 12

"And as for Seth, to him also a son was born; and he named him Enosh. Then men began to call on the name of the LORD." [Genesis 4:26]

Seth was the first man to pray. When he prayed, he had no idea where it would lead him, nor what effect it might have on his own life. Seth's prayer life began as a tiny trickle on the pages of human history, and that is how all who pray begin. We see our influence with God and on world events as insignificant - so small that no-one will ever notice. But every river begins as a trickle high up in the mountains. As it flows, it gathers momentum. Five generations later, Seth had a great, great, great grandson named Enoch who was the first prophet to the human race. Soon after that there was a preacher named Noah. Jesus said that we ought always to pray and not to lose heart [Luke 18:1]. We falter in prayer when we think we are having no effect. There is no more discouraging thought than to think that we live, work, preach, pray and have no influence on those around us. It is knowing that we are making a difference that keeps us going. Here, God lifts the veil for us to see the link between praying people and His activity in the earth. There is no prayer that is not answered. It is one of the foundations of the universe that there is a God in heaven who hears and answers prayer. A Chinese proverb says that dripping water will break a stone; the prayers of God's people - **our** prayers - will shape and change the world, and one day the veil will be lifted and we will see what we have believed.

November 13

"For I think that God has displayed us, the apostles, last, as men condemned to death; for we have been made a spectacle to the world, both to angels and to men."
     [1 Corinthians 4:9]

The word here for a 'spectacle' is the word for a stage in the theatre. Paul here describes his consciousness of living out his life and ministry under the scrutiny of 'the world', which he divides into two groups - angels and men. He was conscious that there were visible and invisible beings watching him. The visible ones watched his outward conduct - and with video cameras everywhere nowadays, never has this been truer! He was also conscious of invisible beings watching him - angels watching his conduct even in the privacy of his own bedroom. He does not here actually mention God, who watches our thoughts and sifts our hidden motives. It is not that we should be always looking over our shoulder to see who is watching. But we must fully face the challenge of being inwardly what we appear to be, when we know people are watching. It is that gap between our public and private world that must be removed. Some people have interpreted this to mean that, if we are harsh and blunt in our thoughts, then we should just express them! On the contrary, if we are unloving at heart, then we must love others by obedience, asking God to change us inside to match our ideals. Christ was genuine pure love, through and through; and unless that becomes more and more the case in us, we will be 'on stage' for the times we are conscious of others, and 'off stage' in our private thoughts. Paul is communicating that there is no 'off stage'. No-one can escape the watchful eye of God and His angels. The key is to live for God first, and realise that every word, thought and motive is in full, plain sight.

November 14

"And He said to them, 'What things?' So they said to Him, 'The things concerning Jesus of Nazareth… But we were hoping that it was He who was going to redeem Israel. Indeed, besides all this, today is the third day since these things happened. Yes, and certain women of our company, who arrived at the tomb early, astonished us. When they did not find His body, they came saying that they had also seen a vision of angels who said He was alive. And certain of those who were with us went to the tomb and found it just as the women had said; but Him they did not see.' " [Luke 24:19-24]

The disciples on the Emmaus road were filled with sadness at Jesus' death, and they simply did not believe He was risen. Jesus began to minister faith to their depressed hearts by asking them a question. He made them speak out what they knew. If they had listened carefully to themselves, they would have realised that God was doing something wonderful. The cure of our unbelief is in our own mouths if we will go over what God has done in our lives till now. God does not leave a thing half-finished - He will surely complete it. The supernatural is so strange to us that every time God does something beyond our power to explain, we tend to doubt it. There is no rational reason why there cannot be angels, or why Jesus Christ cannot be risen from the dead. Listen to yourself speak, and realise that God's answer is not in adding to what you already know, but in causing you to see what you know from His point of view. Jesus lived in supreme consciousness of the supernatural. He became 'naturally supernatural' and He expects the same of us. Linguists talk of passing a barrier in learning a foreign language, when they begin to think in it. The realm of faith is a language

208

all believers speak, but we must go further, and begin to think in it.

November 15

"Then Samson said to the lad who held him by the hand, 'Let me feel the pillars which support the temple, so that I can lean on them.' .. And he pushed with all his might, and the temple fell on the lords and all the people who were in it. So the dead that he killed at his death were more than he had killed in his life." [Judges 16:26,30]

The main subject of the Bible is Christ and His death and resurrection. It is like a vein of purest gold that runs through the Scriptures and indicates the wealth that is in God Himself. In these verses, Samson is an unlikely type of Christ and His cross. When Jesus was humiliated in His death, He felt the pillars on which the human race was standing. These pillars are the power of sin and death. Christ tasted the awful poison that destroys the human heart from the inside. Then He applied the awesome power of His own sinless life and destroyed the power of evil in Himself, so bringing down the whole kingdom of darkness, by which Satan ruled the human race. In His death, Jesus healed and delivered multitudes, and potentially the whole human race, if only all would believe. His death was thus more important and effective than all His preaching and His ministry. In fact, without His death and resurrection, His teaching and ministry would have given hope, but no power to fulfil that hope. When we consider the cross, we often see it in the light of what **we** feel and what **we** need. We must see it in the light of what **He** endured and felt, and most of all what **He** accomplished. The cross is the greatest act God has ever done or ever will do. It is the flawless jewel that shines out on the darkest background. It is right that we should lay our all at His feet in surrender and worship for who He is and what He has done.

November 16

"So He humbled you, allowed you to hunger, and fed you with manna which you did not know nor did your fathers know, that He might make you know that man shall not live by bread alone; but man lives by every word that proceeds from the mouth of the LORD." [Deuteronomy 8:3]

God's ways with His children are not harsh. They are full of grace and care. Imagine the opposite of the above. It would read something like this: *"So He allowed them everything they wanted, and let them feast on all the food they desired till their appetite for spiritual things was completely spoilt, and they completely lost all thirst for God's Word or Presence."* This would be a supreme tragedy. God shapes our circumstances so that we may hunger for something better than what we have around us. The manna is a symbol of food in another dimension. Spiritual things do not merely involve learning more information or skills, like studying astronomy or languages or plumbing do. Knowing the things of God involves the faculties of our conscience, our spirit and our will. We have to enter into the realm of the Spirit and the Kingdom of God. If we continually feed our bodies and minds to their full capacity with other things, we will find that we have no thirst for the things of God. There will be a dimension we have completely missed. The door to this dimension is the Word of God. Food, intellectual stimulation and entertainment all have their place in a balanced life, but none of them can satisfy our heart's thirst for God. When a child rejects the wholesome food its mother has prepared, she will ask: *"What have you been eating?"* If we have no hunger for God, we need to look at the vain things we have been over-indulging in. If we will not make the right choices, God will lead us into a wilderness where we can no longer find the things we once relied on for our happiness.

November 17

"God is in the midst of her, she shall not be moved; God shall help her, just at the break of dawn." [Psalm 46:5]

We might wish that God would not always wait till the break of dawn, but that is most often what He does. He watched the disciples rowing on the sea with a contrary wind, and came to them in the fourth watch of the night [Matthew 14:25]; that was just at the break of dawn. God allows us to go through things so that our trust and faith in Him grow - that is what He imparts by this process. We often focus on the end of the difficulty itself, but He sees the growth in our inner stature. He cannot leave us or forsake us – water would flow uphill before God would ever be unmindful of His children and not provide for us in our needs and distresses. Though it may seem a long time, hang in, for the intervention of God is just around the corner. In the 19th century, C.T. Studd had given up a fortune and become a missionary to China. His money ran out, and he prayed through the night for the answer to his need. In the morning the mailbag came, but it seemed empty. He shook it again, and out fell an envelope from an engineer named F. Crossley, who had been baptised with the Holy Spirit through Studd's ministry back in England. Some 2 months before this, he had been praying and had received a command from God to send £100 to Studd in China. He had been unable to sleep because of the clear conviction that God was urging him to do this, so he posted the letter with the money the next morning. The letter was 2 months in the post, and arrived on the very morning when Studd so desperately needed it.

November 18

"But He put them all outside, took her by the hand and called, saying, 'Little girl, arise.' Then her spirit returned, and she arose immediately. And He commanded that she be given something to eat. And her parents were astonished, but He charged them to tell no one what had happened."
    [Luke 8:54-56]

God is not in showbusiness! It is always surprising to note how little Jesus used His works of power to advertise Himself. The age of miracles is not past. A friend of mine was a missionary in Papua New Guinea and he had to cross a river to visit a sick man. Returning in the evening, he was swept off his feet and sank under the weight of his backpack. He suddenly felt a mighty hand seize hold of him by the waist and lift him out of the water and place him gently on the river bank. This happened to an ordinary, sane and trustworthy man. Yet God seemingly did not intervene in this miraculous way in order to dazzle or impress anyone, but simply to care for His servant. In fact, this divine discretion seems to be part of His whole way of operating. He does not parade the sufferings of Jesus in order to get sympathy, and He does not perform works of power like a circus. But He does work continually where people put their trust in Him. If we do not know what He is doing, it means that we are definitely reading the wrong books! We will not find God advertised in the daily newspapers. The things of God must be sought out. We must stir ourselves to seek Him. He will not always make it easy for us. We have to lift the latch and push the door, and follow where our thirst for the living God leads us.

November 19

"And Jesus answering said, 'Were there not ten cleansed? but where are the nine? There are not found that returned to give glory to God, save this stranger.' And he said unto him, 'Arise, go thy way: thy faith hath made thee whole.' "
      [Luke 17:17-19, KJV]

Ten lepers were healed, but only one returned to thank Jesus. The other nine treated Jesus like a miracle worker - a divine 'doctor' whom you visit when you have a problem, but whose name you can't remember.   The one who returned had no intention of receiving a deeper blessing – he wanted to give thanks to Jesus. He fell down at Jesus' feet and glorified God, and there he received another word from Jesus, which made him 'whole'. The true need of our hearts is not always what we think it is. Sometimes our true need can only really be met when our other needs have been met. When we are healthy, well-fed and secure, sometimes only then does the question come: what is the purpose of this life?   It is not merely to go to Church and read our Bibles in our spare time. Our purpose is to glorify God and enjoy Him for ever. Our purpose is to surrender our lives to Jesus and allow Him to rule over us. Only then do we know a real 'wholeness' - in the soaring worship we were created for. An eagle is not 'whole' because it has no sickness; it is 'whole' when it comes into its own, soaring on winds high above the mountains. So, too, we are not whole just because our sins are forgiven, or because we have a nice job and a happy family. We are whole because we are living this life of giving ourselves to Jesus in thanksgiving and worship. There we receive the 'second touch', and we are His for evermore.

November 20

"And Jesus, immediately knowing in Himself that power had gone out of Him, turned around in the crowd and said, 'Who touched my clothes?' But His disciples said to Him, 'You see the multitude thronging You, and You say, "Who touched me?" ' " [Mark 5:30-31]

The woman with the flow of blood approached Jesus secretly, hoping just to touch the hem of His garment and then escape without Him noticing! The amazing fact is that Jesus let her do it. When He noticed that power had gone from Him, He turned round and asked who had touched Him. This beautiful detail indicates the non-confrontational way Jesus works with hurting people. It is the same way that God called to Adam in the Garden of Eden. God knew where Adam was, but He did not confront him; He simply called him. Jesus knew who had touched Him, but He had no desire to confront her. Jesus doubtless saw countless desolate, broken people watching Him from afar, fearing to approach Him. His heart would have ached for them. But He would not barge in and confront them; He dealt with them tenderly. There is no-one who can handle us as wisely and tenderly as Jesus. He made us, and He knows and understands us through and through. He knows our need for love; He alone can satisfy that need. The best counsellor is clumsy compared with Him. And He allows us to approach Him secretly and still blesses and heals us. Once, a certain man held back from coming to Christ because he feared telling anyone he had done so. The evangelist told him that he did not need to tell anyone that he had become a Christian. The man was so relieved that he went home to his bedroom, where he knelt and gave his life to Christ. He was so changed and filled with joy that he immediately ran to tell his family what had happened to him!

November 21

"This far you may come, but no farther, and here your proud waves must stop!" [Job 38:11]

During the siege of Dunkirk in 1940, there were some major miracles that saved the British forces from destruction. Hitler's forces had completely surrounded them but, for no apparent reason, Hitler commanded them to stop their advance. The flotilla of small boats that set out from England to rescue the troops was vulnerable to bad weather; but although the weather was bad elsewhere along the coast, between Dunkirk and Dover the sea was calm. Some days earlier, the King and the Prime Minister had led the nation in a day of prayer. God responds wherever and whenever He is invited. This verse in Job shows that it is God who rules over all things, including the boundaries of the sea. The nations may rage and the people of God be assailed by enemies, yet their boundary is set by God and He in His grace will not allow any power or situation to overwhelm us. *"When you pass through the waters, I will be with you; and through the rivers, they shall not overflow you. When you walk through the fire, you shall not be burned, nor shall the flame scorch you."* [Isaiah 43:2]. The human race is powerless against

213

the forces of nature.   Hurricanes, volcanoes, floods and earthquakes are just the reminders of God's awesome power. He and He alone has the power to hold back the forces that can engulf us. In 1904 there was a terrible drought in Australia and the government called for a national day of humbling and prayer. Three days later, rain fell.

November 22

" '...A wicked and adulterous generation looks for a miraculous sign, but none will be given it except the sign of Jonah.' Jesus then left them and went away."
   [Matthew 16:4, NIV]

Paul said that 'the Jews' sought miraculous signs [1 Corinthians 1:22]. This can be taken to include not only Jews, but a certain kind of person.   There are some who are naturally drawn to signs, while others, like the Greeks, are drawn to arguments. The astonishing thing about signs and arguments is that there is an abundance of both. When the Jews asked Jesus to give them a sign, He had just fed the five thousand!   I personally know three trustworthy, rational individuals who have seen angels; I know of two who have heard them singing.   I know many ordinary people who have been healed of incurable diseases by an act of God.   The strange thing is that no amount of miraculous signs or arguments will ever be enough to make people trust God.   Faith in God is a response to His Word and, above all, to the message of the death and resurrection of Jesus. There is something about God's own act of love and mercy in dying for the human race, that creates faith in a way nothing else can. Signs and arguments may impress for a moment, but they cannot replace faith. In the end, we must simply believe. If we examine things carefully, we will discover that we have enough evidence to make faith reasonable. But it is still a moral choice that we must make. We must cease the unbelieving demand for signs and 'proof', and simply put our trust in Him.

November 23

"But those who wait on the LORD shall renew their strength; they shall mount up with wings like eagles, they shall run and not be weary, they shall walk and not faint." [Isaiah 40:31]

The order of effect here in waiting on God is: fly, run, walk. This seems unusual at first glance, since the reverse order would indicate a progression from the ordinary to the extraordinary, from the natural to the supernatural. We might expect that those who are deepest companions of God will be always 'flying' in the rarified atmosphere of His love and holiness. What Isaiah here reveals is that someone who discovers the divine touch, through waiting on God, will feel that their feet have left the ground. The experience of this is more common than we might assume. Many people can look back on their lives and remember moments when their hearts grew still and they were filled with wonder at the Master's touch. But often these moments of exultation do not result in a closer walk with God; we need to let the excitement settle down, and to persist in waiting on God. The result will be a motivation that will cause us to 'run without tiredness'. That is miraculous indeed. Then comes the third stage of a deeper relationship with God, which results in a steady walk. This is like the leisurely enjoyment of two friends who can wander contentedly together and forget time and problems and enjoy each other's conversation. There are fewer emotional highs at this stage, but a deeper sense of well-being. No wonder David exhorted himself to wait patiently [Psalm 62:5] and persistently on the Lord - through the exultant praise and worship, onto the broad uplands of intimate fellowship.

November 24

"....God is love." [1 John 4:8]

This statement identifies the irreducible essence of God. It means that love is not an attribute of God, but that the attributes of God are also attributes of love. God does not 'have' love; He **is** love. The plan of God is not to do something for us, but to **be love** to us. We must get beyond the mechanical view of God, as if He were a Chief Executive Officer or Managing Director running the universe. God can only be Himself to us when we receive Him into our being. Salvation always begins with God doing something for us, but then, as we let Him be the focus of our lives, there comes a moment when we begin to know and to marvel at the ocean of love that He is. The name we give to this experience will endanger it; we may call it 'the baptism with the Holy Spirit'. But it is not an 'it' - it is Him. It cannot be limited to a mere 'label' or something that indicates we are 'deeper' Christians than others. This will result in God being like a membership card to an exclusive club. The whole realm of the Kingdom is God Himself, who is love. As soon as we know Him

215

as love, our hearts will be melted, and we will never be satisfied again with anything less.

November 25

"When Jesus saw their faith, He said to the paralytic, 'Son, your sins are forgiven you.' " [Mark 2:5]

Jesus forgave the paralysed man's sins, and thus healed him first of spiritual paralysis. Guilt paralyses our hearts as nothing else can, and makes it impossible for us to believe, pray, worship or love. Guilt produces fear, suspicion and mistrust. It is a hidden power of destruction in the armoury of the prince of darkness. Forgiveness always breaks his dread grip on situations and individuals. Jesus came to release us from the paralysing burden of guilt by forgiving our sins. In 1963 Kenya received independence from Britain. This had been preceded by years of violence between Mau Mau independence fighters and British colonial forces. The new President, Jomo Kenyatta, had been imprisoned by the British. On independence day, President Kenyatta addressed the newborn nation on Kenyan state radio. He spoke first to the British settlers, remembering many bad things they had done over many years, and then said: *"But I forgive you."* Then he went one step further, remembering the bad things done by the independence fighters, and concluded: *"Please forgive us."* Jomo Kenyatta gave Kenya the new beginning it needed. Forgiveness cannot reverse the effects of sins, but it does break the bitterness and division that flow from guilt. No wonder, then, that Jesus' next words to the paralytic are the physical counterpart of forgiveness: *"...arise, take up your bed, and go to your house"* [Mark 2:11]. We rise from the world of the stress and misery of guilt, into the world of love and acceptance, and then walk home into the loving arms of our heavenly Father.

November 26

"For ye have need of patience, that, after ye have done the will of God, ye might receive the promise."
[Hebrews 10:36, KJV]

The sin of impatience caused untold havoc in the Old Testament. It was through impatience that Abram went into Egypt and got entangled with lies at the court of Pharaoh [Genesis 12:10-20]. It was through impatience that Ishmael

216

came into the world [Genesis 16]. Impatience with ourselves, impatience with God, impatience with those around us, leads us into avenues from which we cannot easily escape. Abraham lived with the consequences of his impatience for the rest of his life. So why is patience so important? It is because it is the result of believing God. If I really believe that God is in control of the details of my life (such as the length of the queue at the supermarket checkout!) then I can step back and enjoy the moment. Faith understands that God will work in His own time, and this takes the stress and hurry out of us. Some tourists are so obsessed with their camera or their guidebook that they don't actually step back and enjoy the sights that are before their eyes. Or we might, for instance, be hurrying to see the crown jewels in the Tower of London, and yet miss the sunlight on a single dewdrop, as it flashes with a momentary brilliance that is unique and intended for our pleasure alone. God is in control of the big things in our lives, and He will not let us down. Though we may sometimes have to wait for what seems a long time to us, it will be worth it when the promise is fulfilled. In the meantime, step back and enjoy each moment that He gives.

November 27

"For since, in the wisdom of God, the world through wisdom did not know God, it pleased God through the foolishness of the message preached to save those who believe. For Jews request a sign, and Greeks seek after wisdom; but we preach Christ crucified, to the Jews a stumbling block and to the Greeks foolishness, but to those who are called, both Jews and Greeks, Christ the power of God and the wisdom of God." [1 Corinthians 1:21-24]

Human wisdom meets a ceiling beyond which it cannot pass. No amount of concentrating, knowledge or learning can penetrate the Presence of God or understand the origins of the universe. No amount of strength, money, or sheer brain power can ever get any of us out of the appalling state of ignorance of God that prevails in human hearts. To do that, we need revelation, and the only thing that can ever get beyond the blank wall of our spiritual emptiness is faith, married with humility. We must come to the humbling realisation that we have been like fools and paupers in God's sight, and that is not easy for competent or wealthy or educated or skilled people to accept as good news! It does not mean that God is trying to humiliate us or push our faces into the dust, but it does mean that we will get nowhere by parading our own abilities. We must bow before the great King, lay down our abilities and achievements before Him, and realise that they count as nothing. As believers, we do not deny the power of logic or intellect, but we realise that there are areas in which we are less than powerless, and that we must bow before God. God is good, and quickly ushers all who seek Him into His loving Presence. God's ways are simple: He resists the proud and gives grace to the humble [James 4:6].

November 28

"But Abraham said, 'Son, remember that in your lifetime you received your good things, and likewise Lazarus evil things; but now he is comforted and you are tormented.' "
[Luke 16:25]

At first sight it may seem that Jesus is saying here that the rich man went to hell for being rich and the poor man (Lazarus) went to heaven for being poor. The truth is that both were judged on the basis of their attitude to the hand of God in their lives. Faith creates a submissive attitude that honours God by the way we live. The rich man hardened his heart to the cry of the poor, and never reflected on the goodness of God in his circumstances. It never occurred to him to share what he had. Though nothing is known about Lazarus' faith, the implication is that suffering had brought him to a brokenness and trust in God in his helpless condition. The balances of God weigh human hearts, both in this life and in the next. Should pain and hardship bring us to our senses, the day will come when we will thank God for it. Should blessing and wealth dull us to our spiritual debt to God, then the day will come when we may wish we had never seen them. Pain and luxury, poverty and riches are all tests. It is God who knows whom He will test - some this way and some that. It is vital to reflect on how God is challenging us by things He has placed in our lives. We cry to God to speak to us, and He answers with a hand that carves our circumstances. At one point in C.S. Lewis' *Chronicles of Narnia*, the intrepid children are searching for some writing, and spend hours walking through deep trenches that are in fact the words themselves, carved in the mountainside, and that can only be read from an elevated position. We are walking through God's word to us, carved out in the circumstances through which we tread.

November 29

"For He taught His disciples and said to them, 'The Son of Man is being betrayed into the hands of men, and they will kill Him. And after He is killed, He will rise the third day. ' .... on the road they had disputed among themselves who would be the greatest." [Mark 9:31,34]

Jesus here taught His disciples that He would die and then rise again. But because they were only familiar with death, their ears and hearts were completely deaf to the hope of resurrection. They understood only with their natural minds, and completely missed the greatness of the Kingdom of God. This kingdom is so powerful and positive, that all that appears to be loss is swallowed up in the great arms of resurrection. The disciples' reaction was to miss the point and discuss the question of succession: which of them would take the place of Jesus after He had gone from the earth? All such disputes are based on the assumption of an absent Jesus. Jesus is not looking for a replacement, but for a yielded life through which He can manifest Himself. The greatest in the Kingdom of God is Jesus, and there is no-one who can replace Him in His ministry and His love, and no-one who is worthy to be worshipped even in the smallest degree. We have to offer up our lives to be filled by Jesus and His glorious life. Paul expresses this when he says: *"I have been crucified with Christ; it is no longer I who live, but Christ lives in me."* [Galatians 2:20]. We are not to look at ourselves or compare ourselves with each other, but to look to the glorious risen Saviour who indwells us.

November 30

"For My yoke is easy and my burden is light."
    [Matthew 11:30]

When my children were little they would often want to join in what my wife or I were doing - genuinely believing they could be of enormous help. As a father, it never seemed right to discourage even their slightest desire to help. On one occasion, I was carrying a heavy piece of wood, and my 3 year-old son offered to help me carry it. He bravely took hold of one end of the piece of wood. He held on to it so tightly that, as I lifted the wood, his feet left the ground, and I was carrying him along with the wood! How easily we think we are carrying really heavy burdens on our shoulders. We go about our business with such a serious expression, and the furrows on our brow are quite genuine. But the burdens that God lays on our hearts are not like burdens that crush and destroy. When He lays a burden on one of His children, it actually 'carries' us, and motivates us to do things that were formerly beyond our power. The burdens God shares with us shape our character and make us into people of compassion. Strangely, this kind of burden doesn't make our steps heavier, but lighter. We find ourselves running to prayer, running to help others, with an energy and drive that we never had before, and part of it is the sheer delight of partnership with God. Jesus finds running the moral, spiritual and physical universe a sheer delight, and He wants to share that delight with us.

December 1

"...My blood is drink indeed." [John 6:55]

This is the centre of the Christian's faith. We celebrate it by the elements of the bread and the wine. A Christian has 'drunk the blood of Christ'. This is of course a shocking image, and it is only the incredible power of habit that robs it of its force. What, then, does it really mean to 'drink His blood'? No-one drank His physical blood, nor ever shall. The answer is that the blood is the essence of Christ. It is what He is on the deepest level. It is what He is when tested to the utmost. It is His deepest instincts, when subjected to the most awful pressure. It is not some passing, superficial whim or thought. No! The blood is pure God, distilled by the fires of suffering, and by the white heat of hell's furious onslaught. The blood is what pours out of God when He is cut to the heart. That is the cup that He places to our lips and invites us to drink deeply. We are to receive into our beings what God is and has always been. This is sobering, for it lifts a human being to fellowship with the Eternal, the Unchangeable. God has opened up His veins and poured out His essence - not merely that His physical blood should stain a piece of wood outside Jerusalem, but that pure God should be poured into our hearts, and wash and cleanse all else by Himself. Do it reverently, do it consciously, do it definitely, do it by faith - drink His blood!

December 2

"They shall be coupled together...." [Exodus 26:24]

The Tabernacle was made of many parts, and of a huge variety of materials - from badger skins to gold, from wood to linen. But all the parts were integrated into one whole. This is a picture of the unity of the Church, and of the need each believer has to be in fellowship with others and to take their place in the body. If we withdraw from the Church, through a sense of its failures and weaknesses, or through personal hurt, we damage ourselves first and the Church too. It is in the Church that we hear faith expressed, and are able to share our struggles with others. Our spiritual life is often impossible to express to those who do not yet have faith. The very act of being with other believers of a like mind should make us breathe a sigh of relief, as we realise that we are not alone. Take time this day, if you can, to fellowship with someone else - by writing a card, making a phone call, or perhaps visiting someone. As you do, your faith will flow through you and will bless that other person, and you will experience the wonder of being a connected part of the people of God.

December 3

"Therefore it was necessary that the copies of the things in the heavens should be purified with these (blood from animal sacrifices)*, but the heavenly things themselves with better sacrifices than these. For Christ has...entered...into heaven itself..."* [Hebrews 9:23-24]

This is a startling revelation - that heaven itself was purified by the blood of Jesus. Sin began in the heart of Lucifer when he was a mighty angel in God's Presence. From his fallen lips came the lie that he uttered from the beginning [John 8:44]. Christ's blood was applied before the throne of God, where the slander had been uttered. What was that lie? It is repeated in a thousand forms through human lips: *"God does not care, God does not love!"* But the blood of Jesus cancels that lie once and for all. Since Christ has died, His blood has cancelled the devil's lie from the highest heaven where it was first spoken, to the lowest hell where it is still repeated. God loves us so much that, despite all our crimes and resistance against that love, He has prevailed and shed the blood of His Son to reconcile us to Himself. Let the blood speak in your heart and purify you from the devil's lie. Declare to yourself and to all who will hear: *"God is good, and has loved the human race with an infinite and everlasting love"*. The sound rings on and will never fade, and the hosts of heaven resound with worship, wonder and praise to the Lamb that was slain to redeem us back to God.

December 4

"...casting all your care upon Him, for He cares for you."
    [1 Peter 5:7]

An African woman once stood by the road waiting for a pick-up truck to come so that she could return to town from her fields carrying all the produce she had harvested. It would cost her just a few cents to get into town. When at last a pick-up came, she clambered into the back but kept the heavy basket of fruit and vegetables balanced on her head. After a mile or so, the driver noticed her in his mirror and, stopping the truck, asked her why she was still carrying her load. *"I don't want to pay for the load"*, she said in a matter-of-fact voice. *"I will carry the load myself."* We may smile at this, but it is astonishing how often we continue to carry heavy loads ourselves, forgetting that we are being carried by the almighty power of God. We were not created to worry - that is both an unnatural use of the human mind, and ultimately a sin against God. But most of all, if we are carrying the 'weight' of our spiritual lives - trying to maintain a life of holiness and devotion by our own strength - then we are continuing in unnecessary strain, since it is Christ Who died for us and Who gives us the strength to live for Him. There are many things He will ask us to do, but none of them will crush us. So lay your burdens down, and enjoy the fact that He cares for you!

December 5

"And it happened after ten days that the word of the Lord came to Jeremiah." [Jeremiah 42:7]

The people were confused and uncertain; they needed a word of guidance from the prophet. Jeremiah agreed to seek the Lord on their behalf, and he prayed. He waited ten days, till at last the word of the Lord came. Why does God wait to speak to us? Isaiah 30:18 teaches that God waits that He may be gracious to us. When we ask God to speak, we are often already conditioned to the kind of thing we want Him to say, and if that is what He wants to say, we are immediately ready to hear. But if He wants to speak something we are not expecting to hear, then He must wait - till frustration and impatience have died down, and our hearts are open to whatever He wants to say. The longer we wait, the more we will be open to hear something that we had not expected. So it was with Jeremiah. He had prophesied for years that the Jews should accept the inevitable and either go into exile in Babylon or die. In Jeremiah 42 the remnant of the people asked whether they should go into exile into Egypt. Jeremiah was given the answer that they were not to go into Egypt, or they would die there! God knows why He waits to speak. He is waiting till things come into the place, either in our circumstances or in our hearts, where we are able to receive His guidance.

December 6

"And it happened after ten days that the word of the Lord came to Jeremiah." [Jeremiah 42:7]

Jeremiah set his heart to listen to God on behalf of the people, and it was only after ten days that God's answer came to him. Patience in listening and looking up are the most precious qualities of the prophet. Patience is a never-failing spring of life for God's people. It is part of the bedrock of our relationship with Him. We know that He hears us, and for that reason we will wait for Him until He answers. I am not to be 'patient' until I have had enough of waiting, and then stomp off in a huff exclaiming: *"I have been patient long enough!"* That is not patience! Patience makes me rest in His love and His faithfulness; it makes me know that I simply have to wait till He chooses, in His wisdom, to answer me. God **has** heard your prayers, now let your heart come to rest in that great comforting fact, and wait for His response.

December 7

"Watch therefore, and pray always that you may be counted worthy to escape all these things that will come to pass, and to stand before the Son of Man." [Luke 21:36]

This is the Son of Man speaking in sober authority. At first sight His words here may seem to roll back all the wonder of grace, and return us to striving under law. But these words are to awaken us to our responsibility to abide in the grace of God. Jesus is not saying that we must pray a lot in order to avoid trouble. The concept of 'praying always' is to direct us into maintaining a clear relationship with God. The life of faith is the only thing that can make us worthy to stand before God. Jesus is the Master of putting His finger on the key issues in our hearts. Don't allow yourself to descend into mere religious habits or forms of Christian life. Keep yourself awake and alert to the voice of the Son of God in your heart. As you do this, His grace will refresh you inwardly and your life will manifest the graciousness and beauty of heaven. Our responsibility is to keep our hearts in tune with our Saviour. How true it is that we are not under law - but it does not mean that we are not under anything! We are under the ministry of Jesus. We have exchanged the tyranny of striving under law, for the loving Lordship of Christ that enables us to be all He asks us to be. Are you worthy to stand before Him now? Don't drift - lift up your heart and receive his goodness and love to empower you today.

December 8

"Then they began to plead with Him to depart from their region. And when He got into the boat, he who had been demon-possessed begged Him that he might be with Him. However, Jesus did not permit him..." [Mark 5:17-19]

How far will I let Him go in my life?
There are two prayers in these verses - one that Jesus would go away, and one to be closer to Jesus. Both prayers are of course answered, but in different and surprising ways. The first prayer draws a line in the sand and pleads with God not to step over it. While we may assume that Jesus was reluctant to answer this prayer, there is no doubt that He instantly took these people of the Gadarene region seriously, and accepted their choice, even though it had tragic consequences for others. We are forced to ask: did these people have no demon-possessed or sick relatives, did they have no need of Him? But whatever their needs, they set the limits on how far He could go with them. Jesus always takes us seriously.   Sometimes we are not conscious of deliberately hindering Him, but we have still set the limits and have determined how far He is useful to us. The scary thing is that He does take us seriously, and it is verses like these that challenge us to make sure that we are allowing Him free access to our entire life. The second prayer was beautiful, and yet Jesus declined to give the man what he asked for. If the man had insisted, Jesus would have yielded and the man would have limited Jesus in his life. But this man was praying from a place of surrender that allowed Jesus to answer as He wished. The man leaped for joy at the honour of representing Christ to others. He allowed Jesus free access to his life, to do with him whatever He wished. Give Him the free reign He seeks in your life; and remember, we determine how far we will allow Him to go.

December 9

"...to create in Himself one new man..." [Ephesians 2:15]

The word 'created' is a word that human beings cannot, strictly, use of their own efforts. A story is told of two scientists who claimed they could create life in the laboratory. God heard of this, and came along to observe. One of the scientists was really hoping to impress God with his skill, and reached for a jar of clay. But God interrupted him and said, *"Excuse Me, that's My clay; use your own!"* Scientists have indeed succeeded in manipulating DNA, but they cannot create life. Spiritually, we may think that we have to make the best of what we are by our natural inheritance. But God answers that He is able to create something in us that was never there before. The Christian life is not just making do with the character and qualities we have inherited naturally. It is letting God have His way, to call things into being that were not there before. God spoke a universe into being, and He works in us in the same way. Don't count on your own resources, or you'll be discouraged. Believe in the Creator God. This is the faith of Abraham, who had to be brought to the end of his own inventiveness. He realised that what God was asking of Him was impossible. But God wanted Abraham to let Him do the impossible, and give him a son through a barren wife in their old age. God waits till all our resources have proved insufficient, and we look to Him to do something that we could never do.

December 10

"For My yoke is easy and My burden is light."
  [Matthew 11:30]

This claim of Jesus is amazing. He had been involved in an extremely busy time of ministry - praying for thousands day after day, casting out demons and even raising the dead. We might think that He was under enormous pressure to keep on satisfying the multitudes that flocked to Him. But then, if a touch can heal the sick, where is the pressure? Isn't it a delight to exercise that power? Ministering to others only becomes stressful to us if we are trying to be something we are not. If we feel we have to make a miracle happen, then praying for the sick becomes the most intolerable burden we can ever imagine. If deliverance depends on us, then praying for the relief of oppressed people becomes a burden that will crush the faith out of our wearied minds. But all these things do not depend on us - they work by the sheer grace and gift of God. It is a delight to pray for people and minister to them because we cannot make it happen, either by becoming intense and serious as we pray, or by raising our voices. It is a delightful wonder that God heals and works through us, and all we have to do is to keep our hearts under His yoke - free and dependent on Him. The worst thing we can do is to pretend we are something we are not. Be yourself, and delight in His grace and goodness to you and through you.

December 11

"...and he (Joshua) said in the sight of Israel: 'Sun stand still over Gibeon; and Moon, in the valley of Aijalon.' So the sun stood still, and the moon stopped, till the people had revenge upon their enemies." [Joshua 10:12-13]

This is one of the greatest miracles of the Old Testament, when God gave to Joshua a longer day. What was Joshua's valiant prayer? It was a prayer against the coming of the night, in which his enemies could flee, regroup and live to fight another day. Joshua prayed for light so that he could fight till the battle was complete, and this same fighting spirit should grip us, as the people of God. Joshua prayed for light to fill the whole scene; he prayed that the light would not sink and fade till every vital victory had been won. We are to pray that God will give us such light, from the death and resurrection of His Son, that all our lives will be transformed and begin to radiate the glory of the love of God. Jesus Christ is light that burns up sin, and we must walk in His light. Light is not given for us to pursue our selfish lives; it is given for us to get everything right with God. God pours forth light by His Spirit and by His word. There are times in each of our lives when we are convicted of what can be done in the light that God gives. When God shines in your life, act, obey, put things right. The light is the opportunity to tie up loose ends, to get things ready. The night of temptation must come, and you will have to live then by the things you have attained to in the light. The night will test what you did in the light, when Christ touched you with His word and His love.

December 12

"The virgin, the daughter of Zion, has despised you, laughed you to scorn; the daughter of Jerusalem has shaken her head behind your back!" [Isaiah 37:22]

When Isaiah said this of God's beloved Israel, neither the king nor his armies were feeling at all exultant. They were shaken by the threat of the Assyrian armies camped at the gates of Jerusalem. The Assyrian generals had shouted lies and abuse at the people of God, and Hezekiah's response to the danger had been to make a desperate plea to God for help and advice.

227

While Hezekiah and the people feared the worst, yet they would not give up hope, but prayed, although they felt so weak in prayer. And that is exactly what trouble and temptation do to us. They wear us down and demoralise us; we feel weak and pathetic, and our praise and worship seem dull and powerless. But God views things in a totally different way. When we pray in desperate moments, when we praise feeling as if our lips were swollen and our tongues heavy like lead, God values that praise as worth more to Him than all the dancing and praising we offered to God when all was well and life was easy. God here teaches us that prayer from a weak heart that turns, helpless, to God, is heard like a great shout of victory in heaven. It is the response all heaven awaits, and the trigger for the great interventions of God in human lives. Though Hezekiah didn't yet know it, he was shaking his head at the devil with the boundless joy of victory. Don't condemn yourself if you feel your responses to God are weak, for the fact that you respond to God in weakness is what makes your prayer so pleasing to God and so certain of victory.

December 13

"There was a little city with few men in it; and a great king came against it, besieged it, and built great snares around it. Now there was found in it a poor wise man, and he by his wisdom delivered the city. Yet no one remembered that same poor man. Then I said: 'Wisdom is better than strength. Nevertheless the poor man's wisdom is despised...'." [Ecclesiastes 9:14-16]

Solomon here told a whole epic story in a few words - it is intriguing, and it would be very interesting to know more details. The fact is that when a righteous man or woman walks with God, they have an impact on the world around them far out of proportion to what others notice, or history records. God said to Abraham that He would not destroy Sodom if He found ten righteous people there. If He had found them, those ten would never have known in this life that their presence had turned aside God's wrath. God says often in the Old Testament that He sought for a single person to stand in the gap. One man or woman who walks with God can turn the tide of evil in a place. That individual can prick the conscience of multitudes who will never mention it – they may, for instance, challenge traders to be truthful, or gossips to hold their tongues. Politics is the art of managing a nation's defences, finances, schools and so on. But the defence of a nation is not ultimately in the hands of

228

governments - it is in the hands of God, and He looks to righteous people to determine what He will do. A righteous person is righteous because they have been reconciled with God. They have touched reality through repentance and faith. How the world mocks and demons sneer at the righteous, but do not be discouraged and do not expect applause. Follow through and be a delight to God. He will stand with the righteous; a world without you would be a dark and hopeless place.

December 14

"So then it is not of him who wills, nor of him who runs, but of God who shows mercy." [Romans 9:16]
"For 'whoever calls upon the name of the Lord shall be saved'." [Romans 10:13]

The Bible assures us, in these verses, both of our free will and of the sovereignty of God. How is this possible? The answer is that our free will is real, but it is a gift from God. It does not put us in the driving seat. It is our free will to co-operate with the driver of the car, not to take control of it! When we understand the grace of God in granting us freedom to choose our destiny, we should be humbled, and fear Him. People today easily imagine God as a being like a rather old-fashioned, unpopular teacher who should be grateful that we are his friends, given his reputation. In the eyes of many people today, it is God who should do the pleading, and we who should offer Him grace! But once stated like this, it is clear how awful this attitude is. The fact is, God can say 'No' to us at any time, because we have not merited His grace. He has no reason to answer our cries for help, other than that He is kind, loving and gracious. It is not that God wants us to grovel, but He hates arrogance and will not respond to those who talk down to Him. The amazing fact of Calvary is that God has gone into the very dust of death to obtain our forgiveness. His mercy has gone lower than we ever will. God is not reluctant - Calvary proves that beyond all doubt. But God will not pander to our pride. You have freedom of will; thank God for it, and make sure you are not trying to be in the driving seat!

229

December 15

" 'Who will ascend into heaven?' (that is, to bring Christ down from above) or 'Who will descend into the abyss?' (that is, to bring Christ up from the dead)." [Romans 10:6-7]

The redemptive work of Christ stretches from the highest throne of holiness and bliss to the deepest hell of God-forsaken misery that human beings could ever imagine. We know so little of these extremes. We know little of where we came from, or how we were individually made. There is mystery on every side. But these verses tell us that Christ has come down from on high, and has plumbed the depths of sin and death and hell. As one poet put it:

"Dying Jesus, going down,
Deeper than a man can drown,
Deeper, darker, further, far,
Than ever fell the morning star.
Jesus Lord! My spirit saith:
'Bury me within thy death!' "

Here is the marvellous love of God that reaches us wherever we are, and lifts us to know the life and the love that are His for eternity. There are conflicts too severe for our human minds, there are choices too heavy for us to bear, but Jesus made the whole matter easy for us. We must choose Him and embrace Him who reached down and paid the price for our redemption. Thank God that there is a Saviour who takes all the burden and enables us to partake of that immense life that spans the creation, and redeems us from sin.

December 16

"And God raised us up with Christ and seated us with him in the heavenly realms in Christ Jesus." [Ephesians 2:6, NIV]

As Christians, we stand between two worlds. We live a normal earthly life, with our feet firmly on the ground. But we have a soaring spirit. We have been introduced to something that is holy and exalted. We cannot see the glory of God with our physical eyes, but our inner eye is aware of something that we cannot put into words. This is why we need the testimony of people who have seen more than others. Paul was granted to hear unspeakable words [2 Corinthians 12:4], as was the apostle

John [Revelation 10:4], and yet the Bible does not bid us seek similar experiences. Paul is here saying that, while we may not all have the same privilege of seeing God's unveiled glory, yet we are all made partakers of the same heavenly life. In our spirits we are seated in that glory, and that is why we can allow our spirits to soar. We can soar in thinking spiritually, because then our thinking will match what God has done for us. We can soar morally, because then we will reveal the righteousness of the Kingdom of God. Living for God is a moral and spiritual adventure, and those who follow this path need the inspiration of the few who can put these mysteries into words. Christian discipleship is not tediously following an impossible goal. It is catching the wind of the spirit - catching the glory of Christ in His heavenly life and His matchless victory. Christians are 'of resurrection' [Romans 6:5], and we must never forget that we are a window on heaven to a dull and lifeless world all around us.

December 17

"The glory of the LORD shall be revealed, and all flesh shall see it together; for the mouth of the LORD has spoken."
      [Isaiah 40:5]

This is the announcement by Isaiah of the coming of Messiah. The entire world shall see the glory of God through Him. Jesus Christ is the perfection of all things. In Him we see God perfectly revealed. It is the most amazing fact in the history of this earth, that the baby born in Bethlehem was God in human form. This makes it the most wonderful event that we could ever imagine. God did not want anyone to misunderstand Him. People may complain about preachers, Churches, or religious attitudes that have grown up around Jesus Christ. But the way through all the fog of religion is to focus clearly on Him. He is faultless, His teaching is perfect, His character is attractive and appealing. His teaching is not merely good - it is from God, without dilution or alteration. God wanted us to be absolutely sure about the Truth, so He came Himself. Isaiah 40:9 proclaims, *"Behold your God!"* Jesus Christ is God, and it is in looking at Jesus and listening to Him that we know exactly what God is like - both by His words and by His tones. Although the Gospels are not audio recordings, you cannot read them without sensing the greatness of the person of Christ. Einstein said of Jesus:

"...I am enthralled by the luminous figure of the Nazarene. ... No one can read the Gospels without feeling the actual presence of Jesus. His personality pulsates in every word. No myth is filled with such life."

It is when we believe that the connection is made between us and the living Christ, and when the connection is made, the power of His life flows into us every time.

December 18

"But when the fullness of the time had come, God sent forth His Son, born of a woman, born under the law, to redeem those who were under the law, that we might receive the adoption as sons." [Galatians 4:4-5]

The *"fullness of the time"* refers to the point in human history when everything was ripe for the appearance of God's Son on the stage of world history. His life is the centre of all history, yet there was nothing in His earthly life of the kind of 'greatness' that fascinates historians. He commanded no armies, and aspired to no throne on earth. He never fought anyone, and never led any movement for social or political reform. His heart and mind were full of compelling focus, but that focus was on redeeming individuals. He was a good listener, and answered questions with keen interest in the motive and inner thoughts of the questioner. The great and famous personalities of history were often concerned with occupying the centre of power in nations; but Christ is interested in the 'little' people, and the details of people's lives. He is interested in shaping and building our individual lives into the pattern that pleases God and brings blessing to us. God in Christ is about the business of making us into His sons. This is the detail that goes unnoticed by historians, but will one day be revealed as the only really important matter in everyone's life. All of us will answer to God for what we have built in our character. Christ has come to adopt us into His family so that we might bear His family likeness. We human beings are ruined by sin, but Christ takes us up and slowly and carefully restores us into the image of God. He came to impart the glory of His life.

December 19

"He has put down the mighty from their thrones, and exalted the lowly. He has filled the hungry with good things, and the

232

rich He has sent away empty." [Luke 1:52-53]

Mary prophesied in this prayer concerning the whole character of her Son and of the Kingdom of God. Christ was born with a cross in His heart – that is, He naturally followed the way of humility and selfless sacrifice. It was natural to Him. Right through His earthly life and ministry, Jesus never grasped at anything as being His right. He displayed the life of someone who sought no fame or wealth or personal comfort. Yet to Him all thrones will be given; all wealth and riches will be laid at His feet. This is spiritual law - it is the law of God's nature and God's kingdom. The hallmark of Jesus' teaching is that it always exalted God and His ways. He asked Peter for the favour of entering and using his boat, when He could command myriads of angels. When invited to a banquet, He would take the lowest seat. When hosting a banquet, He would invite the beggars and the unwanted people. When visiting a city, He would go to tea with the least respected citizen (Zacchaeus). When receiving friends, He would make sure He washed their feet. Jesus would always do these things, because not only did He die on the cross, He also lived a crucified life. He delighted in taking the lowest path, and He found perfect joy and ease there. There were no crowds to impress and no reputation to lose there, anyway. There was also no morbid sense of self-conscious sacrifice in Him. Can you hear Him laugh as He takes the lowest path and delights in the kind of people He finds there? Go with Him - it is the way of joy.

December 20

"Then the lame shall leap like a deer, and the tongue of the dumb sing. For waters shall burst forth in the wilderness, and streams in the desert." [Isaiah 35:6]

This chapter describes the full effect of the Messiah's ministry. How can lame people leap and dumb people sing? The answer is that, wherever Messiah appears, the effect is the reversal of all that hindered and destroyed the lives of sinners. These verses prophesy the literal healing of broken bodies - and this ministry continues today; but how much more wonderful that the healing also refers to broken hearts and damaged emotions. Messiah brings a fountain of bliss, and our voices, once despairing and sorrowful, can now sing like a lark. What is your experience of the boundless joy of His Presence? Bliss means joy unspeakable and full of glory. Bliss is when you realise that the gulf of

233

darkness that threatened you has been swept aside for ever. Bliss is when you realise that God's love and supply of strength will never fail you. Bliss is when you have to pinch yourself to remind you that this is really happening to you. How easily we fall back into old patterns of thought and feeling. Don't let that happen. The world changed for ever when Christ died, rose again and sent the Holy Spirit. Your world has changed for ever, and wherever people realise who He is and what He has done, lame people dance and dumb people sing. Multitudes stop and stare at the power of Him who reverses years of stiffness and shyness, and the heaviness of a world that had no Messiah, to exchange them for the bliss of the Kingdom of God.

December 21

"So he was there with the Lord forty days and forty nights; he neither ate bread nor drank water. And He wrote on the tablets the words of the covenant, the Ten Commandments."
  [Exodus 34:28]

Moses was one of the few men ever taken up into the world beyond. This was not merely heaven - it was the direct Presence of God. Moses did not eat or drink, but that does not mean that his body grew weak and thin - it is not surprising that we often think in natural ways, but God is better food than bread, and better drink than water. We do not even know whether we will need to breathe in heaven, because God is better oxygen than anything we know down here. We always tend to think of God as somehow a part of the physical world He made, rather than as the author of it. He makes the rules, and so He is the best interpreter of them. This is the truth for our whole life. If we can only get into His Presence, we will find that we are sustained with a life that is always fresh and always supplies our mental and spiritual needs. When Jesus said, *"I am the bread of life"* and *"I have bread to eat you know not of"*, He was referring to the great sustenance of the Presence of God to the human soul. We will always need our daily bread on earth, just as He did; but we need to pass beyond the world we can see, into Christ, into God - into the world that needs no supports or supply. The New Creation is of a different order from the old one, for it does not need the light of the sun [Revelation 21:23]. God will ultimately gather all things into Himself, Who is the source of all life, and that is where we must learn to live right now. Faith goes beyond the things made, to the One who created them by His word.

December 22

"And let them make Me a sanctuary, that I may dwell among them." [Exodus 25:8]

This verse expresses God's great longing to dwell amongst the human race. This is in one way the greatest declaration of His love, in that it is not some great act that He has done, but His desire to be in a permanent relationship with us that is as close as marriage. God looked down on the camp of Israel and said to Moses, *'Make Me a tent; I'm coming down to live with you.'* God's desire to live with us could only be truly fulfilled through Christ - His incarnation is a statement of the heart of God towards each one of us. And this desire is perfectly fulfilled in the New Creation, when it says that God Himself shall dwell with His people on earth [Revelation 21:1-3]. God is not a distant God; it is our sin that separates us from Him. God is a Father and He loves to be with us. The birth of Christ was the key step in the fulfilment of the Father's longing, and constitutes an unimaginable sacrifice on the Father's part, because He knew what would happen to His Son. It was allowing a Lamb to enter the wolf's lair. For God so loved the world that He gave His Son, to be our nearest neighbour, our closest friend and advisor. God came down to earth to live in all the rough and tumble of a normal family, and to suffer all the misunderstandings of a religious system that had grown cold. Jesus Christ came down, embracing the inevitable suffering, because He loves each one of us and is determined to fulfil the dream of eternal life with us. On Calvary He died for us; in Bethlehem and Nazareth He became our closest relative, ready to live with us for ever.

December 23

"And the dragon stood before the woman who was ready to give birth, to devour her Child as soon as it was born."
    [Revelation 12:4]

Christ's birth into this world was as momentous an event as the creation of the world itself [John 1:1 and Genesis 1:1]. When Christ was born on earth, the devil knew that this meant the end of his kingdom and power. Mary yielded her body to the Holy Spirit to become the channel for Christ to have a body in this world. In spiritual terms, the same is true of each individual believer. We are to yield our bodies to the Holy Spirit so that

Christ may be formed in our lives. Christ came to be the firstborn of many sons and daughters of God. That this is opposed by Satan should not surprise us, since every believer who realises their inheritance in Christ is part of the fulfilment of Christ's victory. Satan will oppose and discourage us, he will make us think our lives are without ultimate purpose, and try to make us live for empty, childish games that are not worthy of the Son of God. The thing that sets Christ and all His followers apart is that our lives are at the forefront of the defeat of the powers of darkness. For each believer, the fiercest battle is to overcome the enemy's attempts to hinder us from becoming a mature warrior in the Kingdom of God. Every time you set your heart to go on with God, that very thought is opposed by Satan. You are a king and a priest, with a great and high calling. While there will always be a difference between Christ and His Church (Christ is God and the Church is not!) yet there is no difference between the resources available to us and those that were available to Christ on the earth. It is thus within your power to throw off the attacks of the wicked one, and to allow the Son of God to be manifest in your life in His fullness.

December 24

"Salmon begot Boaz by Rahab, Boaz begot Obed by Ruth, ... David the King begot Solomon by her who had been the wife of Uriah." "...Hezekiah begot Manasseh..."
[Matthew 1:5-6,10]

The genealogy of Jesus Christ was far from illustrious. If we look at it carefully, we find some spiritual giants, but also some base and sinful people. Rahab was a prostitute. Manasseh was a mass murderer. The wonderful truth is that the genealogy has a redemptive dimension. Jesus Christ was not grafted into the human race, to receive the 'sap' of the human 'tree' into Himself, but rather the human race was grafted into God through the incarnation and the cross. The sap that is in God made all those who receive Christ clean and pure. God does not look at our qualifications of birth, education or upbringing. God cuts us off from our past and plants us in Christ. Christ's birth in Bethlehem means that the human race was planted back into God. His birth was the first step in our redemption. The cross is the culmination of His birth. By His cross He has taken our lives and planted them into the 'new man' [Ephesians 2:15]. By the cross, we are grafted into Him and we begin life anew. We are not physically children of God, but spiritually we have

236

made a completely fresh start. Christ has created in Himself a new humanity from the materials of the old humanity. In Christ is perfect redemption: our past is swallowed up, and the life of Christ is our future in this life and for all eternity.

December 25

"...He is not ashamed to call them brethren, ..."
    [Hebrews 2:11]

In the incarnation, God humbled Himself to reach the human race. Imagine for a moment some highly privileged person, such as the Queen of the England, volunteering to clean the filthy public toilets in a rundown and dangerous area of an inner city. God not only did the equivalent of that - He felt at home doing it. God is not naturally a palace-dweller. He loves to be with poor, deprived people. He is most at home there, drawing them and bringing them to His heaven, where kings wash their servants' feet. That the King of heaven should lie as a baby in a feeding trough is not remarkable only by the sheer paradox of it. It is most remarkable because it is the expression of God's ways - it is the most perfect revelation of heaven on earth. To the angels and beings in heaven, it is not unusual to see their King humbled. Christ fitted into humanity like a hand in a glove. God did not display His glory by a remarkable one-off visit to the poor. He displayed His glory by doing what He always does. God was at home in Bethlehem, and in the manger we learn to see the glory that is enthroned on high. Oh come, let us adore Him!

December 26

"Now there were in the same country shepherds living out in the fields, keeping watch over their flock by night." [Luke 2:8]

These shepherds were not seeking revelation from God. They were faithfully and diligently fulfilling their rather mundane calling - to care for sheep. That God should choose these men to receive the announcement of Messiah's birth is full of symbolism. And that is the way Scripture is written - to picture aspects of God's heart. We may assume that these shepherds had some spiritual stature as well as merely agricultural skills! But the words *"living out in the fields"* speak to us also of evangelists seeking the lost, or of missionaries pioneering new regions. The words *"keeping watch...by night"* speak to us of pastors labouring in prayer for their congregations, or of mothers and fathers, sleepless with longing for their children to know God. When Samuel came to Bethlehem to anoint the new king of Israel, David was at first absent - he was also caring for sheep, and yet he was God's choice as king [1 Samuel 16:11-13]. God does not only answer intense desire and fervent prayers - God answers the life that is laid down for others, and tending sheep symbolises this. He reveals Himself to the person who loves others sacrificially. God does not look on the earth for people who are ambitious for fame or greatness - even spiritual greatness. God looks for people who will lay their lives down for others. He sees the wisp of prayer that rises in the heart of those who are weary through labouring for others. He responds by opening heaven and giving a brief glimpse into a glory that transforms our lives for ever.

December 27

"And the Word became flesh and dwelt among us...."
    [John 1:14]

Greek philosophers wrote of their quest for the 'logos', which was the unifying force or theory that held the whole universe together. They believed this 'logos' was a force or a mathematical equation. Einstein knew that his discoveries fell short of this 'logos'. But John here tells us that the 'logos' is a person, named Jesus Christ. He is the unifying personality that holds together the mystery of the created universe, the mystery of moral conscience, and the love of God that gives purpose to everything. Without Jesus, we would know that the Creator is intelligent, and we would have a keen sense of right and wrong through our conscience. But these are not enough. We need to know what God is like. Christ reveals God in the most perfect way that He could ever be revealed. He is the exact, accurate expression of God's heart and of God's ways. As we look on Jesus Christ, we understand that God is merciful to sinners and to people who fail. We see that He is forgiving and humble. We see that He has a servant heart and is happy washing the feet of people who have argued through selfish pride. We see that God is inexpressibly perfect, good and loving. We also see that He has total authority over the universe, and is able to change our lives and heal whoever comes to Him. In Christ we see the wonder of grace and truth, humility and majesty, love and power, all in one perfect Person.

238

December 28

"Now therefore, give me this mountain..." [Joshua 14:12]

Here we see Caleb's fighting spirit of faith! There is a strength and a boldness in true faith that is the opposite of passivity. It is not right to exalt passivity - simply accepting all our circumstances with resignation. God has made promises, and He is determined to fulfil them. Christ came actively to seek and to save that which was lost. As believers, we must wholeheartedly lay hold of God for His promises. This does not mean that we are fighting God, for we should always be careful to acknowledge God's sovereign hand in our lives. But neither does it mean that we look at our weaknesses, sins and sicknesses as if God is unable to do anything for us. God is all-powerful, and He desires to use His power and authority on behalf of those who love Him. Caleb looked at the mountain which was occupied by giants, and his faith rose to the challenge and declared that this was the very kind of situation where the glory of God could be made known. Whatever your mountain, and whatever the giants, boldly claim God's help to overcome and stand victorious in the fight. Whatever the outcome, we are to be victors, not victims - rejoicing in God's comfort and help in the midst of battle.

December 29

"But you have come to Mount Zion..." [Hebrews 12.22]

How wonderful that, by the work of Christ in our hearts, we have already attained the goal. It is like someone who starts a degree course, and is granted the certificate at the beginning of the course, not at the end. It is the difference between taking the lift up the Empire State Building and taking the stairs. God has done it! We have attained the blessed Presence of God with all the saints of old, and the holy angels. When we pray, we should not think of struggling up a steep mountain to come into God's Presence; no - we only need to think of a curtain being swung back to reveal that we have been brought into His Presence with Christ, in the power of His resurrection. There are mountains to climb and rivers to cross during our lives, but the purpose of these is not so that we might merit heaven or the Presence of God. The Christian life is one of gift, not merit, and the grace is unspeakably great - so much so that it does not really seem 'fair'. This is so that all the merit goes to Jesus. It also ensures that even the weakest believer is accepted. Thank God for His gift of grace.

December 30

"I know, O LORD, that Your judgments are right, and that in faithfulness you have afflicted me." [Psalm 119:75]

None of us like pain or affliction, but no-one can read the pages of the Bible without realising that God allows these things in our lives. He allows them in order to purify, change and mature us as people who know and trust Him. Here the Psalmist not only recognises the hand of God in his afflictions, but goes a step further – he says that the afflictions we pass through are a mark of God's love and faithfulness to us. They are gifts of grace and love, and marks of God's kindness. Why? Does God enjoy our afflictions? By no means - He weeps with us in our pain. But He has a greater end in view than we do. We see the immediate discomfort, but God sees the things that He can only bestow upon us if our hearts are prepared to receive them. God is preparing us to share His authority and His rule, but most of all to be vessels of His love and mercy to others. God uses various methods to make us vessels of honour in His house [2 Timothy 2:20-21], but His ultimate goal is always the same - that we should be filled to overflowing with all the goodness and Presence of our wonderful Father.

December 31

"...and He indicated that He would have gone farther." [Luke 24:28]

The hearts of the two disciples on the Emmaus road burned in them as Jesus drew near [Luke 24:32] - but not as much as His heart burned. He is filled with desire to 'take us further' - to show us more, to release us from tiredness and burdens and enlarge our capacity. He is not disappointed in you - that is not the basis on which He appeals to you to go further – it is because He has great plans for you, and longs to fulfil them in your life. *"He indicated..."* - in other words, He touched their hearts and gave them the option. Perhaps He pointed ahead, or opened another avenue of Scripture in their minds that they had never noticed before. But they declined to respond to His prompting. No doubt they were interested, but not interested enough to pursue the matter with Him there and then. The Lord wants to take you further. There are so many things that we can't even guess are just around the corner, if we will only throw off our petty feelings and follow Him. There is a great new door opening - don't hesitate, go through it with Him.

SCRIPTURE INDEX

Old Testament

Isaiah 41:1	March 11	Matthew 7:1	January 3
Isaiah 43:16,19	August 19	Matthew 7:13	Feb 26
Isaiah 53:6	January 2	Matthew 7:28-29	August 22
Isaiah 53:7	August 5	Matthew 8:2-3	May 23
Isaiah 55: 8-9	May 7	Matthew 9:14-15	October 20
Isaiah 64:3-4	August 18	Matthew 9:17	July 10
Jeremiah 20:18	November 7	Matt 10:16	July 26
Jeremiah 23:18	April 18	Matthew 11:30	November 30
Jeremiah 33:3	Feb 17	Matthew 11:30	Dec 10
Jeremiah 42:7	Dec 5	Matthew 13:3	May 27
Jeremiah 42:7	Dec 6	Matthew 13:19	April 26
Daniel 1:8	January 22	Matthew 13:33	October 22
Daniel 3:24	August 23	Matthew 15:26	May 26
Hosea 6:3	July 19	Matthew 16:4	November 22
Jonah 4:4	May 4	Matthew 16:4	November 22
Jonah 4:10-11	May 2	Matthew 17:24-27	May 30
Habakkuk 1:2	June 29	Matthew 18:10	November 5
Habakkuk 2:4	September 10	Matt 18:18-20	June 1
Zechariah 14:13	April 9	Matthew 19:25-26	Feb 16
Malachi 3:13	Feb 9	Matthew 25:24	January 25
Malachi 3:16	Feb 10	Matthew 25:24	September 6
		Matthew 27:29	April 8
New Testament		Matthew 28:20	April 7
		Mark 1:17	June 13
Matthew 1:5	Dec 24	Mark 2:4	October 15
Matthew 3:11	April 23	Mark 2:5	November 25
Matthew 5:3	October 1	Mark 2:5	April 27
Matthew 5:4	October 2	Mark 2:23 and 27	April 28
Matthew 5:5	October 3	Mark 5:17-19	Dec 8
Matthew 5:6	October 4	Mark 5:30-31	November 20
Matthew 5:7	October 5	Mark 5:35	April 22
Matthew 5:8	October 6	Mark 5:35	September 8
Matthew 5:9	October 7	Mark 5:41	July 12
Matthew 5:10	October 8	Mark 8:35	August 31
Matthew 5:11-12	October 9	Mark 9:31 & 34	November 29
Matthew 6:3	January 18	Mark 10:16	September 9
Matthew 6:5	September 2	Mark 12:43-44	October 21
Matthew 6:6	April 17	Mark 14:38	August 6
Matt 6:6	June 9	Luke 1:13	March 25
Matt 6:6	June 10	Luke 1:20	April 29
Matthew 6:9	January 27	Luke 1:52-53	Dec 19
Matthew 6:9	March 17	Luke 2:8	Dec 26
Matthew 6:9	March 18	Luke 2:45	Feb 7
Matthew 6:10	March 19	Luke 3:21-22	July 8
Matthew 6:10	March 20	Luke 4:1-14	June 16
Matthew 6:10	March 21	Luke 5:3	November 9
Matthew 6:11	March 22	Luke 5:3	October 27
Matthew 6:12	March 23	Luke 5:8	October 28
Matthew 6:13	March 24	Luke 7:6	Feb 29
Matthew 6:24	September 3	Luke 8:22-23	July 25
Matthew 6:25-26	September 1	Luke 8:54-56	November 18

Luke 10:42	July 23	John 18:25	April 5
Luke 11:13	July 7	John 20:15	March 27
Luke 14:33	April 4	John 20:22	June 5
Luke 16:25-26	November 28	John 20:27	November 4
Luke 17:17-19	November 19	John 21:3, 9	September 14
Luke 21:36	Dec 7	Acts 1:5	November 10
Luke 21:37	April 13	Acts 2:1	April 14
Luke 22:28-30	June 11	Acts 2:2	April 15
Luke 23:34	April 19	Acts 2:4	June 6
Luke 23:42	March 26	Acts 2:32-33	October 12
Luke 24:17	Feb 27	Acts 2:39 J	une 3
Luke 24:19	March 6	Acts 2:42	October 11
Luke 24:19-24	November 14	Acts 2:43	Feb 6
Luke 24:28	Dec 31	Acts 3:6	March 10
Luke 24:34	April 21	Acts 3:6	September 27
John 1:1 and 9	June 23	Acts 3:16	August 16
John 1:14	Dec 27	Acts 4:13	August 7
John 1:1 and 18	June 21	Acts 4:31	April 20
John 1:18	September 20	Acts 8:36	September 7
John 3:16	March 8	Acts 11:8	September 22
John 3:35	October 26	Acts 13:27	September 11
John 4:24	July 5	Acts 16:13 & 16	July 31
John 5:19	July 29	Acts 16:31	July 14
John 5:22	Feb 15	Acts 19:2	July 6
John 5:32 and 37	January 19	Acts 28:3, 5	September 26
John 5:25	January 20	Romans 1:1	June 12
John 6:19	July 30	Romans 4:3	June 27
John 6:55	Dec 1	Romans 5:1	January 5
John 7:37	June 4	Romans 5:1-2	October 31
John 7:53-8:1	January 14	Romans 5:20	Feb 21
John 8:7	January 21	Romans 6:3	October 25
John 8:23	June 22	Romans 6:5	September 29
John 9:6	May 25	Romans 8:16	January 28
John 10:27	October 10	Romans 9:1	October 19
John 10:41	August 13	Romans 9:16; 10:13	Dec 14
John 11:14-15	July 13	Romans 9:20	April 25
John 11:27	July 24	Romans 10:6-7	Dec 15
John 12:1-2	August 2	Romans 14:17	July 21
John 12:2-3	August 3	Romans 14:17	September 13
John 12:35-36	July 15	1 Cor 1:21-24	November 27
John 13:3	Feb 24	1 Cor 1:28	June 15
John 13:3-4	October 30	1 Corinthians 2:10	September 18
John 13:36	April 6	1 Corinthians 4:9	November 13
John 14: 4-5	October 29	1 Cor 12:17, 29-30	August 12
John 14:5	October 16	1 Corinthians 13:14	September 15
John 14:17	May 15	2 Cor 5:2	May 11
John 14:17	May 16	2 Cor 5:21	May 18
John 14:26	Feb 1	2 Corinthians 8:9	October 18
John 14:26	June 8	Galatians1:15-16	May 14
John 17:1	October 24	Galatians 2:11	October 23
John 17:5	March 9	Gal 2:15	June 30

CPSIA information can be obtained at www.ICGtesting.com
Printed in the USA
LVOW121318161112

307659LV00005B/15/P

9 781467 976466